TRYING TIMES

South Florida-Rochester-Saint Louis
Studies on Religion and the Social Order
EDITED BY

Jacob Neusner   William Scott Green   William M. Shea

TRYING TIMES
Essays on Catholic Higher Education
in the 20th Century

edited by
William M. Shea
with
Daniel Van Slyke

TRYING TIMES

ESSAYS ON CATHOLIC HIGHER EDUCATION IN THE 20TH CENTURY

edited by
William M. Shea
with
Daniel Van Slyke

Scholars Press
Atlanta, Georgia

TRYING TIMES
Essays on Catholic Higher Education
in the 20th Century

edited by
William M. Shea
with
Daniel Van Slyke

Published by Scholars Press
for the University of South Florida, University of Rochester,
and Saint Louis University

Funds for the publication of this volume were provided by
The Tyson and Naomi Midkiff Fund for Excellence of the Department of Religious Studies at the University of South Florida, The Max Richter Foundation of Rhode Island, and
The Tisch Family Foundation of New York City

Library of Congress Cataloging-in-Publication Data

Trying times : essays on Catholic higher education in the 20th century
/ edited by William M. Shea.
        p.   cm. — (South Florida-Rochester-Saint Louis studies on
religion and the social order ; 26)
    ISBN 0-7885-0586-6 (cloth : alk. paper)
    1. Catholic universities and colleges—United States.
2. Education, Higher—Social aspects—United States. I. Shea,
William M., 1935–   . II. Series: South Florida-Rochester-Saint Louis
studies on religion and the social order ; v. 26.
LC501.T79   1999
371.071'2'73—dc21   99-44120
                                CIP

08 07 06 05 04 03 02 01 00 99   5 4 3 2 1

Printed in the United States of America
on acid-free paper

Contents

Acknowledgements   vii

Introduction
Sandra Yocum Mize, University of Dayton   ix

Conference Papers

1. Catholic Colleges and Civil Law: Burdens and Benefits
   Charles H. Wilson, Bazelon Center   1

2. Changing Conceptions of Catholic Theology/Religious Studies
   Patrick W. Carey, Marquette University   65

3. Protestant Colleges, 1960-1990
   Richard T. Hughes, Pepperdine University   85

Seminar Papers

4. American Catholic Higher Education: An Experience of Inculturation
   Alice Gallin, O.S.U., Saint Louis University   99

5. Saving Truth: Catholic Universities and their Tradition
   James F. Hitchcock, Saint Louis University   121

6. The Message and the Messenger: The Untold Story of Father
   Claude Heithaus and the Integration of Saint Louis University
   Paul J. Shore, Saint Louis University   135

7. The Ethical Eloquence of the Silenced:
   A Levinasian Reading of Teilhard de Chardin's Silencing
   Michael D. Barber, S.J., Saint Louis University   153

8. Catholic Higher Education in the Public Sphere:
   Tensions and Possibilities
   William R. Rehg, S.J., Saint Louis University   173

vi

9. Jesuits and Scholarship: A Reading of the Macelwane Report
    William M. Shea, Saint Louis University   195

    Contributors   221

ACKNOWLEDGMENTS

Alice Gallin received four years of support from the Lilly Foundation to write a history of Catholic higher education since 1960. In doing that work she was able to spend an academic year at Saint Louis University where, as visiting professor of theological studies, she organized and directed a two semester seminar for the faculty of the university. She was able, with the help of the Lilly Foundation, to invite scholars to a conference concluding her stay. The essays in this volume are from the seminar and conference participants in support of her project, written at her request.

Her stay with us was a source of great enlightenment. By the time she arrived in the Fall of 1996 she had been at work several years on her project, had finished a volume on the vast institutional changes in Catholic higher education in the late sixties (*Independence and a New Partnership in Catholic Higher Education*), and was full of more knowledge than anyone else in the country about the three decades since 1960. She was ready (as she always is!) to share it with all comers. Her time here was as well a source of interpersonal and spiritual joy to all who worked with her and under her guidance.

There are many people to thank. Jacob Neusner every year finds financial support for this series (and several others) and so makes it possible for good scholarly work with a limited audience to find its way to the shelves for other scholars to read. Jeanne Knoerle of the Lilly Foundation approved and supported Alice's work at Saint Louis University, and joined us for the two conferences. Richard Breslin, the Provost and Vice President of the university, and Shirley Dowdy, the Dean of the College of Arts and Sciences, pulled together the resources to make the seminar and the conferences possible. University president Lawrence Biondi, S.J., who worked with Alice many years ago when she directed the ACCU and he served on its board, welcomed her here with enthusiasm and graciousness. James Blumeyer, S. J., the university's Vice President for Mission and Ministry, supplied funds from the Marchetti Fund, a gift of the Jesuit community to the university, to enable faculty members to attend the seminar and engage in research. The university's School of Business and Administration invited us to use one of their well-appointed seminar rooms and supplied us with cookies and soft drinks each week. Jeffrey Marlett worked for the year as the graduate student assistant to the seminar, and did a yeoman's job of organizing and keeping us on track. To all of them we owe our thanks.

Paul Reinert, S.J., was president of the university through that dark period when it seemed that many of the Catholic colleges and universities could not go on. His national leadership through the sixties and seventies helped them survive, and his work for Saint Louis University saved it from dissolution. This extraordinary man, who embodies Jesuit ideals and dedication, spent an afternoon with the seminar in its first semester during which he recounted his understanding of the rebirth of the urban universities and colleges. That visit alone was worth the efforts and expense of the year!

Gratitude is also due to Daniel Van Slyke with whose help this volume was prepared for publication. He was assigned to this task as a graduate assistant and carried it through admirably as an editor and an intellectual colleague.

The contributors to this volume, and indeed the entire community of American Catholic higher education, are indebted to Alice Gallin for her leadership of the Association of Catholic Colleges and Universities and for her half century of service to the church as a member of the Order of Saint Ursula. In her work and her friendship she has been a sister to us all.

William M. Shea
Saint Louis University

Introduction

Sandra Yokum Mize
University of Dayton

Ambiguity. Tensions. Change. Turmoil. Silencing. Segregation. Flux. Fragmentation. Burdens. Crises. Such words appear with some regularity in the titles and the bodies of essays contained in this volume. On occasion these words expressing uncertainty, conflict, and even disintegration have more affable companions as in the pairing of "ambiguity" with "interaction," "burdens" with "blessings," "fragmentation" with "integration," "tensions" with "possibilities." From several vantage points, the story of Catholic higher education in the twentieth century ought to feature the latter half of each pair to convey a classic American tale of success — the poor unrefined immigrant grows into a respectable middle class citizen. As commentators (Alice Gallin among them) have often noted, a significant majority of the Catholic colleges and universities founded since the mid-nineteenth century have survived and adapted to the exigencies of the "Modern World," the context that has shaped all existing American institutions of higher learning. Today's Catholic colleges and universities, for the most part, interact positively with the wider culture, academic and otherwise, and enjoy the blessings that social establishment brings to all accredited institutions of higher education.

The descriptors used to open this introduction belie the surviving institutions' success in becoming contributing members within the modern forms of higher education. Yet the words chosen to express critical concerns about Catholic higher education discussed in this volume do not really reflect the thrust of modernity. If modernity were the focus, terms like "specialization," "disciplinary integrity," and, for Catholics, "secularization" would have headed the list. The catalogue of concerns listed in the previous paragraph's opening line has more in common with post-modernity: preoccupied with ambiguity, fragmentation, flux, and the power to control and silence. These preoccupations emerge, at least in part, from a heightened awareness of the significance of "social location" for every venture — intellectual, political, cultural. To become aware of and then to analyze the impact of one's own and others' often disparate and always multiple social locations is to realize that all human endeavors remain limited and partial. From the most noble to the very least, all undertakings, expressed as ideas or actions, reflect the interests and assumptions of the communities which initiate and promote them. These essays taken as a whole reflect the multiple social locations in which Catholic higher education has expressed and acted upon its points of view in the United States. Broadly identified, these "locations" include the church, the academy, and U.S. political, economic, social, and cultural contexts. Attempts to negotiate the complex relationships among these varied social locations can understandably produce experiences of ambiguity, fragmentation, flux, tensions, and conflicts of authority.

I find it useful for the purposes of this introduction to borrow from Thomas Landy's description of his essay and to consider the other authors' essays as snapshots as well. Some, like Charles Wilson's essay on "Catholic Colleges and the Civil Law," resemble a retrospective series on a particular theme, in this instance, federal legal decisions that have transformed Catholic higher education. Others, such as Michael Barber's ethical reflections on Teilhard de Chardin's silencing, are more like a portrait that effectively conveys not merely its subject's visage but also the person's passions which enkindle his or her deepest commitments. Brought together into a single album, these varied "snapshots" of Catholic higher education present the multiple contexts in which any contemporary Catholic college or university must operate to continue to exist as a credible institution of higher learning with a recognizable Catholic identity.

Credibility as institutions of higher education has been an ongoing concern of Catholic colleges and universities in the United States. William Shea's essay, "Jesuits and Scholarship: A Reading of the Macelewane Report," corroborates this claim with its focus upon an internally generated critique of Jesuit graduate education completed in 1932. Shea focuses upon two central sources that marked the identity of this particular manifestation of graduate education, "Jesuits" and "Scholarship." "Jesuit" signifies, obviously, a religious order which bears a complex set of relationships with and within the Roman Catholic church. Similar to other religious orders which have colleges and universities, the Jesuits, on the one hand, provide a distinctive identity for a subset of Catholic universities and colleges in the United States but, on the other hand, have a mission that significantly exceeds higher education in the United States. The Jesuits' transnational identity, in fact, played a key role in generating the 1932 critique of graduate education in these U.S. schools. The initiation of the Macelewane report on graduate education and its implementation came from the Father General in Rome rather than Jesuit leaders in the United States.

Interestingly enough, the implementation of the report's recommendation came only after a 1934 American Council of Education report omitted all of the Jesuit institutions' graduate programs from their list of approved doctoral programs. This point highlights the other and more common source of credibility in U.S. graduate education — the accrediting agencies of the wider academy. Research receives the designation, "scholarship," when it meets the standards of excellence generated by the wider academy whose orientation was and still is quite distinct from, though not necessarily contradictory to, that of a religious order. Shea considers the difficulties in reconciling the identity of the research scholar with the "religious" and "practical" vocation of the Jesuit.

> . . . though every Jesuit, in the ideal order, ought to be a trained scholar, the Jesuit mission is soul-saving, character formation, and the transformation of cultures. The tension becomes acute in a Jesuit whose dedication to scholarship may seem inimical to the corporate and institutional goals or in a Jesuit whose dedication to the corporate mission threatens to outweigh his responsibility to scholarship.

Shea ends the essay with more questions than answers and offers no resolution to the particular quandary of the "Jesuit scholar," especially in light of what is described in the essay as a strong strain of anti-intellectualism among today's Jesuits. This somewhat ominous conclusion is, however, tempered by his recognition of the significant advances in Jesuit-sponsored graduate education that have occurred since the submission of the Macelewane report over sixty years ago.

James F. Hitchcock's "Saving Truth: Catholic Universities and Their Tradition" raises serious questions about the credibility of Catholic colleges' and universities' commitment not to scholarship but to a meaningful Catholic identity. As described in his essay, Catholic institutions of higher education, especially in the period from 1965 through 1970, implemented reforms modeled after the practices of prestigious secular universities. What Hitchcock highlights is "an atmosphere of crisis for the Church and the whole of Western society" in which these reforms occurred. He pinpoints the Second Vatican Council as catalyst for the ecclesiological identity crisis in which familiar "spiritual and intellectual landmarks . . . seemed suddenly to be swept away." A more sweeping indictment identifies "the delayed but inevitable effects of the spirit of modernism" as source of the wider crisis. Within the academy, the triumph of "skeptical modernism" generated an identity crisis on secular campuses of a magnitude equal to that of the church.

Hitchcock characterizes the eventual outcome of the Catholic institutional reforms as a "liberal Catholic synthesis." Indicative of the identity crisis which informed the synthesis has been and continues to be a complete inattentiveness in the hiring of Catholic faculty members committed to the institution's religious mission. Coupled with the repercussions of indifference in faculty hiring has been the curricular impact of the loss of a "normative standing" for the Catholic tradition in the curriculum, even in a theology. What emerges from this synthesis is the "final logic of the liberal position," a subjective relativism in which religious commitment is reduced to personal preference based upon "experience." Within such a context, Hitchcock argues that ". . . ultimately, there are no compelling reasons to assert even an attenuated Catholic identity." He makes very clear that to be "Catholic" is to belong to a community that exceeds the local one, whether the local refers to the United States or even more particularly a university or college community. "What it means to be Catholic is finally the decision of popes and councils, not of university faculties and boards of trustees." Hitchcock concludes that given the separation of university governance from ecclesial authority, the existence of a U.S. Catholic university "in the full sense" is highly unlikely.

Despite his negative assessment of the possibility of a juridically definitive Catholic university, Professor Hitchcock does end his essay with a constructive suggestion. He suggests a revision of the highly contested liberal arts curriculum, recognizing its centrality in modernism's influence and then appeals to Christopher Dawson's proposal, "that an undergraduate curriculum be built around the study of 'Christian culture,' approached almost as an alien reality." This course of studies, formulated in the 1950's, has, according to Hitchcock, real merits for a 1990's Catholic undergraduate curriculum, in part for a quality much revered in the contemporary academy — an inclusive approach. The curriculum, as Dawson conceived it, incorporates several disciplines including art, literature, philosophy, theology, history, politics, and even science, allows for ecumenical studies since 'Christian culture' includes Protestant and Orthodox, and encourages trans-cultural analysis not limited to Western Europe. It also accepts the current reality of faculty demographics since both non-believers as well as believers could teach.

The crucial difference from current programs lies in the curriculum's embodiment of the principle of unity underlying Christian culture, even as it explores diverse expressions of it. In championing this particular focus on Christian culture, Hitchcock even finds a certain commonality with advocacy scholars, in feminist and African American studies, whom he earlier had located squarely within the crisis in academia. He does make clear, however, that the social location of his advocacy lies beyond any special interest group and certainly beyond the university. He is advocating the truth of divine revelation. Hitchcock simultaneously calls Catholic colleges and universities to save the truth, articulated in and through the Catholic tradition, and embedded in Christian culture; and by saving this truth, Catholic colleges and universities can "offer authoritative guidance to the larger culture" through their teaching about "the possibility of the saving truth." Given the depths of the crises in the Church and the university, at least as Hitchcock describes them, it remains difficult to understand how one could convince any faculty to cooperate in such profound curricular reform or who within the secular academy would deem such reform as an offer of "authoritative guidance."

Professor Hitchcock is certainly correct in noting that the curricular reforms of the late sixties profoundly affected the teaching of theology at Catholic colleges and universities. Patrick Carey carefully traces some of the effects in his "Conceptions of Catholic College Theology/Religious Studies." Perhaps no other discipline has felt the impact of the dramatic shifts in Catholic education over the past thirty years as has the study and teaching of theology/ religious studies. As the principal location for the study of Catholic theology moved from the seminary to the university, so too did the principal adjudicator of legitimacy shift from the church to the academy. Prior to 1960, religion courses at Catholic colleges and universities had as their principal aim to foster faith either through a teaching of apologetics or through a fostering of Catholic character formation. After 1960, the emphasis was on "the academic study of religion with a host of internal methodologies and disciplinary specialties."

Carey's discussion rightly emphasizes the introduction of required theology/religious studies courses as a distinctive feature of an undergraduate's academic program at a Catholic college or university. What may be surprising to those unfamiliar with the history of the discipline of theology/religious studies is what an innovation these required courses were. The innovation was justified by claiming that all students, regardless of religious conviction, should study religion as a universal human phenomenon. New approaches to theology based upon "a revolutionary turn to the subject and to history in Catholic theology" justified in turn this new universalist and pluralistic view of religion. Professors of theology/religious studies at Catholic colleges and universities no longer locate the authority or standards for the discipline in a "sacred order," but rather in methodologies and disciplinary specializations. Carey traces the results, evident in most Catholic undergraduate theology/religious studies programs, namely, fragmentation in curriculum. Compared to other disciplines within a college, theology/religious studies lacks coherence. Students choose courses on a purely elective basis and do not progress through a body of knowledge as they would in other disciplines. Carey identifies theology/religious studies faculty's inability to defend the coherence of their discipline to members of other departments as a motivating factor in their reconsidering and reconstructing the required course of studies. The intent is to provide a more integrative approach to the study of theology/religion as an academic discipline without abandoning the necessary specialization and recognition of religious pluralism.

The public debates about the nature and aim of theology/religious studies stand in sharp contrast to the personal acquiescence of many twentieth century Catholic intellectuals, theologians and others, to their religious superiors' demands of silence. Two essays in this collection provide portraits of two Jesuits, the unknown Claude Heithaus and the famous Teilhard de Chardin, who obeyed such commands. Both must be seen within the context of their religious vocations expressed in their unfailing commitments to the Society of Jesus. These two men thus shared a common vow, obedience; yet, the context in which that vow was put to the test varied radically.

The little-known Claude Heithaus, son of German immigrants, a member of the Jesuits' Missouri province, had a promising career as a scholar of archeology at Saint Louis University. The conflicts between himself and his superior arose not over his scholarship but rather his political commitments. Heithaus publicly supported integration of the University. President Patrick Holloran and the Missouri Provincial Joseph P. Zuercher denounced his interference and eventually removed an unrepentant Heithaus from his university position. Aside from the inherent drama of the story, the incident points to the complexities in the relationships among various contexts in U.S. Catholic institutions of higher learning.

On the one hand, Heithaus made his appeal for integration based upon certain basic Catholic principles of social justice as well as the practices of a global church; he even appealed to Pius XII's appointment of black bishops. On the other hand, his superiors appealed to the long tradition of holy obedience within a religious order. The urgency with which Heithaus's superiors demanded obedience arose not simply from concern for preserving a Catholic tradition but from concern for preserving a Catholic institution dependent on the tuition of white middle class students who were born and raised in a racist society. As the essay notes, fear of anti-Catholic backlash, deeply embedded in the collective memory of the Missouri province Jesuits, also contributed to the rejection of Heithaus's call for racial integration. Changing social contexts, especially on university campuses, and changing notions of Jesuit identity transformed the Jesuit villain into a hero. In 1970, Pedro Arrupe, S.J., the Father General, commended Heithaus for his "efforts on behalf of civil rights." The religious order had been transformed from the site of this Jesuit's humiliation to the site of his glorification.

In a far more dramatic way, the fortunes of Teilhard de Chardin have changed over the last thirty years — from an intellectual silenced to an intellectual much proclaimed. Michael Barber, S.J. takes his readers beyond consideration of this familiar story into the ethical implications of Teilhard's acceptance of his silencing. Certainly the immediate context for Teilhard's obedience was his loyalty to the Jesuits. Yet Barber takes us much further into the ecclesiological context to consider the scholar's relationship to "the tradition" or rather to the community which bears that tradition and preserves its vitality through beliefs and practices. Using a Levinasian ethical framework, Barber interprets Teilhard's response to his being silenced within a context of "face-to-face ethical relationship." What is especially provocative in Barber's analysis is his highlighting Teilhard's deep commitment to the Catholic tradition and his acknowledging that Teilhard's own "reasoning about Christian faith arises out of a pre-theoretical context of communal-historical practices that cannot be easily or completely rationalized."

The French Jesuit conceded in a letter that "'the church has the right to expect our compliance in some things, because in the current that she represents she is the vehicle of more truth than any one of us in his slender individuality.'" Teilhard never forsook his convictions but acquiesced to the prohibition of their publication for the sake of that community whose tradition he embraced and sought to uplift. Barber finds Teilhard's willingness to accept his silencing for the sake of the "other," i.e. the Catholic community, to be instructive with respect to academic freedom in a Catholic university setting. The "ethical relationship of the face to face" calls not only scholars and university administrators but also ecclesial authorities to consider "the other" in all controversies that test academic freedom. This essay's ethical thrust raises important questions concerning the "ends" or teleology which situates and defines an intellectual's identity.

Teilhard's end, uplifting the tradition, followed from what he identified as his principal location — the Catholic community; most scholars in the university context identify their principal location as the academy whose primary commitment or end is maintaining the individual scholar's academic freedom. The question remains whether it is ever necessary to abandon one of these ends for the sake of the other, and which one a Catholic university or college ought to abandon for the sake of situating and defining its intellectual identity.

William Rehg, S.J. suggests yet another *telos* for Catholic higher education — the promoting and effecting of social justice through engagement in the public political life of the nation. Rehg places this appeal within a broader context of Jesuit education by invoking the memory of six Jesuits, their cook, and her daughter who were murdered on the grounds of the University of Central America in San Salvador. By offering this particularly poignant example as his introduction, Rehg challenges other Jesuit universities in the Americas to consider their own responsibilities as public institutions with a clearly enunciated religious identity.

Rather than focusing on a particular university or college, Rehg presents a panoramic view of the Catholic university situated in a particular *polis*, the United States, that permits a plurality of public discourse. Rehg appeals to current political theory on "deliberative democracy," which promotes the retrieval of rational discourse among various informal publics in an attempt to identify specific common goals that promote justice. He then uses the peace and economic pastorals of the U.S. bishops as examples of explicitly Catholic contributions to deliberative democracy. Even with their commitment to an open deliberative process, however, the bishops remain constrained by their ecclesial role as representatives of the Roman Catholic church. The Catholic university, even more than the episcopal-sponsored forum, is the logical site for ongoing Catholic-informed contributions to deliberative democracy, reasoned public discourse promoting the common good. Rehg sees the university's commitment to academic freedom as making for a qualitatively different kind of discussion than that of the bishops, since Catholic voices exist as only one of many on most campuses. While Catholics still form the majority on most campuses the opportunities to include more diverse participants have significantly increased over the past thirty years. To accept the tensions inherent in this growing plurality provides possibilities for dialogue that better reflects the reality of deliberative democracy in the United States.

The inclusion of Richard T. Hughes' essay, "Protestant Colleges, 1960-1990" in a volume on Catholic higher education confirms an expansion of the dialogue to include "the Other" who has been featured throughout much of U.S. Catholic history. Hughes gently reminds his Catholic readers that "the Protestant" of so much U.S. Catholic rhetoric does not exist in practice. Rather, "Protestant" encompasses a variety of faith traditions of which Hughes provides examples from three: Anabaptist, Lutheran, and Reformed. Hughes's article brings into focus the wider pluralism operative in U.S. culture and its translation into higher education. By laying out the distinctive focus of each of the institutions which he examines, Hughes also underscores each faith tradition's recognition of the value of a distinctive education as an important expression of a faith community's vitality. Hughes describes how the distinctive theological commitments inform the choices made in shaping each of the three colleges' educational missions. The narratives concerning the three institutions make very clear that, like their Catholic counterparts, these religiously affiliated colleges have had to struggle with financial difficulties and respond to the changing market of Christian higher education. Unforseen circumstances demand in some cases an adjustment and in others a complete change in the school's mission. While sometimes competitors in promoting the benefits of an education at a private institution, Catholic and Protestant colleges and universities are in many more ways compatriots. They learn from each other their own distinctive contributions to Christian higher education, and they share many common concerns as religiously affiliated institutions of higher learning attempting to be a Christian witness of the intellectual life within a highly secularized culture.

The U.S. legal system is one context in which Catholic and Protestant colleges and universities have many common interests. Charles H. Wilson alludes to this shared fate in his masterful treatment of the federal court cases which transformed the federal government's involvement in higher education, including that located at Catholic-affiliated institutions. Wilson first focuses upon those federal cases situated in this nation's ongoing discourse on the separation of church and state. The primary legal questions of the last thirty years have centered around whether federal funding for Catholic higher education necessarily violated the non-establishment clause of the First Amendment. Certain decisions resulted in significant benefits, including funding for new buildings used for non-religious purposes, and financial aid to individual students who could use the money to attend a Catholic college or university. As Wilson notes, accepting these benefits meant living with "the burdens" of federal laws and regulations. In examining "the burdens," Wilson first discusses the civil court's role in unraveling the union movement among faculty. He then examines anti-discrimination cases involving two hotly debated issues on today's Catholic campuses. The first is the hiring and tenuring of faculty, and the other concerns the official approval of student groups, most notably gay, lesbian, and bisexual groups. In the former, an appellate court has allowed for preferential hiring of religious from an institution's founding community. In the latter, the supreme court upheld Georgetown's right to refuse official recognition to an organization at odds with its mission.

These two issues accentuate the contested notions of identity that Catholic universities and colleges still face. To be a university in the United States is to defend academic freedom and maximize a plurality of views; to be a Catholic is to claim a particular identity delineated by certain beliefs and practices, even if both are defined broadly. Is it defensible in a university to implement a policy of preferential hiring to promote a particular identity? Would it apply only to qualified members of an institution's founding religious order or to Catholics in general? What about hiring a Catholic faculty member who takes controversial positions on delicate subjects? Then of course what about those students or faculty who wish to establish organizations that directly contradict official Catholic teaching? These questions remain unresolved, and controversies surrounding these issues erupt on a regular basis on Catholic campuses. One can be certain that these ongoing controversies will provide new civil suits to be decided in the court of law.

Despite these controverted issues, as Alice Gallin rightly points out in her essay, "American Catholic Higher Education: An Experience of Inculturation," Catholic colleges and universities have adapted rather well to their American context. To frame her narrative describing the adaptation, Gallin chooses two descriptors, "ambiguity" and "interaction." This pair arises from recognizing the difficulties inherent in the American Catholic university's mission of inculturation, a mission that John Paul II has recently assigned to every Catholic university within its particular culture in the much discussed document, *Ex corde ecclesiae.*

To provide a better understanding of these difficulties, the careful historian, Gallin, provides a succinct account of key developments in American higher education that have resulted in "a wonderfully diverse, sometimes contentious mixture of private and public universities. . . ." Quoting William Shea, Gallin also makes very clearly that despite the distinction won by the designation "private," "'American Catholic higher education is already public'." It accepts the criteria of excellence of the secular academy, uses federal funding and therefore abides by governmental regulation, and imposes no religious test on a faculty or students.

Catholic higher education has, Gallin concludes, succeeded in Americanizing itself. It has adopted many of the distinctive features of almost every American institution of higher education, whether public or private.

> To sum up, the impact of the American experience (as distinct from the European) on Catholic higher education can be seen in the commitment to an education that focuses on the student, on the conviction that advanced research and undergraduate education are complementary and can coexist, that voluntary associations can set standards for academic excellence, and that institutional autonomy and academic freedoms are basic to higher education.

The remainder of the essay addresses the controverted issue of maintaining a credible Catholic identity in the colleges and universities who have successfully participated in American higher education.

While she approves of the institutions' successes, Gallin contends that more is demanded of Catholic higher education than simple accommodation. The Catholic intent in interacting with the culture is adaptation not simply for the sake of survival but for the sake of inculturation. She explains, "Inculturation has two stages: the first is the effort to enter into and understand the culture into which one is moving; the second is to bring about interaction between the culture and one's own so that the values of both can be promoted." Of course, success in this first stage may inevitably lead to failure at the second stage, especially if Catholic higher education mimics the Protestant institutions' secularization as outlined in George Marsden's *Soul of the American University* or as decried in the often referenced *First Things* articles, "The Decline and Fall of the Christian College," by James T. Burtchaell, C.S.C.

Gallin argues that successful adaptation does not necessitate the secularization of Catholic colleges and universities, as Marsden and Burtchaell describe. While Gallin does not shy away from citing five clear similarities between mainstream secularized institutions, formerly affiliated with particular

Protestant denominations, and contemporary Catholic colleges and universities, she also articulates five crucial differences between them. First and foremost, she notes that "timing was very important." Twentieth-century Catholics, in comparison to nineteenth-century Protestants, have been adapting to the demands of secular education defined by a very different historical context. Gallin also notes the varied and complex relationships that Catholic colleges and universities have had with their church. Many of these ties have no parallel in the formerly Protestant-affiliated institutions. Most notable is the Catholic institutions' founding by religious orders whose affiliation with the church is clear but quite distinct from that of the hierarchy. Even the gradual diminishment of the orders' influence with the adoption of lay boards of trustees drew upon an ecclesial context for support, namely the Vatican II emphasis on the importance of the laity's participation in all sorts of Catholic institutions. Despite the diminishment of the direct influence of a canonically recognized ecclesial body, i.e., the religious order, "the church universal" has remained an important interlocutor, especially in the recent challenges laid before the leaders of American Catholic universities to examine and articulate the Catholicity of their mission. Finally, Gallin notes that Catholic universities have integrated theology/religious studies into their curriculum. Even with the limited success of this integration, the decision permitted theology to claim a legitimate place within the university. Protestant institutions, by way of contrast, relegated such study to separate divinity schools or seminaries.

As Gallin reminds her readers, Catholics' exclusion from the mainstream academy until very recently also remains a significant factor in understanding the relationship between Catholic institutions and American culture. With the Vatican II call for universities to respond to "the signs of the times," Catholic colleges and institutions have an even greater obligation to promote the research necessary for bringing their influence to bear on American higher education. And even though Catholic institutions of higher education have yet to produce influential scholarship in various disciplines rooted in the Catholic tradition, Gallin finds hope in their long-term commitment to maintaining a distinctive Catholic identity. Such an identity, Gallin believes, also serves as a positive starting point for fruitful dialogue within the pluralistic American culture with those as firmly grounded in their own traditions, both secular and religious.

Though Alice Gallin ends on this hopeful note of interaction, the ambiguity remains. Within a highly secular academy skeptical of all traditions, can disciplinary scholarship rooted in the Catholic tradition ever be influential? Who will choose the arbiters of excellence, and by what criteria will the chosen arbiters determine real contributions? If the standards of institutional excellence are determined by those institutions of higher education who have always been the gatekeepers of academic prestige, can Catholic colleges and universities ever expect to be permitted into the ranks of the prestigious? Conversely, if the standards are set by the ecclesiastical institution, can Catholic colleges and universities maintain the intellectual dynamism wrought through academic freedom? On a more practical note, if ecclesiastical authority determines academic excellence, can Catholic colleges and universities still qualify for the federal funding so necessary to their survival? These varied questions arise out of the multiple social locations within which Catholic institutions of higher education operate.

To juxtapose the central points in some of these essays underlines not only the multiplicity of locations but also their divergence. To cite but one dramatic example, if the highest academic value is an individual researcher's freedom of expression, then Teilhard de Chardin's acceptance of his silencing for the sake of the community stands in direct opposition to the academy's commitment. Yet, Catholic colleges and universities recognize in both the researcher's freedom of expression and in the acceptance of silence their own identity. Given the tension between these two views, this identity will remain disputed both within and without Catholic higher education. I do think, despite the ambiguity, tensions, change, turmoil, silencing, segregation, flux, fragmentation, burdens, and crises, Catholic institutions of higher education have done a remarkable job of educating a significant number of students from quite diverse backgrounds. While continuing to note all the shortcomings, I also want to suggest that there is much in Catholic higher education that deserves the designation "excellent." Excellence arises at least in part from ongoing attempts to put into practice the "both/and" of Catholic higher education—both the freedom grounded in scholarly research and the freedom grounded in well done Catholic beliefs and practices. May we all learn how to bring our practices closer to perfection from the examples set forth in this volume.

1

Catholic Colleges and Civil Law

Benefits and Burdens

Charles H. Wilson

José A. Cabranes, a federal appellate court judge, was, prior to being appointed to the bench, the first general counsel of Yale University. Several years ago, he said that, during his time as Yale's general counsel, he would describe himself as "the lawyer for a corporation in a regulated industry."[1] Continuing in that hyperbolic vein, he added that, "in the period since the early 1960s, colleges and universities had become one of the nation's leading regulated industries."[2]

I suggest that Judge Cabranes was engaging in hyperbole because, no matter how heavy the regulatory burden imposed by government on institutions of higher education seems to be,[3] it does not even begin to approach the burdens borne by such regulated industries as electric and gas utilities, radio and television stations, railroads, airlines, banks, etc. Nevertheless, hyperbole serves a rhetorical purpose. If Rip Van Winkle had earned his Ph.D. in 1945 from a Catholic university, fallen immediately into a deep slumber and awakened today,

---

[1] J. A. Cabranes, *American Higher Education and the Law: Some Reflections on NACUA's Silver Anniversary*, 12 JOURNAL OF COLL. & UNIV. LAW 261 (1985).

[2] *Idem.*

[3] Judge Cabranes was participant in a symposium sponsored by the National Association of College and University Attorneys, an organization of lawyers representing both public and private institutions. Public universities, being creatures and organs of the state, are more heavily regulated than private colleges. To the extent that Judge Cabranes's remarks included the regulatory problems facing public institutions, the hyperbole was not as great. This paper focuses on the legal issues confronting the Catholic segment of private higher education and, from that perspective, the hyperbole is at its strongest.

1

he would likely be astounded by the importance that government has assumed in the operation of Catholic and other independent institutions of higher education.

In this paper, I will trace some of the significant developments of that governmental involvement in Catholic higher education over the past 35 years or so. That involvement has been of two types: (1) the extension of financial assistance in the form of institutional grants, research funds and student aid, which is the focus of the "benefits" phase of this paper; and (2) the enactment of laws and regulations addressing such issues as union organizing and anti-discrimination obligations, which is the focus of the "burdens" phase of this paper.

The increase in the federal government's involvement in matters affecting higher education has been dramatic. While most states have been involved directly in higher education for many years by establishing and operating their own universities and colleges, the federal government's involvement in higher education is relatively recent. Prior to 1945, and with the exception of the assistance it provided to land-grant colleges and the establishment of the various military academies, the federal government had virtually no role in higher education. Thus, the evolution of the federal role in higher education occurred roughly in the time period that is of interest to this colloquium.

The "burdens" phase of this paper will focus on federal laws and regulations because they apply uniformly across the country. To the extent that states have acted in ways that burden Catholic higher education during the same period, there are wide variations among the states. Consequently, it is simpler to generalize about the growth of federal involvement in higher education.

In the "benefits" phase of this paper, federal institutional and student aid programs have had the most dramatic impact on Catholic higher education. However, as we will see, government aid to religiously affiliated institutions raises significant constitutional questions, and some state aid programs have contributed significantly to the evolving constitutional standard. Supreme Court decisions clarifying the constitutional standard are the unifying force in the "benefits" area.

I.

Government Benefits to Catholic Higher Education

The Legal Perspective

When religiously affiliated institutions participate in a public aid program, the most common legal challenge to such participation is made under the

Establishment Clause[4] of the First Amendment to the United States Constitution. In the most general of terms, the Establishment Clause prohibits "sponsorship, financial support, and active involvement of the sovereign in religious activity."[5]

When the federal government embarked in 1944 on its first significant aid program that benefited higher education, including the church-affiliated sector, the Supreme Court had not yet undertaken the task of construing the intended reach of the Establishment Clause. Indeed, the Court did not issue its first significant Establishment Clause decision until 1947.[6] For that reason and others, the early federal programs that benefited Catholic higher education did not face the obstacle of legal challenges.

However, the pace of Establishment Clause adjudication began to accelerate in the 1960s, and cases challenging the constitutionality of aid to church-related education at all levels contributed significantly to the evolution of the Supreme Court's Establishment Clause jurisprudence. Of the higher education aid cases that were part of that evolution, only one—the landmark case of *Tilton* v. *Richardson*—involved a federal aid program, the Higher Education Facilities Act of 1963. Two other significant aid cases involved aid programs enacted by the Maryland legislature. Moreover, the two most significant student aid cases challenged state programs in Tennessee and Washington. Nevertheless, in all of those cases there was a federal unifying feature. The Supreme Court is the final arbiter of the meaning of the Establishment Clause, and its decisions, irrespective of whether federal or state programs are at issue, are the law of the land.

---

[4] "Congress shall make no law respecting an establishment of religion . . . ." CONSTITUTION, AMEND. I.

[5] *Walz* v. *Tax Commission*, 397 U.S. 664, 668 (1970).

[6] *Everson* v. *Board of Education*, 330 U.S. 1 (1947) (upholding a New Jersey program that reimbursed the parents of Catholic school students for the cost of bus fares to send them to school). The Court had issued an obscure Establishment Clause decision at the close of the nineteenth century. In *Bradfield* v. *Roberts*, 175 U.S. 291 (1899), a federal taxpayer challenged a congressional grant of funds to Providence Hospital, which was located in the District of Columbia and which was owned and operated by a Catholic order of nuns. The Court found no constitutional impediment to such a use of federal funds. It ruled that the only relevant inquiry was the nature of the institution being assisted. Finding that Providence Hospital had been chartered by the federal government as a hospital, it ruled that the Establishment Clause did not prohibit federal assistance to hospitals. That the hospital was owned and operated by women of a particular religious faith who had committed themselves to the religious life was of no constitutional concern to the Court.

Early Federal Aid Programs

Many date the onset of federal assistance to higher education, including the Catholic segment, in the 1960s because the Higher Education Facilities Act[7] was signed into law in December 1963. That aid program was challenged in the federal courts on constitutional grounds, a challenge that was resolved in a landmark decision, *Tilton v. Richardson*.[8]

In fact, however, significant federal involvement in higher education began almost two decades earlier when Congress passed the Serviceman's Readjustment Act of 1944,[9] more popularly known as the "G.I. Bill of Rights." The educational benefits made available to returning World War II veterans under the G.I. Bill of Rights had a profound and enduring impact on American higher education.

Thousands of World War II veterans took advantage of the educational benefits of the G.I. Bill of Rights to attend college, something they otherwise might not have done. Equipped with college degrees, they were able to obtain higher-paying jobs than they might otherwise have aspired to. And, in keeping with the American dream of the upward mobility of succeeding generations, the children of those original G.I. Bill of Rights recipients—the so-called "baby boomers"—flooded college campuses in the 1960s, prompting Congress to enact the Higher Education Facilities Act in 1963 to assist colleges and universities to expand their facilities to accommodate the new wave of enrollments.

The educational benefits of the G.I. Bill of Rights were awarded based on a veteran's service in World War II, and he was able to use those benefits at any college he chose. Many chose to use the benefits to attend Catholic colleges and universities, and those institutions benefitted accordingly. Indeed, some veterans used their G.I. Bill of Rights benefits to attend Catholic seminaries and become priests.

While the absence of any Establishment Clause precedent is one probable explanation for the lack of constitutional challenges to that use of G.I. Bill of Rights funds, there are surely other more pragmatic explanations. We had not yet become a litigious society, and rushing to court to challenge what we did not like had not yet become a reflexive response. Moreover, this country's participation and success in World War II had aroused deep feelings of patriotic pride among the American people. One can only imagine the public ire that would have

---

[7] 77 U.S. Statutes 364, codified at 20 U.S.C. § 721 *et seq.*

[8] 403 U.S. 672 (1971).

[9] 58 U.S. Statutes 284. That Act has been amended many times since 1944 and has gone through many permutations as the nation has engaged in various post-World War II conflicts. Educational benefits now available to military veterans are codified at 38 U.S.C. §§ 3201 *et seq.*, and §§ 3451 *et seq.*

descended on any person or organization that might have had the temerity to mount a legal challenge to the G.I. Bill of Rights.

The next significant federal program of aid to higher education was the National Defense Education Act of 1958 (NDEA). The impetus for that program was the successful launch of Sputnik by the Soviet Union and the resulting fear among Americans that our country was losing the space race. The NDEA authorized grants to colleges and universities to improve the teaching of science at all levels of education. Catholic colleges and universities received grants under that program.

Although the Supreme Court had decided three important Establishment Clause cases by the time NDEA was enacted,[10] there was no legal challenge to NDEA grants to Catholic institutions. While there is no way to *prove* why NDEA escaped judicial scrutiny, one suspects that considerations of patriotism may again provide an explanation. The Cold War was in full bloom in the late 1950s and the fear of nuclear confrontation was palpable. That the Soviet Union might dominate space exploration (using space as a platform for launching nuclear weapons) and outstrip the United States in scientific advancement was a source of genuine concern, a concern that the NDEA addressed in the name of national security. Anyone who filed a legal challenge to such legislation would surely have incurred the wrath of the American people.

For whatever reason, neither the G.I. Bill of Rights nor the NDEA was subjected to Establishment Clause scrutiny, despite the tangible benefits that both programs conferred on church-related higher education. The Higher Education Facilities Act of 1963 would meet a different fate.

The Horace Mann Case

President Johnson signed the Higher Education Facilities Act (HEFA) into law in December 1963. Three months earlier, however, the first shot in the coming church-state wars was fired in Annapolis, Maryland, when the Horace Mann League filed a lawsuit in the Circuit Court for Anne Arundel County. The suit challenged four state legislative grants, with a total value of $2.5 million, to four church-related colleges in Maryland for the construction of academic facilities, the precise form of aid available under HEFA. Those grants, the Horace Mann League alleged, violated the Establishment Clause because the four recipient

---

[10] Everson v. *Board of Education*, see note 6, *supra*; *McCollum* v. *Board of Education*, 333 U.S. 203 (1948) (The Establishment Clause prohibits programs under which religious instructors came on public school premises during regular school hours to offer religious instruction to children who chose to participate); *Zorach* v. *Clauson*, 343 U.S. 306 (1952) (There is no Establishment Clause prohibition of programs under which public school children who chose to participate were excused from school early once a week to attend religious instruction off the public school premises).

colleges were pervasively sectarian.[11] The four colleges were named as defendants in the lawsuit.[12] Two were Catholic—the College of Notre Dame of Baltimore and St. Joseph's College of Emmitsburg—one was Methodist—Western Maryland College of Westminster—and the fourth was affiliated with the United Church of Christ—Hood College of Frederick.

The trial judge in the *Horace Mann* case was Circuit Judge O. Bowie Duckett, and he ruled in favor of the colleges. Leo Pfeffer, the plaintiffs' attorney who was also a college professor and a leading theorist of the Religion Clauses of the First Amendment, had argued that the determinative question was whether, in their orientation and operation, the four colleges were too "pervasively sectarian" to qualify for public funds. Judge Duckett framed the central issue differently. For him, the decisive question was "whether the primary effect of providing the means [public funds] for the construction of secular buildings at these Institutions advances religion."[13] Judge Duckett ruled that religion was not advanced by the challenged grants, which were to be used for the construction of science buildings (at Notre Dame, Western Maryland and St. Joseph's), a dining hall (at Western Maryland) and a classroom building (at

---

[11] Since the decision in the case of *Zorach* v. *Clauson* (note 10, *supra*), the Supreme Court had decided four additional Establishment Clause cases: *McGowan* v. *Maryland*, 366 U.S. 420 (1961) (upholding Sunday closing laws); *Torcaso* v. *Watkins*, 367 U.S. 420 (1961) (striking down a provision of the Maryland Constitution that required appointees to state offices to affirm a belief in God); *Engle* v. *Vitale*, 370 U.S. 421 (1962) (invalidating a state-composed prayer that public school students in New York had to recite at the start of the school day); *Abington School Dist.* v. *Schempp*, 374 U.S. 203 (1963) (invalidating a practice in Pennsylvania and Maryland public schools of starting the school day with devotional readings from the Bible). Thus, while the pace of Establishment Clause adjudication was quickening, the 1947 decision in *Everson* v. *Board of Education* (see note 6, *supra*) remained the only Supreme Court decision addressing the validity of extending public benefits to children attending church-related schools.

[12] The colleges were not necessary defendants in the case. The core claim in the case was that the challenged grants violated the Establishment Clause. The various clauses of the First Amendment only restrain governmental action; a private entity cannot violate the Establishment Clause. For that reason, the four colleges could have moved successfully to be dismissed as defendants because no relief could be granted against them. However, all four chose to remain as defendants. The allegations of the complaint made clear that the colleges' religious affiliations and activities would be the centerpiece of the evidence offered by the plaintiffs. By remaining as defendants, the colleges, through their attorneys, could participate in the evidentiary process and present facts about their educational programs and processes that could balance the one-sided portrait that Leo Pfeffer and his co-counsel intended to present.

[13] The written opinions of circuit courts in Maryland are not published. The parties in the *Horace Mann* case reprinted Judge Duckett's opinion in the Joint Record Extract they filed with their appellate briefs. That Extract is part of the official record of the case in the Maryland Court of Appeals.

Hood). The result would have been different, he wrote, if any of the grants had been used to build a chapel.

The trial judge also specifically rejected Pfeffer's contention that the perception of the intensity of a college's religious orientation should control. "If we distinguish between church-related colleges on the basis of the degree of their relationship to a particular denomination, we would discriminate between religions, which is likewise prohibited by the First Amendment." He also noted that the Maryland Court of Appeals, the state's highest court, in previous cases had made "little or no distinction between a sectarian or secular institution, provided the money is used to perform a public service such as, for example, the health, education and general welfare of our citizens."

Pfeffer appealed the trial court's judgment to the Maryland Court of Appeals, and by the narrowest of margins, 4 to 3, he successfully challenged the grants of three of the four defendant colleges.[14] Only the grant to Hood College survived review by the Court of Appeals.

Sadly, the Court of Appeals's majority opinion, written by Chief Judge Stedman Prescott, has a decidedly anti-Catholic flavor. For example, at the start of his Establishment Clause analysis, Chief Judge Prescott asserted that

> ...it will be unnecessary to include an extended historical background of the First Amendment . . . . However, it seems appropriate to set forth a sketchy outline of some of the facts which the Framers of our Federal Constitution and the First Amendment had in mind when the Amendment was added.[15]

Then, after recounting in one paragraph the persecution of Christians by the Roman Emperor Trajan in the second century, Chief Judge Prescott devoted almost four pages of his opinion[16] to such matters as the Crusades and their abuses, the "horror and perfidies" of the Spanish inquisition, the conflict between King Henry VIII of England and the Papacy, the relationship between Queen Elizabeth and the established church in England, the Thirty Years' War between German Protestants and Catholics, and the harsh treatment of the Huguenots by Catholics in France. No historic horror that could be attributed to the Roman Catholic Church escaped mention in Chief Judge Prescott's "sketchy outline."

Reading the minds of the Framers of the Constitution and the Bill of Rights is necessarily a difficult exercise, especially from a distance of two centuries or more. Yet it is an exercise in which the Supreme Court has frequently engaged when construing the Establishment Clause. But the Supreme

---

[14] *Horace Mann League* v. *Board of Public Works*, 220 A.2d 51 (1966).

[15] 220 A.2d at 55-56.

[16] 220 A.2d at 56-59.

Court has been more interested in the colonial experience with religious persecution than with the Crusades and the Inquisition.

For example, in *Everson* v. *Board of Education*,[17] the Court's first extensive examination of the reach of the Establishment Clause, Justice Hugo L. Black, writing for the majority, devoted one paragraph of his opinion to summarizing the religious persecution in Europe that drove the first settlers to this country.[18] In that paragraph, Justice Black declined to point to any particular religion as the villain. He noted that "at various times and places, Catholics had persecuted Protestants, Protestants had persecuted Catholics, Protestant sects had persecuted other Protestant sects, Catholics of one shade of belief had persecuted Catholics of another shade of belief, and all of these had from time to time persecuted Jews."[19]

Justice Black seemed far more concerned with the colonial and pre-Constitution experience with religious persecution as the relevant backdrop for the Establishment Clause. After reciting briefly the nature of the religious persecutions in Europe, he said, "These practices of the old world were transported to and began to thrive in the soil of the new America."[20] He then traced the practices of established churches in the various colonies and their repression of minority religions.[21]

Justice Black also noted that the opposition that developed against the established churches in the colonies "reached its dramatic climax in Virginia in 1785-86," on the eve of the Constitutional Convention.[22] The Virginia experience to which he referred was the effort by the Virginia legislature to renew a tax levy for the benefit of the established Anglican Church and the vigorous opposition by James Madison and Thomas Jefferson to that proposal. Madison wrote his famous *Memorial and Remonstrance Against Religious*

---

[17] 330 U.S. 1 (1947).

[18] 330 U.S. at 8-9.

[19] 330 U.S. at 9. While Justice Black spread the historical blame for religious persecution, the dissenting opinion by Justice Robert H. Jackson made an odd observation about American public schools: "Our public school, if not a product of Protestantism, at least is more consistent with it than with the Catholic culture and scheme of values." 330 U.S. at 23.

[20] 330 U.S. at 9.

[21] 330 U.S. at 9-11. One of the colonial practices was Maryland's prohibition of the public celebration of Mass. *See* C.J. Antieau, A. T. Downey & E.C. Roberts, *Freedom from Federal Establishment* (Milwaukee, WI: Bruce Publishing Co., 1963) 25; W. W. Warner, *At Peace with All Their Neighbors: Catholics and Catholicism in the National Capital, 1787-1860* (Washington, DC: Georgetown University Press, 1994), 44.

[22] 330 U.S. at 11.

Assessments that helped defeat the tax levy, and Jefferson drafted the "Virginia Bill for Religious Liberty" that the Virginia legislature eventually adopted. [23]

Thus, the historical emphasis that Chief Judge Prescott chose in his *Horace Mann* opinion is far off the constitutional mark. One cannot help wondering whether some form of bias was operating when Chief Judge Prescott decided to stress only the abuses of power by the Roman Catholic Church in Europe in his exegesis of the Establishment Clause. Certainly the result reached by the majority in the Maryland Court of Appeals was not encouraging for Catholic higher education.

The essential point of disagreement between the Court of Appeals and the trial court in *Horace Mann* was whether the nature of the public aid at issue or the nature of the recipient institutions was controlling. For the trial court, the fact that the challenged state funds would assist in the construction of academic facilities to be used for purely secular instruction was dispositive. For Chief Judge Prescott and his colleagues in the majority, the determinative inquiry was whether a recipient college was so pervasively religious in its orientation and operations that it could be considered "legally sectarian." If so, according to the majority, the state could not, consistent with the Establishment Clause, give public funds to such an institution, irrespective of the use to be made of those funds.

The majority adopted that analytical approach despite conceding that determining "whether or not an educational institution is sectarian in such a legal sense *is a rather elusive matter, being somewhat ephemeral in nature.*"[24] To conduct that inquiry, the majority adopted and embraced verbatim six general criteria urged by Leo Pfeffer in his appellate brief. Those criteria examined (1) the college's stated purpose, (2) the degree of religious control exercised over the institution's governing board and administration, (3) the college's other relationships with religious organizations, (4) the place of religion in the college's program, (5) the "outcome" of the college's program, as measured by accreditation and activities of alumni, and (6) the image of the college in the community.[25]

Chief Judge Prescott had little trouble concluding that the grants to Notre Dame and St. Joseph's were constitutionally impermissible.[26] At the outset of his

---

[23] Supreme Court opinions have frequently referred to the Virginia experience and the efforts of Madison and Jefferson as critical to understanding the Establishment Clause, e.g., *Reynolds* v. *United States*, 98 U.S. 145, 164 (1878); *Davis* v. *Beason*, 133 U.S. 333, 342 (1890); *Flast* v. *Cohen*, 392 U.S. 83, 103-04 (1968).

[24] 220 A.2d at 69 (emphasis added).

[25] 220 A.2d at 65-66. While there were six general criteria stated, sub-criteria in each category required examining more than 20 aspects of each college's operation.

[26] *See* 220 A.2d at 70-72.

legal analysis, the Chief Judge stated: "In setting forth the facts relevant to each [college], we have followed, in considerable measure, appellants' brief with reference to some of the schools, after carefully checking the same with the evidence."[27] With respect to Notre Dame and St. Joseph, Chief Judge Prescott did more than follow Leo Pfeffer's brief "in considerable measure." Virtually every sentence in the majority opinion that recites facts about the two Catholic colleges was copied verbatim from Pfeffer's brief. That approach to opinion writing is, at the very least, questionable.

We have only Chief Judge Prescott's word that he checked "carefully" to see if the factual representations in Pfeffer's brief were supported by the evidence. But that is not the problem. The prosecution of a lawsuit, whether at the trial or appellate level, is an adversary process. Pfeffer's objective in the *Horace Mann* case was to portray all four colleges as thoroughly religious in their orientation and operation. The evidence he presented in the trial court concerned only the religious aspects of the four colleges, and his brief on appeal recited only facts related to the religious aspects of the schools.

The lawyers for the four colleges sought to balance the record by offering considerable evidence about the educational and other non-religious aspects of the institutions. By following Pfeffer's brief "in considerable measure" for an account of the evidentiary record, Chief Judge Prescott totally disregarded the countervailing evidence offered on behalf of Notre Dame and St. Joseph's and summarized in the briefs filed on their behalf in the Court of Appeals. Faced with such a stacked deck, those two colleges had no hope of prevailing on appeal.

Such an approach would not suffice for the two Protestant colleges— Hood and Western Maryland. It is painfully apparent to one familiar with the *Horace Mann* case and its evidentiary record that Chief Judge Prescott and his colleagues in the majority believed they could not strike down the grants for the two Catholic colleges and allow the two Protestant institutions to walk away from the case unscathed. To do so would invite accusations of religious bias. Consequently, the majority sacrificed Western Maryland College and allowed Hood College to retain its grant.

But it could not reach that result factually by reading only Pfeffer's brief, for Pfeffer tried to portray the two Protestant colleges as being as intensely religious as Notre Dame and St. Joseph's. For Western Maryland College, the majority recited a few evidentiary facts not found in Pfeffer's brief, enough to suggest that college was not as intensely religious as the Catholic schools but sufficiently religious to fall on the wrong side of the constitutional line it had drawn. For Hood College, the majority relied on very few of the facts contained in Pfeffer's brief, but rather drew on other evidentiary facts to portray an

---

[27] 220 A.2d at 66.

institution that it felt could receive public funds without violating the Establishment Clause.

A casual reader of the majority opinion in *Horace Mann* would be puzzled by the distinctions drawn between Western Maryland and Hood.[28] What seemed to doom Western Maryland was that the majority of the Court of Appeals detected "a decidedly religious 'flavor'" at that institution.[29] For no apparently principled reason, Hood survived judicial scrutiny and Western Maryland did not. The constitutional line that the majority had drawn was indeed "ephemeral" and "elusive." Both sides in the *Horace Mann* case sought Supreme Court review, but the Supreme Court declined to hear the case.[30]

The Maryland Court of Appeals issued its *Horace Mann* decision on June 2, 1966. The timing for Catholic higher education could not have been worse. Vatican Council II had ended a year earlier, and the leadership of Catholic higher education in this country had begun the process of trying to determine how their institutions should respond to the Council's various decrees and declarations. The *Horace Mann* ruling was the only decision by an American appellate court that had addressed the question of the eligibility of Catholic colleges for public aid. The deliberations prompted by Vatican Council II were not directly concerned about the public aid issue. However, it was an issue that could not be ignored as the deliberations proceeded, and *Horace Mann* hung like a storm cloud over the deliberations.

By June of 1966, HEFA had been in effect for two and one-half years, and Catholic colleges and universities were among the institutions of higher education that had begun to receive HEFA grants. Indeed, in the 1967 fiscal year, Catholic institutions of higher education would receive $125 million in federal funds.[31] If courts generally were to adopt the *Horace Mann* analytical approach, those grants could be in jeopardy. The express purpose of HEFA, after all, was to allow existing colleges and universities to expand their facilities to accommodate the soaring growth in college enrollments in the 1960s. If a court of competent jurisdiction were to reach the same result as the majority in *Horace Mann* and declare Catholic colleges and universities constitutionally ineligible for HEFA grants, the consequences for those institutions could have been

---

[28] For example, the majority noted that Hood received only 2.2 percent of its operational budget from the United Church of Christ. 220 A.2d at 67. The majority considered the financial contribution of the Methodist Church to Western Maryland to be "considerable," but only between two and three percent of its operational budget came from church sources. *Idem* at 68.

[29] 220 A.2d at 69.

[30] 385 U.S. 97 (1966).

[31] William P. Leahy, S.J., *Adapting to America: Catholics, Jesuits, and Higher Education* (Washington, DC: Georgetown University Press, 1991), 134.

devastating. Supreme Court Justice Byron R. White observed several years later: "Without federal funding to provide adequate facilities for secular education, the student bodies of those [church-related] institutions might remain stationary or even decrease in size and the institutions might ultimately have to close their doors." [32]

That there was no concerted effort by Catholic colleges to make sweeping changes in their overall structure and programs to conform to the Hood College model, and thus assure eligibility for public funding, is clear. But it is also clear that concern about the impact of the *Horace Mann* case insinuated itself into discussions in the late 1960s about the American Catholic higher education community's response to Vatican Council II. Sister Alice Gallin's recent study of the changes in governance of Catholic colleges during that time notes, for example, that the attorney for the College of New Rochelle was influenced by *Horace Mann* in the advice he gave on the governance issue and that the administration of New York's Bundy Law was also affected by the Maryland decision. [33]

The Catholic higher education community would not receive definitive guidance on the constitutional criteria for eligibility for public funds until 1971 when the Supreme Court decided the case of *Tilton* v. *Richardson*. [34]

The Tilton Case

HEFA was not challenged in the courts until almost five years after it was signed into law. The reason for that delay was a formidable jurisdictional barrier that the Supreme Court had erected to suits challenging the constitutionality of acts of Congress.

In 1923, the Supreme Court ruled that federal taxpayers did not have "been standing" to maintain lawsuits in federal courts to question the constitutionality of federal statutes. [35] Article III of the Constitution limits the jurisdiction of federal courts to cases and controversies. One aspect of the "case-

---

[32] 403 U.S. at 664. The quoted language comes from Justice White's separate opinion in the cases of *Lemon* v. *Kurtzman*, 403 U.S. 602 (1971), and *Tilton* v. *Richardson*, 403 U.S. 672 (1971). Those two case were argued together and decided the same day. Justice White was the only dissenter in *Lemon* that held violative of the Establishment Clause programs in Pennsylvania and Rhode Island that provided state funds to Catholic parochial and other religious schools to subsidize the salaries of teachers of secular subjects. Justice White concurred and provided the critical fifth vote in *Tilton* that upheld the constitutionality of HEFA grants to four Catholic colleges in Connecticut.

[33] A. Gallin, *Independence and a New Partnership in Catholic Higher Education*, (Notre Dame, IN: University of Notre Dame Press, 1996). 32-33, 91-92, 119.

[34] 403 U.S. 672 (1971).

[35] *Frothingham* v. *Mellon*, 262 U.S. 447 (1923).

and-controversy" doctrine, as it has evolved in the Supreme Court, is that a person filing a lawsuit in a federal court must have been standing to maintain the suit. To have been standing, a litigant must have a sufficient personal stake in the outcome of the case to assure "that concrete adverseness upon which [federal courts] so largely depend for illumination of difficult constitutional questions."[36] The standing requirement seeks to assure that federal courts will be asked to redress particularized harm and not to arbitrate generalized grievances. Resolving generalized grievances is more appropriate for the legislative branch in our separation of power's scheme.

If making grants of public money to church-affiliated institutions offends the Establishment Clause, it is difficult to identify any person in society who suffers particularized harm from that governmental action. Certainly such an action would be a misuse of tax funds, but the impact of that misuse is felt equally by all taxpayers.[37] For these reasons, at the time that HEFA was signed into law, those who might want to challenge the constitutionality of federal grants to church-related colleges could, with some justification, fear that federal courts[38] would not entertain a suit challenging the constitutionality of HEFA.

---

[36] *Baker* v. *Carr*, 369 U.S. 186,204 (1962); *see also Flast* v. *Cohen*, 392 U.S. 186 (1968).

[37] It is true that taxpayers who identify themselves with an absolutist interpretation of the Establishment Clause that would bar government from providing any form of assistance to church-affiliated institutions would be more deeply offended. But those feelings derive not from their status as taxpayers but from their agreement with a particular interpretation of a clause in the constitution.

[38] Because Article III addresses only the jurisdiction of *federal* courts, state courts are not so constrained in entertaining taxpayer suits challenging the constitutionality of state spending programs. Indeed, the *Horace Mann* case was a state taxpayer suit. Judge Duckett, in fact, ruled that the Horace Mann League did not have standing in that case because it was a nonprofit corporation that did not pay taxes. But he found that, under relevant state law, the individual plaintiffs could maintain the suit as state taxpayers. The Article III case-and-controversy doctrine, however, governs whether state taxpayers can file their challenge in a federal court and whether, in a state taxpayer suit properly entertained in the state courts, the losing party can appeal a final judgment to the United States Supreme Court. *See Doremus* v. *Board of Education*, 342 U.S. 429 (1952).

However, on June 10, 1968, in the case of *Flast* v. *Cohen*,[39] the Supreme Court carved a narrow exception to the general rule that federal taxpayers could not sue in federal court to contest the constitutionality of an act of Congress. Relying on its perception of the particular evils the Establishment Clause was intended to prohibit, the Court ruled that federal taxpayers had the standing to challenge an act of Congress as unconstitutional as long as the taxpayers challenged legislation enacted under the Taxing and Spending Clause of Article I of the Constitution[40] and as long as the challenge was based on claims that the Establishment Clause prohibited the spending program in question.

With the jurisdictional hurdle removed, Leo Pfeffer, the attorney for the plaintiffs in *Horace Mann* and the attorney for the successful appellants in *Flast*, filed the *Tilton* v. *Richardson* lawsuit, a federal taxpayer suit, in the federal district court in Hartford, Connecticut, on September 25, 1968, alleging that HEFA grants to four Catholic colleges in Connecticut violated the Establishment Clause.

The Supreme Court decided a second case on June 10, 1968, that influenced how the parties in the *Tilton* case framed their arguments. In *Board of Education* v. *Allen*,[41] the Court considered an Establishment Clause challenge to a New York program that lent textbooks without cost to students in grades 7 through 12 in public and private schools, including those with church affiliations. It was only the second time that the Court had considered a challenge to an aid

---

[39] 392 U.S. 83 (1968). The *Flast* case involved an Establishment Clause challenge to Title I of the Elementary and Secondary Education Act of 1965. Under Title I, the federal government provides money to local school district to provide remedial educational services to children who were economically and educationally disadvantaged. The statute requires that children attending private schools, including those with church affiliations, who have the same level of economical and educational disadvantage as public school students receive services comparable to those provided public school students. Title I has been the subject of considerable litigation. For example, in *Wheeler* v. *Barrera*, 417 U.S. 402 (1974), the Supreme Court, in effect, upheld the requirement that private school children, including those attending church-affiliated schools, receive Title I services comparable to those provided to public school students. In *Aguilar* v. *Felton*, 473 U.S. 402 (1985), the Court ruled unconstitutional the practice of sending public school Title I teachers onto the premises of church-affiliated schools to provide the remedial instruction. And this very Term of the Court, it has agreed to hear arguments in *Agostini* v. *Felton*, Nos. 96-552 and 96-553, that its decision in *Aguilar* should be overruled.

[40] Several years later, the Court provided an example of how this requirement restricted federal taxpayer suits. In *Valley Forge Christian College* v. *Americans United*, 454 U.S. 464 (1982), the taxpayer plaintiffs sought to block the transfer of surplus federal property to the college at a price far below its market value. The Court ruled that taxpayers had no standing because the legislative authorization for the transfer was under Congress's Article I power over federal property, and not under the Taxing and Spending Clause of Article I.

[41] 392 U.S. 236 (1968).

program that benefited students in church-affiliated schools.[42] By a 6 to 3 vote, the Court upheld the program, and the ground for its decision would be significant in the defense of the Catholic colleges sued in the *Tilton* case.

The New York textbook loan program prohibited the lending of religion books or books to be used in a course in religious instruction. With that limitation, the Court construed the program as aiding only the secular instructional program of church-affiliated schools. Acknowledging affirmatively that church-affiliated schools performed dual and separable functions—secular education and religious instruction—the Court ruled that public aid restricted to the secular educational functions of such schools did not violate the Establishment Clause.[43]

The Catholic institutions named as defendants in the *Tilton* case were Fairfield University, Sacred Heart University of Bridgeport, Albertus Magnus College of New Haven, and Annhurst College of South Woodstock. Also named as defendants in the suit were the United States Secretary of Education[44] and the chairman of the Connecticut agency that administered HEFA grants awarded to colleges in that state. The complaint had one peculiar feature. It alleged affirmatively that Trinity College and Wesleyan College, two private schools in Connecticut with Protestant affiliations, were eligible for HEFA grants. [45]

While the plaintiffs had a leading Establishment Clause theorist—Leo Pfeffer—as their lead attorney,[46] the four Catholic colleges retained Edward

---

[42] The first was *Everson* v. *Board of Education*, 330 U.S. 1 (1947).

[43] Such a rationale completely refutes Leo Pfeffer's argument of pervasive sectarianism. That argument necessarily proceeds from the assumption that the secular and religious are so intertwined in the pervasively sectarian school that it is not possible to aid the secular educational function without also aiding the religious function. The *Allen* analysis is, in effect, the analysis employed by the trial court in *Horace Mann*.

[44] When the lawsuit was filed, Wilbur Cohen was the Secretary of Education, and the case was styled *Tilton* v. *Cohen*. When the federal district court issued its decision, Robert Finch was Secretary of Education, and the case was styled *Tilton* v. *Finch*. When the Supreme Court issued its decision, Elliot Richardson was Secretary of Education, and the case finally became styled *Tilton* v. *Richardson* for all time.

[45] That allegation was "peculiar" because, if Leo Pfeffer did believe that Trinity and Wesleyan could constitutionally receive HEFA grants, he need not have referred to them in the complaint. By vouching for their constitutional eligibility, he seemed only to highlight that his attack was directed only at Catholic colleges. The attorneys for the defendant colleges in *Tilton* would turn the allegations about Trinity and Wesleyan against Pfeffer by placing in evidence documents from those colleges that suggested they did not differ in any material way from the Catholic colleges that had been named as defendants.

[46] When Pfeffer appeared in various church-state cases, he did so as an attorney for the American Jewish Congress. He would always associate with him lawyers from the state in which the suit was filed and those lawyers were usually recruited by public interest organizations, such as the American Civil Liberties Union, that espoused a theory of strict

Bennett Williams, a Jesuit-educated Washington attorney who was among the best trial lawyers and Supreme Court advocates in the country, to represent them. Those who understood the stakes in the *Tilton* case looked forward to the ultimate confrontation of those two advocates in the Supreme Court.

The court convened to hear the case consisted of a judge of the United States Court of Appeals for the Second Circuit (in New York City) and two Connecticut United States District Court judges. A federal statute that was then in effect but that has since been repealed[47] required the convening of such three-judge courts for cases that challenged the constitutionality of federal or state statutes. The advantage of that procedure was that judgments issued by such three-judge federal courts could be appealed directly to the Supreme Court, thus eliminating the delay that would otherwise result from an appeal to an intermediate federal circuit court of appeals.

Pfeffer saw the *Tilton* case as a way of getting the federal courts to place their imprimatur on the criteria of sectarianism he had successfully promoted in the *Horace Mann* case. He alleged that the defendant Catholic colleges were pervasively sectarian educational institutions, as measured by the criteria adopted by the Maryland Court of Appeals in *Horace Mann*, and that the Establishment Clause prohibited the federal government from giving HEFA grants to pervasively sectarian educational institutions.

The principal argument advanced by the colleges' attorneys was predicated on the ruling in *Board of Education* v. *Allen*. The HEFA grants awarded to those colleges were to aid in the construction of a science building (Fairfield University), two libraries (Fairfield and Sacred Heart Universities), a fine arts building (Annhurst College), and a language laboratory (Albertus Magnus College). Noting that the educational functions those buildings would assist were strictly secular, the colleges argued that they, like the church-affiliated schools that benefited from New York's textbook loan program, offered a secular educational program that was separable and distinct from their religious instruction and other religious activities. Consequently, the colleges argued that the *Allen* reasoning controlled and whether they were religiously affiliated or oriented was constitutionally irrelevant under *Allen*.

The colleges also made a fallback argument. If the court were to consider the intensity of their religious orientations to be controlling, the colleges argued they were not the pervasively religious institutions that the plaintiffs' complaint

---

separation between church and state. The ACLU affiliate in Hartford, for example, provided the attorneys who assisted Pfeffer in *Tilton*. Those lawyers were not merely names on pleadings to satisfy local bar admission rules. Leo Pfeffer was a theorist and not a trial lawyer. Pfeffer would develop the legal theories and write the trial and appellate briefs in his cases. But the task of conducting discovery and presenting evidence in court fell to the local lawyers.

[47] 28 U.S.C. §§ 2281, 2282, 2284.

depicted. Rather, they were educational institutions that offered secular educational programs in the liberal arts tradition. Their religious orientations were simply an added dimension that enhanced, but did not distort, their total educational program.

The case went to trial before the three federal judges in Hartford on December 2, 1969, and the evidentiary hearing lasted three and one-half days. The plaintiffs' evidence, which examined only the religious aspects of the colleges' programs, consisted almost exclusively of documents from the institutions.

The federal and state governments did not put on any evidence. They took the position that HEFA did not permit them to draw distinctions among colleges that applied for grants based on perceptions of how intensely religious they are, or even to make inquiries into such religious matters.[48] Consequently, the role of the federal and state lawyers in the case was limited to entering into a stipulation with the plaintiffs about how HEFA was administered at the federal and state levels. That position by the governmental defendants made the colleges' active participation in the evidentiary process critical to offering the court a balanced account of how they carried out their educational functions.

The evidence offered by the defendant colleges consisted of the testimony of 23 witnesses and additional documents.[49] The witnesses included the presidents of the four institutions, other administrators and faculty members. Their testimony established, *inter alia*, that the facilities constructed with their HEFA grants would be used strictly for secular purposes. They would argue in their post-trial brief that that was the only relevant constitutional inquiry under *Board of Education* v. *Allen*.

However, to counter the distorted account of their educational programs in plaintiffs' evidence, they also offered evidence of their total operations. That additional evidence tended to show that no religious restrictions were placed on the admission of students or the employment of faculty, that the courses they

---

[48] The lawyers for the federal and state governments were correct in asserting that HEFA required them to be officially ignorant about the religious orientation of church-related colleges that applied for HEFA grants. Eligibility for such grants was based on religiously neutral criteria set forth in the statute, and institutions qualified for grants by satisfying those criteria. (The statute did prohibit any facility constructed with a HEFA grant from being used for a religious purpose, but there was no presumption that a church-related college could not comply with that requirement.) The position of the government lawyers in *Tilton* vindicated the decision of the defendant colleges to participate actively in the case. *See* note 12, *supra*. Absent the evidence they presented about how they carried out their educational missions, the record in the case would depict the colleges according to the highly distorted image that Leo Pfeffer's evidence suggested.

[49] Included among the additional documents were several catalogs of Trinity and Wesleyan Colleges. *See* note 45, *supra*, and accompanying text.

offered, including theology, were taught according to the requirements of their disciplines and without the inclusion of irrelevant religious considerations, that the curriculum was not used to indoctrinate students in religion, that the institutions subscribed to accepted standards of academic freedom, and that no students were forced to participate in religious activities against their will.

After receiving post-trial briefs and hearing post-trial arguments, the three-judge court issued its decision on March 19, 1970. The court rejected Pfeffer's position and embraced unanimously the legal arguments of the defendant colleges based on the *Allen* decision. The court ruled that the only relevant inquiry was whether the academic facilities constructed by the defendant colleges with the HEFA grants would be used solely for secular educational purposes. Finding that the facilities in question satisfied that constitutional requirement, the court entered judgment for the defendants. Its opinion did not discuss the conflicting evidence about the religious character of the defendant colleges, and it made no findings of fact on that issue. [50]

Leo Pfeffer promptly filed his notice of appeal to the Supreme Court and, on June 22, 1970, the Court agreed to hear the appeal.[51] But, before the appeal was heard, three other cases that would have a direct bearing on the issues on appeal in *Tilton* were decided.

While the *Tilton* case was working its way through the federal district court in Hartford, suits were filed in the federal district courts in Philadelphia, Pennsylvania, and Providence, Rhode Island, challenging the constitutionality of aid programs in those states that benefited Catholic parochial schools. Leo Pfeffer was the attorney for the taxpayer plaintiffs in both cases.

The Pennsylvania case was styled *Lemon* v. *Kurtzman*.[52] At issue was a state program that reimbursed [53] nonpublic elementary and secondary schools, including those with church affiliations, for the cost of teaching certain specified subjects: mathematics, physical science, physical education, and modern foreign languages.[54] The program was obviously structured to bring it within the ruling in *Board of Education* v. *Allen*. The three-judge federal court agreed, by a 2 to 1 vote, that the Pennsylvania program satisfied the constitutional requirements of *Allen*, and it entered judgment for the defendants.[55] Pfeffer promptly appealed,

---

[50] *Tilton* v. *Finch*, 312 F. Supp. 1191 (D. Conn. 1970).

[51] 399 U.S. 904 (1970).

[52] 310 F. Supp. 42 (E.D. Pa. 1970).

[53] The program was called a "purchase of services" to comply with a state constitutional limitation on granting public funds to private entities.

[54] The limitation of foreign language instruction to "modern" languages excluded reimbursement for instruction in Latin. The legislature apparently believed that instruction in Latin came too close to the religious functions of Catholic schools.

[55] The proceedings in *Lemon* differed from those in *Tilton*. There was no evidentiary

and the Supreme Court would hear that appeal the same day that it heard arguments in *Tilton*.

In the Rhode Island case, *DiCenso* v. *Robinson*,[56] the challenged state pro-gram provided a salary supplement to teachers in private and church-related schools that amounted to 15 percent of the salaries paid to public school teachers. To qualify for the salary supplement, private school teachers had to teach strictly secular subjects and not engage in the religious instruction and activities at their schools.

That program was a response to the difficulties the private schools were having in attracting qualified teachers because of the pay differential between public and private school teachers. The problem was particularly acute in Catholic parochial schools that were beginning to feel the impact of the decline in vocations. Rhode Island has the highest percent of Catholics of any state in the union. When the salary supplement program was enacted, more than one-third of all Rhode Island elementary school-aged children attended Catholic parochial schools. The Rhode Island legislature was concerned that such a substantial segment of the state's elementary school population might be receiving their instruction from teachers who were not fully qualified. [57]

The *DeCienso* lawsuit was filed by Leo Pfeffer, with assistance from the ACLU of Rhode Island. The only named defendants were the state officials responsible for administering the aid program. The law firm of Edward Bennett Williams[58] was retained by the Roman Catholic Bishop of Providence, and it represented Catholic school teachers who qualified for the salary supplement.

---

hearing in *Lemon* and no evidence about the religious orientation and activities of church-affiliated schools that benefitted from the challenged program. Rather, the defendants filed a motion to dismiss the complaint as their response to the complaint, and the three-judge court granted that motion. Such a motion tells the court that, even if all of the factual allegations of the complaint are true, the moving parties are entitled to judgment as a matter of law because there is no violation of law. The effect of that motion in *Lemon* was that the defendants did not challenge factually Pfeffer's allegations that Catholic parochial schools were pervasively sectarian. The only information in the record of the case about the church-affiliated schools that benefitted from the Pennsylvania program were the untested allegations of Pfeffer's complaint.

[56] 316 F. Supp. 112 (D.R.I. 1970).

[57] In fact, because the Catholic elementary schools could not pay its teachers salaries that were competitive with those paid to public school teacher, the Diocese of Providence did not require that its elementary school teachers have a college degree. To qualify for a salary supplement under the Rhode Island program, the Catholic school teachers had to have a college degree.

[58] The firm's name was, and is, Williams & Connolly. While Williams would argue the Rhode Island case in the Supreme Court, he was not involved in the trial court phase of the case. The lawyers from the firm who handled trial court proceedings were Jeremiah C. Collins, a graduate of Georgetown University and its law school, and the author of this paper.

The teachers intervened as defendants to protect their interests. Like the *Tilton* case and unlike the *Lemon* case, the *DiCenso* case involved an evidentiary hearing that examined how the salary supplement program was administered and the educational process in the Catholic parochial schools. The evidentiary hearing ended on March 19, 1970,[59] and the three-judge court took the case under advisement. Before that court issued its opinion, however, the Supreme Court decided an important Establishment Clause case that would drastically alter the legal assumptions on which *Tilton*, *Lemon* and *DiCenso* had been tried.

In *Walz* v. *Tax Commission*,[60] the Court considered whether the tax exemption that states and municipalities granted to churches violated the Establishment Clause. In resolving that issue, the Court identified a type of Establishment Clause concern that had not previously been specifically articulated. To decide whether the challenged tax exemption violated the Establishment Clause, the Court said, it had to determine whether the effect, or end result, of the exemption, created "excessive government entanglement with religion." [61]

Stating that the newly identified test was "inescapably one of degree," the Court noted that the choice facing government was either to tax churches or exempt them from taxation. The Court conceded that both options involved some government involvement with religion. But eliminating the exemption "would tend to expand the involvement by giving rise to tax valuation of church property, tax liens, tax foreclosures, and the direct confrontations that follow in the train of those legal processes."[62] Consequently, because the exemption option involved a lesser degree of government entanglement, the challenged tax exemptions survived constitutional scrutiny.

On the surface, there would seem to be little, if any, connection between the tax exemptions approved in *Walz* and the aid programs challenged in *Tilton*, *Lemon* and *DiCenso*. But the Court's opinion in *Walz* contained the following sentence:

> Obviously a direct money subsidy would be a relationship pregnant with involvement and, as with most governmental grant programs, could encompass sustained and detailed administrative relationships for enforcement of statutory or administrative standards, but that is not this case.[63]

---

[59] That same day the three-judge federal court that heard the evidence in the *Tilton* case issued its opinion.

[60] 397 U.S. 664 (1970).

[61] 397 U.S. at 674.

[62] 397 U.S. at 674.

[63] 397 U.S. at 675. On April 22, 1970, just two weeks before it issued the *Walz* decision, the Court agreed to hear the appeal in *Lemon* v. *Kurtzman*. One is left to wonder

The parties in the *DiCenso* case would soon learn how the issues in their case were connected to the *Walz* ruling.

Just seven weeks after the *Walz* decision the three-judge court in Providence issued its decision in *DiCenso*. That court ruled unanimously[64] that the salary supplement posed a serious risk of excessive government entanglement with religion. Because the statute required that teachers receiving salary supplements not teach religion, the court believed that state officials administering the program would have to monitor classroom instruction by the subsidized teachers, particularly those employed by religiously affiliated schools. That form of government involvement with religion was precisely what the excessive entanglement doctrine prohibits, the court ruled.

The state defendants and the intervening teachers promptly appealed that decision, and the Supreme Court set the *DiCenso* case for argument with *Tilton* and *Lemon*. The Court heard arguments in the three cases on March 2 and 3, 1971, and it issued its opinions in the cases on June 28, 1971. The Court decided the Pennsylvania and Rhode Island cases in a single opinion, styled *Lemon* v. *Kurtzman*,[65] striking down the salary subsidy programs, with only Justice White dissenting. In *Tilton* v. *Richardson*,[66] the Court, by a 5 to 4 vote, upheld the constitutionality of HEFA and the HEFA grants to the four defendant Catholic colleges. Justice White cast the decisive vote in *Tilton* in a separate opinion. Because the Court used the *Lemon* case to announce a new Establishment Clause test that would control challenges to church-related education in the future, that opinion requires brief examination.

With Chief Justice Warren E. Burger, the author of the *Walz* decision, writing the majority opinion, the Court in *Lemon* distilled from the "cumulative criteria" it had developed in Establishment Clause cases over the years a three-part test by which to measure the claims in the Pennsylvania and Rhode Island cases:

> First, the statute must have a secular legislative purpose; second, its principal or primary effect must be one that neither advances nor inhibits religion; finally, the statute must not foster 'an excessive government entanglement with religion.'[67]

---

whether the sentence of dictum just quoted was inserted in Chief Justice Warren E. Burger's majority opinion in *Walz* in anticipation of the *Lemon* appeal.

[64] One member of the panel (Judge Pettine) said he would have upheld the program under *Board of Education* v. *Allen* had the *Walz* decision not intervened.

[65] 403 U.S. 602 (1971).

[66] 403 U.S. 672 (1971).

[67] 403 U.S. at 612-13 (internal citations omitted). The purpose and effect branches of that test had first been articulated in *Abington School Dist.* v. *Schempp*, 374 U.S. 203, 222

The Court held that the challenged salary subsidy programs manifestly had a secular purpose—"to enhance the quality of secular education in all schools covered by the compulsory attendance laws."[68] The Court did not pause to consider whether the programs had valid primary effects because it felt that neither program could survive scrutiny under the excessive entanglement analysis.

To decide whether excessive entanglement existed, the Court examined "the character and purposes of the institutions that are benefited, the nature of the aid that the State provides, and the resulting relationship between the government and the religious authority."[69] Those three factors in combination convinced the Court that the Pennsylvania and Rhode Island programs presented a substantial risk of excessive government entanglement with religion.

The problem, according to the Court, began with the schools benefiting from the programs. The Court characterized the schools as "an integral part of the religious mission of the Catholic Church" and as "a powerful vehicle for transmitting the Catholic faith to the next generation." The schools' ability to achieve that latter goal was "enhanced by the impressionable age of the pupils, in primary schools particularly." The Court characterized the schools as involving "substantial religious activity and purpose." [70]

The problems were, according to the Court, exacerbated by the form of aid at issue—public subsidies to the teaching processes in those schools. It drew a contrast with the form of aid approved in *Board of Education* v. *Allen*. The books at issue in that case could rather easily be checked for content, a content that did not vary. But, the Court said, a teacher's handling of a subject is not easily ascertainable. "We cannot ignore the danger that a teacher under religious control and discipline poses to the separation of the religious from the secular aspects of *pre-college* education."[71]

(1963), and subsequently applied in *Board of Education* v. *Allen*, 392 U.S. 236, 243 (1968). The entanglement branch, of course, derives from *Walz*.

[68] 403 U.S. at 613.

[69] 403 U.S. at 615.

[70] 403 U.S. at 616.

[71] 403 U.S. at 617. The underscored word hints at the types of distinctions the Court would draw in its *Tilton* decision: Colleges are different from parochial elementary schools. The quoted language is also a denigration of the professionalism of parochial school teachers. Later in its opinion, the Court noted that several Catholic school teachers had testified that they did not inject religion into their secular instruction or otherwise teach religion. 403 U.S. at 618. The Court then observed:

> We need not and we do not assume that the teachers in parochial schools will be guilty of bad faith or any conscious design to evade the limitation imposed by the statute and the First Amendment. We simply recognize that a dedicated

Because of those dangers, the Court foresaw the need for the state to engage in extensive and continuous surveillance of the parochial schools to assure that the subsidized teachers would not engage in forbidden religious instruction. Justice William J. Brennan, in his concurring opinion in *Lemon*, raised the specter of "state inspectors prowling the halls of parochial schools and auditing classroom instruction."[72] For these reasons, the Court held that Pennsylvania and Rhode Island programs flunked the entanglement branch of its new three-part test.[73]

In the *Tilton* case, Pfeffer attempted to portray church-related colleges as in-distinguishable from the parochial schools described in the *Lemon* decision. He did so, not by drawing on the evidence presented in the trial in Hartford, but rather by constructing a "composite profile" of what he called a "typical sectarian" institution of higher education.[74] His "composite profile" was an effort to deflect the Court's attention from the evidentiary record,[75] and the Court refused to be deflected.

The Court began its analysis in *Tilton* by noting some significant differences it perceived between colleges and universities, on the one hand, and elementary schools, on the other. At some length, the Court observed:

> There are generally significant differences between the religious aspects of church-related institutions of higher learning and parochial elementary and

religious person, teaching in a school affiliated with his or her faith and operated to inculcate its tenets, will inevitably experience great difficulty in remaining religiously neutral. Doctrines and faith are not inculcated or advanced by neutrals. With the best of intentions such a teacher would find it hard to make a total separation between secular teaching and religious doctrine. *Idem* at 618-19.

That language does not seem to ameliorate the slur on the professionalism of teachers in Catholic parochial schools.

[72] 403 U.S. at 650.

[73] Justice White accused the majority of creating "an insoluble paradox" in its application of the primary effect and entanglement branches of its new test. 403 U.S. at 668. The primary effect branch requires that any public aid given to church-related schools be limited to secular functions performed by those schools so that the program does not "advance religion." But, if the state seeks to act to assure compliance with such limitations, the message of the *Lemon* decision is that the program will run afoul of the prohibition against excessive entanglement.

[74] 403 U.S. at 682. Among the characteristics that he attributed to his "composite" institution was that such an institution restricted admission based on religion, required attendance at religious activities and compelled adherence to the doctrine of the sponsoring religious denomination.

[75] For example, despite the fact that there were several catalogs from the defendant colleges in the evidentiary record, Pfeffer quoted from a catalog of Wheaton College in Illinois to illustrate how his composite sectarian college would describe its religious purposes.

secondary schools. The 'affirmative if not dominant policy' of the instruction in pre-college church schools is 'to assure future adherents to a particular faith by having control of their total education at an early age.' . . . There is substance to the contention that college students are less impressionable and susceptible to religious indoctrination. . . . The skepticism of the college student is not an inconsiderable barrier to any attempt or tendency to subvert the congressional objectives and limitations. Furthermore, by their very nature, college and postgraduate courses limit the opportunities for sectarian influence by virtue of their own internal disciplines. Many church-related colleges are characterized by a high degree of academic freedom and seek to evoke free and critical responses from their students.[76]

The Court then turned to the evidentiary record in *Tilton* to describe the defendant colleges.

The Court found that those four colleges admitted non-Catholics as students and employed non-Catholics as faculty. None required its students to attend religious services. While the colleges required students to take theology courses, those courses were taught as academic disciplines and not to indoctrinate.[77] In addition, the theology courses covered a range of human religious experiences and were not limited to courses about the Roman Catholic religion. Moreover, the colleges subscribed to a well-established set of academic freedom principles. "In short," the Court said, "the evidence shows institutions with admittedly religious functions but whose predominant higher education mission is to provide their students with a secular education." [78]

The Court dealt summarily with Pfeffer's proposed "composite profile." Perhaps some church-related colleges fit the pattern [of the composite profile] that appellants describe. . . . But appellants do not contend that these four institutions fall within that category. Individual projects can be properly evaluated if and when challenges arise with respect to particular recipients and some evidence is then presented to show that the institution does in fact possess those characteristics. We cannot, however, strike down an Act of Congress on the basis of a hypothetical 'profile.'[79]

---

[76] 403 U.S. at 685-86 (internal citations and footnotes omitted). While Justice White concurred in the result in *Tilton*, he was unimpressed by the distinctions drawn in the language just quoted. "Surely the notion that college students are more mature and resistant to indoctrination is a make-weight . . . . If religious teaching in federally financed buildings was permitted, the powers of resistance of college students would in no way save the federal scheme." 403 U.S. at 668.

[77] The Court noted that required theology courses at two of the colleges were taught by rabbis.

[78] 403 U.S. at 687.

[79] 403 U.S. at 682. The Court did, however, rule that one feature of HEFA was unconstitutional. In the statute, Congress declared that the federal government would have an "interest" in buildings constructed with HEFA grants for a period of 20 years. After that period, the federal interest expired and colleges could use the buildings for any purpose they

Thus, while the four Connecticut Catholic colleges were ruled eligible for HEFA grants, the *Tilton* decision was not a sweeping victory for church-related higher education. The Court had not accepted the trial court's ground for decision—that the secular nature of the federal aid should be controlling and that the religious character of the defendant colleges was constitutionally irrelevant. Rather, it accepted Pfeffer's theory, if not his precise argument, that the religious character of the recipient colleges was the central inquiry. Moreover, the Court left open the possibility that, at some church-related colleges, religion could be so pervasive that grants to them would carry the same Establishment Clause risks as grants to the parochial schools in *Lemon.*

The HEFA grants to the defendant colleges in *Tilton* survived constitutional scrutiny because the evidence showed that their secular educational functions were separable and, in fact, separate from their religious functions. Presumably other church-related colleges with characteristics similar to those of the four Connecticut Catholic colleges would survive constitutional scrutiny in the future. But there remained the possibility of further litigation, depending on which institutions might be targeted by the opponents of public aid programs that benefited church-related higher education.

The Roemer Case

There was another feature of HEFA that could have limited the significance of the *Tilton* decision—the type of aid involved. HEFA grants were "categorical"—that is, grants made for a specific purpose. Recipient institutions used HEFA grants for the construction of academic facilities that would be used for secular educational purposes. The legislative grants challenged in *Horace Mann* were of the same character.[80] By their very character, categorical grants are relatively

---

chose. Because the Court believed the buildings would have a useful life that exceeded 20 years and because the Court feared that a church-related college might convert a building to a religious use after 20 years, it declared that limiting the period of federal interest to 20 years was unconstitutional. Consequently, the federal government would have to monitor the use of such buildings as long as they were occupied and used by the colleges. *Idem* at 682-84. There is nothing in this part of Chief Justice Burger's plurality opinion to indicate whether the Court gave any thought to the "entanglement" implications of that ruling.

[80] In addition, the Supreme Court in 1973 had upheld in the face of an Establishment Clause challenge a South Carolina program that assisted private colleges construct academic facilities through low-interest financing by issuing tax-exempt revenue bonds. *Hunt* v. *McNair,* 413 U.S. 734 (1973). The issuance of revenue bonds for construction of an academic facility at a South Carolina Baptist college prompted the lawsuit. While the method of financing used in *Hunt* differed from that in *Tilton,* the end result of the two programs was the same: public subsidy of the construction of academic facilities at church-related colleges.

easy to monitor to assure that their use is limited to secular purposes. At a church-related college where HEFA buildings could not be used for religious purposes, a simple inspection of only that facility could assure compliance with that requirement. There is no need for government to examine the total operations of the institution. Thus, the potential for excessive government entanglement with religion is reduced.

Would non-categorical—or cash—grants to church-related colleges be treated differently? The Supreme Court would answer that question in a case five years after it decided *Tilton*.

That case was *Roemer* v. *Board of Public Works*.[81] At issue was a Maryland program[82] that gave annual grants to qualified private colleges[83] for each of their students who were Maryland residents in an amount equal to 15 percent of the state's appropriation for each student in the state's college system.[84] Students enrolled in seminarian or theological academic programs were excluded from the computation. The state funds could be used for any purpose the recipients chose, except that the statute prohibited using the funds for "sectarian purposes." [85]

Thus, the Maryland non-categorical aid differed significantly from the categorical grants at issue in *Tilton* and *Horace Mann*. The *Roemer* case differed from *Horace Mann* in two other respects. First, it was filed as a state taxpayer suit in the federal district court in Baltimore, rather than in a state court. Second, Leo Pfeffer did not appear as the lawyer for the federal taxpayer plaintiffs. Lawrence Greenwald, a young lawyer with a Baltimore law firm, represented the plaintiffs.[86]

Three of the colleges named as defendants were familiar. They were the three church-related colleges declared ineligible for public aid in *Horace Mann*:

---

[81] 426 U.S. 736 (1976).

[82] The program is codified at Md. Code, Art. 77A, §§ 65 *et seq.*

[83] To be eligible, a college had to have maintained, prior to July 1, 1970, one or more associate of arts or baccalaureate degree programs, refrained from awarding only seminarian or theological   degrees, and agreed to submit all new programs and major alterations of programs to the Maryland Council for Higher Education for review and recommendations.

[84] The computation formula was an acknowledgement that the private colleges were relieving the state of the significant burden that the state would incur if all state residents enrolled in private colleges in the state had to be educated at state institutions totally at public expense.

[85] The original authorizing legislation had no such restriction. However, in 1972, after the Supreme Court issued its decisions in the *Lemon* and *Tilton* cases, the statute was amended to provide for the prohibition on the use of the state funds for sectarian purposes.

[86] The organizations supporting the litigation on behalf of the plaintiffs were the Maryland affiliates of the American Civil Liberties Union and Americans United for Separation of Church and State.

College of Notre Dame, St. Joseph's and Western Maryland. Two other Maryland Catholic colleges were also named as defendants: Loyola College in Baltimore and Mount Saint Mary's College in Emmitsburg.

Notre Dame, St. Joseph's and Western Maryland retained the same law firms that had represented them in the *Horace Mann* case. Loyola and Mount Saint Mary's retained Edward Bennett Williams's Washington firm, Williams & Connolly. The lawyers from that firm who did the courtroom work for those two colleges were Paul Connolly and the author of this paper. Connolly, a graduate of Loyola who had received his law degree from Georgetown University, handled the evidentiary hearing for his alma mater, and the author did the same for Mount Saint Mary's.

The *Roemer* case was assigned to a three-judge federal court in Baltimore,[87] and the evidentiary hearing took place intermittently over a period of five weeks.[88] After hearing post-trial arguments, the three judges voted 2 to 1 to uphold the Maryland program and the grants to the colleges.[89] The plaintiffs appealed directly to the Supreme Court. The Court, again by the narrow margin of 5 to 4,[90] upheld the Maryland program and the grants to the defendant colleges.

The Court, in its primary effect analysis, described the defendant colleges as substantially similar to the colleges in *Tilton*, but with three significant differences.

First, the Court noted that the three-judge lower court had been unable to conclude whether the theology courses taught at the colleges were taught as academic disciplines. The lower court had said there was a "possibility" that those courses "could be devoted to deepening religious experiences in the particular faith rather than teaching theology as an academic discipline." Consequently, that court had ruled that no state funds received by the defendant colleges could be used to support theology and religion courses. Because of that

---

[87] In the *Tilton* and *DiCenso* cases, all three judges attended the evidentiary hearings. In *Roemer*, because a longer trial was anticipated, the parties agreed to allow a single judge to hear the evidence to avoid consuming unnecessarily the time of all three judges. However, all three judges were present for the post-trial legal arguments in the case.

[88] One week was assigned to each college, and the evidence for each college took from two to three days to present.

[89] *Roemer* v. *Board of Public Works*, 387 F. Supp. 1282 (D. Md. 1974). Because the three colleges that were declared constitutionally ineligible for public fund in *Horace Mann* survived constitutional scrutiny in *Roemer*, the *Horace Mann* decision became little more than a historical anomaly.

[90] Justice Harry A. Blackmun wrote the Court's plurality opinion, which Chief Justice Burger and Justice Lewis F. Powell joined. Justice White, joined by then Justice William H. Rehnquist, concurred to provide the majority. However, Justice White's concurring opinion was a far stronger affirmation of the right of church-related colleges to participate in public aid programs than was Justice Blackmun's plurality opinion.

ruling and because the colleges had not appealed the ruling, the Supreme Court came to no conclusion concerning the theology courses,[91] and the nature of the theology courses had no bearing on the outcome of the case.

Second, the Court noted that the "Church" was represented on the governing boards of the Catholic colleges. For example, the Archbishop of Baltimore was an *ex officio* member of the Mount Saint Mary's Board of Trustees. But the Supreme Court accepted the lower court's finding that "no instance of entry of Church considerations into college decisions was shown." [92]

Third, one or more of the colleges gave preference to members of the sponsoring religious orders in hiring decisions. However, the Court viewed that practice as having an economic, rather than religious, motivation: The religious on the faculties, because of their vows of poverty, were paid less than a full salary.[93] For that reason, the Court gave no significance to that hiring preference.

Despite these departures from the characteristics of the colleges described in the *Tilton* case, the Court ruled that the grants to those institutions did not have the primary effect of advancing religion. The Court made the following observation about how it approached the primary effect analysis in *Roemer*:

> To answer the question whether an institution is so 'pervasively sectarian' that it may receive no direct state aid of any kind, it is necessary to paint a general picture of the institution, composed of many elements. The general picture that the District Court has painted of the appellee institutions is similar in almost all respects to that of the church-affiliated colleges considered in *Tilton*. . . . [and we] find no constitutionally significant distinction between them, at least for purposes of the 'pervasive sectarianism' analysis.[94]

That statement was a clear signal that the Court would not approach the analysis of church-related colleges that benefit from public aid programs with the dogmatic rigidity that is evident in parochial school cases. [95]

---

[91] 426 U.S. at 756 n.20.

[92] 426 U.S. at 755.

[93] 426 U.S. at 757.

[94] 426 U.S. at 758-59.

[95] As noted, the Supreme Court in *Tilton* refused to evaluate the eligibility of the defendant Catholic colleges for HEFA grants based on the hypothetical and composite profile of a pervasively sectarian college constructed by Leo Pfeffer. 403 U.S. at 687. However, two years after it decided the *Lemon* case, the Court in fact adopted a "composite profile" constructed by Pfeffer to describe the essential functions of Catholic parochial schools. According to that "profile," those schools "(a) impose religious restrictions on admissions; (b) require attendance of pupils at religious activities; (c) require obedience by students to the doctrines and dogmas of a particular faith; (d) require pupils to attend instruction in the theology or doctrine of a particular faith; (e) are an integral part of the religious mission of the church sponsoring it; (f) have as a substantial purpose the inculcation of religious values; (g)

Because the challenged Maryland program was non-categorical and because it involved annual grants, the Court found the potential entanglement issues "more difficult" than those in *Tilton*.[96] For example, in *Tilton* the Court seemed to minimize the potential entanglement issue with HEFA grants by labeling them "one-time, single-purpose" grants, a feature that the taxpayer plaintiffs in *Roemer* emphasized in their Supreme Court brief. But Justice Harry M. Blackmun, who wrote the plurality opinion, noted that, in the administration of the HEFA program, the government had to engage in continuous monitoring of HEFA-subsidized academic facilities for their entire useful lives to assure that none was converted to a religious purpose.[97]

At root, the same considerations that led to the no-entanglement ruling in *Tilton* led Justice Blackmun to the same ruling in *Roemer*. There was at the defendant colleges in *Roemer* a clear demarcation between the secular and religious functions, presenting a lesser risk that administration of the program would involve the state with the religious activities of the institutions.[98] While conceding that occasional audits would be required to assure there was no diversion of state funds to religious activities, Justice Blackmun agreed with the lower court that such audits would be "quick and nonjudgmental." [99]

But the most telling statement in Justice Blackmun's opinion was the following: "[I]f the question is whether this case is more like *Lemon* or more like *Tilton*—and surely that is the fundamental question before us—the answer must be that it is more like *Tilton*."[100] With that statement, Justice Blackmun confirmed what had seemed implicit in the Supreme Court's public aid decisions: For purposes of Establishment Clause analysis, there is a wide constitutional gulf between Catholic colleges and Catholic parochial schools.

The *Roemer* case was the last in which the Supreme Court would consider the constitutionality of institutional aid programs that benefited Catholic colleges and universities. Those institutions had been carefully scrutinized in *Tilton* and

---

impose religious restrictions on faculty appointments; and (h) impose religious restrictions on what or how the faculty may teach." *Levitt* v. *Committee for Public Education*, 413 U.S. 472, 476 (1973). That "profile," or elements of it, would be repeated in subsequent cases to describe Catholic parochial schools in cases challenging public aid programs. *See, e.g., Meek* v. *Pittenger*, 421 U.S. 349 (1975). Despite obvious differences in their educational approaches, the Court also draws no distinction between Catholic elementary schools and Catholic secondary schools. *See Zobrest* v. *Catalina Foothills School Dist.*, 509 U.S. 1 (1993).

[96] 426 U.S. at 762.

[97] 426 U.S. at 764.

[98] 426 U.S. at 762.

[99] 426 U.S. at 764.

[100] 426 U.S. at 763-64.

Roemer and, despite the close votes in both cases, they had been found constitutionally indistinguishable from other institutions in the independent sector of American higher education.

The Student Aid Issue

Tilton and *Roemer* had resolved the institutional aid issue in favor of Catholic colleges. In the 1970s, however, at both the federal and state levels, the emphasis in public aid to higher education shifted from institutional aid to student aid. At the time that the *Roemer* decision issued, no court had ruled on whether public aid extended directly to students attending church-related colleges would survive a constitutional challenge.

Presumably, students attending Catholic colleges that were constitutionally eligible for institutional aid could receive student aid without creating a constitutional problem.[101] But what of students attending colleges that would be considered "pervasively sectarian"?[102] That issue would be considered and resolved in two cases involving state student aid programs in Tennessee and Washington.[103]

The challenge to the Tennessee Tuition Grant Program, which provided grants to students in public and private colleges, followed a tangled procedural path. The initial lawsuit was styled *Americans United* v. *Dunn.*[104] The three-judge federal court in that case ruled that some of the 39 private colleges and universities in Tennessee were "pervasively sectarian" institutions. Because the enabling legislation for the tuition grant program did not restrict the use of tuition grants to

---

[101] *See Smith* v. *Board of Governors*, 428 F. Supp. 871 (W.D. N. Carolina), *aff'd summarily*, 434 U.S. 803 (1977). That case was limited to the assistance given to students at only two of the state's church-affiliated colleges, Belmont Abbey College and Pfeiffer College. The constitutional challenge was rejected in large part because the three-judge federal court found that "there appears no material distinction between the Maryland colleges [in *Roemer*] and Belmont Abbey and Pfeiffer College." *Idem* at 878.

[102] There are, of course, such institutions in this country. For example, one college that the author represented in a western state required faculty members to sign and express agreement with a doctrinal statement that reflected the beliefs of the sponsoring denomination. Not surprisingly, 95 percent of the faculty members belonged to that denomination. In addition, students to graduate had to take and pass a doctrinal examination that confirmed their understanding of the belief system of the sponsoring denomination. These and other features, such as compulsory chapel attendance, put that institution closer to the parochial schools described in *Lemon* v. *Kurtzman* than to the Catholic colleges described in *Tilton*.

[103] As was true of the educational benefits available under the G.I. Bill of Rights, the federal programs of grants and loans to college students were never constitutionally challenged.

[104] 384 F. Supp. 714 (M.D. Tenn. 1974).

strictly secular purposes,[105] the three-judge court held the tuition grant program unconstitutional. The state appealed that decision to the Supreme Court,[106] and the Supreme Court agreed to hear the case. However, before the writing of briefs could begin, the Tennessee legislature amended the statute to require that tuition grant funds be confined to secular purposes. Since the omission of such a provision had been the fatal defect found by the three-judge court, the state promptly notified the Supreme Court of that development. The Court vacated as moot its previous order agreeing to hear the appeal and remanded the case to the three-judge court for further proceedings.

The lower court ordered the prompt submission of new briefs to evaluate the effect of the recent legislative amendment on its previous ruling. However, before that court could issue a new ruling, the Tennessee legislature adjourned in the late spring of 1975 without appropriating funds for the Tuition Grant Program for the next fiscal year, meaning there would be no Tuition Grant Program for that year. Apparently for that reason, the three-judge court did not issue a new decision.

While the parties to the lawsuit were awaiting further action by the three-judge court, the Tennessee Council of Private Colleges successfully promoted legislation that repealed the Tuition Grant Program and enacted a new Student Assistance Program. Under the former program, the state each year wrote a check to private colleges enrolling students who qualified for the tuition grants. The checks were in the amount of the total grants (of up to $1,000 per student) for the students at particular colleges. The colleges would then credit the accounts of tuition grant recipients in the appropriate amounts. That process gave the appearance that the colleges were the real beneficiaries of the program. To eliminate that appearance, the new Student Assistance Program required that the tuition grants be paid directly to the students who qualified for them.

When the new program became law, the state filed a motion with the three-judge court, claiming that the repeal of the former Tuition Grant Program had rendered the case moot. The court agreed and dismissed the original complaint. Three weeks later, the original plaintiffs filed a new complaint challenging the constitutionality of the Student Assistance Program. In its new incarnation, the case was styled *Americans United* v. *Blanton*.[107]

---

[105] Because the Supreme Court had invalidated the 20-year limitation on the HEFA grants at issue in *Tilton* (see note 79, *supra*), courts subsequently considered that a statutory provision confining the use of public funds to purely secular uses was essential to the statute's constitutionality. That rule, however, emerged from institutional aid cases, and the *Dunn* court gave no consideration to whether it was equally applicable to student aid cases.

[106] The state was the only defendant in the case. In the second phase of the case, the Tennessee Council of Private Colleges retained counsel, and its lawyer brought a number students who had received tuition grants into the case as intervenors.

[107] 433 F. Supp. 97 (M.D. Tenn. 1977).

The same three-judge court convened to hear the case, and the plaintiffs and defendants remained the same. But there were differences in the new case. The challenged state program was new and different, and students in both public and private schools who qualified for the new tuition grants intervened in the case to protect their interests. In addition, the court was presented with new legal arguments.

The new arguments derived from the fact that the students would now receive their tuition grants directly from the state. Since the principal relationships created by the new program were those between students applying for grants and the state, there would be virtually no basis for the state to become excessively entangled with the colleges they attended, whether those colleges were church-related or not.

Moreover, the primary effect inquiry could also be recast. The state was seeking to advance the educational opportunities available to qualified students and not advance the programs and purposes of particular church-related colleges. It was true that church-related colleges might benefit from the program by enrolling students who, without the tuition grants, might not be able to afford to attend those institutions. But the Supreme Court has consistently refused to stop challenged aid programs because of such incidental effects that might aid religious institutions.[108]

These new arguments would be advanced on behalf of the student intervenors. But first there was an evidentiary hearing, at which the plaintiffs offered evidence concerning three Tennessee colleges they claimed were pervasively sectarian. Each college was represented by its own lawyer. The intervenors objected to the evidence as irrelevant because they, as students, and not the colleges, were the true beneficiaries of the program. The court, however, allowed the evidence.

Following post-trial briefing and argument, the three-judge court that had decided the *Dunn* case issued its decision in the new *Blanton* case. This time it upheld the Tennessee program unanimously, accepting for the most part the arguments offered on behalf of the student intervenors. The plaintiffs appealed to the Supreme Court and, by a 6 to 3 vote, the Court summarily affirmed the decision of the three-judge court.[109] While that summary affirmance had precedential effect and could be cited as the Supreme Court's express approval of

---

[108] "Whatever may be its initial appeal, the proposition that the Establishment Clause prohibits any program that in some manner aids an institution with a religious affiliation has consistently been rejected." *Hunt* v. *McNair*, 413 U.S. 734, 742 (1973).

[109] A challenge to a similar student aid program in Arkansas was in litigation while the Tennessee case was before the three-judge court. A three-judge federal court upheld that program unanimously, but there was no appeal to the Supreme Court. *Lendall* v. *Cook*, 384 F. Supp. 971 (E.D. Ark. 1977).

Tennessee's student aid program, the Court itself did not write an opinion. It would do so nine years later in a case from the State of Washington.

In *Witters* v. *Washington Dept. of Service for the Blind*,[110] the petitioner had been denied educational benefits under a state program to assist visually handicapped persons because he planned to use those benefits to attend a Bible school to prepare himself for a career as a pastor, missionary or youth director. Washington's highest court ruled that use of state funds violated the primary effect branch of the *Lemon* three-part test. The Supreme Court disagreed and reversed.

Like the student aid program upheld in *Blanton*, the challenged educational benefits were paid directly to the person qualifying for them, and that person decided at which institution the benefits would be used. Under those circumstances, the Court unanimously sustained the benefits to Mr. Witters.

> Any aid provided under Washington's program that ultimately flows to religious institutions does so only as a result of the genuinely independent and private choices of aid recipients. Washington's program is 'made available generally without regard to the sectarian-nonsectarian, or public-nonpublic nature of the institution benefited,' and is in no way skewed toward religion.[111]

Thus, the Court made the religious character of educational institutions attended by the beneficiaries of student aid programs constitutionally irrelevant. [112]

Retrospective on the Aid Issue

Litigation on the broad issue of the right of church-related institutions of higher education to benefit from programs of public aid had run its course with the *Witters* ruling, and Catholic colleges and their students had emerged with a

---

[110] 474 U.S. 481 (1986).

[111] 474 U.S. at 488 (internal citation omitted).

[112] The Court subsequently applied the *Witters* reasoning to uphold furnishing under a federal program a sign language interpreter to a deaf student attending a Catholic high school. *Zobrest* v. *Catalina Foothills School Dist.*, 509 U.S. 1 (1993). The federal Individuals with Disabilities Education Act ("IDEA") authorized such aid for students with disabilities attending both public and private schools. The school district initially denied Zobrest the services of an sign language interpreter because it believed placing the interpreter in a Catholic high school would violate the Establishment Clause. Among the interpreter's duties would be to transmit to Zobrest the religious instruction offered at the school. The Supreme Court, however, viewed IDEA as "a general government program that distributes benefits neutrally to any child qualifying as 'handicapped' under [the statute], without regard to the 'sectarian-nonsectarian, or public-nonpublic' nature of the school the child attends." 509 U.S. at 10. The interpreter worked in a Catholic school only because of the private decision made by the student's parents to send him to that school, and the Supreme Court ruled that there was no Establishment Clause barrier to the school district furnishing a student in a Catholic school with a form of assistance authorized by statute.

judicial imprimatur of eligibility. A significant fact was that the litigation had come to an end without the lengthy process of a college-by-college test of eligibility that the *Tilton* decision had presaged. In retrospect, the reason that process did not materialize is easily explained.

Suits challenging the eligibility of church-related institutions and their students for public aid are, for the most part, sponsored by organizations that advocate an Establishment Clause theory of strict separation between church and state. Those organizations include the American Jewish Congress, on behalf of which Leo Pfeffer brought his cases, Americans United for Separation of Church and State, and the American Civil Liberties Union.[113] Those organizations generally sponsor only "impact" cases—that is, cases that will have a major impact on the development of constitutional law issues. They have neither the resources nor the institutional inclination to pursue the type of college-by-college evaluations that the *Tilton* decision seemed to invite. Once the Supreme Court in *Tilton* rejected the notion that colleges fitting Pfeffer's "composite profile" should be constitutionally excluded from public aid programs, those organizations turned to other items on their agendas. Without the backing of such organizations, taxpayers offended by public aid going to particular colleges or universities were unable to pay the significant costs that such litigation involves.

Another remarkable facet of the court battles over the eligibility question was that Catholic colleges had survived without being unfaithful to their perceived missions. There is no question that the *Horace Mann* decision caused concern within the Catholic higher education community. The predicted rapid increase in college enrollments was well underway when that ruling issued, and the ability of Catholic colleges to expand rapidly enough to accommodate additional students depended in large part on their ability to qualify for HEFA grants. The reasoning of the majority opinion in *Horace Mann* was hostile to Catholic colleges and, if adopted by other courts, could have jeopardized their eligibility for HEFA grants.

Nevertheless, although it caused many moments of anxiety, the *Horace Mann* decision prompted very few Catholic colleges to make significant changes in their religious orientations. For example, in her recent study of the changes made in the governance of Catholic colleges in the 1960s, Sister Alice Gallin reports that the process of laicizing governing boards may have been accelerated by concerns over the *Horace Mann* decision, but that the process would have occurred even in the absence of that ruling.[114]

---

[113] For example, the Maryland affiliates of Americans United for Separation of Church and State and of the American Civil Liberties Union sponsored the *Roemer* litigation. In addition, the Tennessee affiliate of Americans United sponsored the challenge to that state's student aid program in *Blanton*.

[114] Alice Gallin, *Independence and a New Partnership in Catholic Higher Education* (Notre Dame: University of Notre Dame Press, 1996), 124-5.

It was certainly true that the four Catholic colleges named as defendants in the *Tilton* case had made no changes of significance in response to *Horace Mann*. Moreover, once they were sued, they could not, as a practical matter, make any significant changes in their operations. Changes made after litigation is initiated in areas that are significant to the case are viewed with suspicion. Consequently, those institutions were frozen in time when the lawsuit was filed, and they were evaluated at the stage of development they had reached simply by then. They were assessed as they were and, as they were, they were found eligible for HEFA grants.

A footnote to the *Roemer* case provides a striking contrast to the Catholic college response to *Horace Mann* case. As noted above, Western Maryland College, the Methodist college that was found ineligible for public funds in *Horace Mann*, was the only Protestant college named as a defendant in the *Roemer* case. That college put on evidence at the trial of the *Roemer* case to demonstrate that it was not a pervasively sectarian institution. When the three-judge district court issued its decision, it ruled that Western Maryland, as well as the four Catholic colleges, was eligible to receive grants under the challenged Maryland program.

However, when the plaintiffs appealed that decision to the Supreme Court, Western Maryland College dropped out of the case. It did so by reaching a settlement with the plaintiffs. The terms of the settlement required the college to divest itself of most of the characteristics that stamped it as a church-related college. For example, it agreed to dilute the power of members of the United Methodist Church on its Board of Trustees and to add two non-Methodists to its Religious Studies Department by a certain date. It also agreed to remove all visible religious symbols from its campus.[115]

There was no formal public announcement of the settlement. So one must necessarily speculate as to why Western Maryland College took that action when it did. But it is fair to suggest that the college was concerned about its prospects on appeal. After all, it had been burned in the *Horace Mann* case when it had been thrown into the same pot as the two Catholic colleges. During the pre-trial phase of *Roemer*, the attorneys for the state and for the various colleges agreed to coordinate their activities as closely as possible so that the defense of the Maryland program would be presented through a united front. But the relationship between the lawyers for the Catholic colleges and the lawyers for Western Maryland always seemed uneasy. The settlement following the favorable trial court ruling no doubt reflected the fear of Western Maryland's lawyers that the defendant Catholic colleges faced a serious risk of losing on appeal and that Western Maryland would share the same fate as those colleges.

---

[115] The plaintiffs graciously allowed the college to store the religious symbols on campus for six months while it found ways to dispose of them.

With the benefit of hindsight, one can now say confidently that Western Maryland indeed would have shared the fate of the Catholic colleges in the appeal of the *Roemer* case. But that fate would have been to survive judicial scrutiny and to remain eligible to receive annual grants under the Maryland program. The settlement also preserved Western Maryland's eligibility for state funds. But, as the price for that settlement, it had to strip itself of all vestiges of its affiliation with the United Methodist Church, an affiliation that had enriched its educational programs and traditions.

II.

Government Burdens on Catholic
Higher Education

The Legal Perspective

Government attempts to interfere with the operations of private colleges and universities go back to the early days of the republic. In the early 19th century, the New Hampshire legislature attempted, in effect, to transform Dartmouth College into a public institution by amending the college's charter to add public members to the institution's board of trustees in sufficient numbers to give them the controlling votes on the board. The college, with Daniel Webster as its advocate, carried its challenge to that legislation to the Supreme Court. In case of *Trustees of Dartmouth College* v. *Woodward*,[116] the Supreme Court ruled that the legislature's action violated the Impairment of Contracts Clause of the Constitution.[117]

The action by the New Hampshire legislature was heavy-handed, and there has been no governmental interference with the independent sector of higher education of that magnitude since. However, in the second half of the 20th century, the number of federal statutes and regulatory actions that impose burdens of varying degrees on independent colleges and universities has grown significantly.

The "burdens" that this paper will consider are those incurred by complying with government laws and regulations. They are not burdens that necessarily accompany benefits that an educational institution accepts from government. Those burdens, such as keeping HEFA buildings free of religious use or complying with the accountability requirements of the authorizing statute, are assumed voluntarily by a college when it decides to accept a HEFA grant. If a college wants to avoid those burdens, it can simply refrain from accepting public financial

---

[116] 17 U.S. (4 Wheat.) 518 (1819).

[117] Article I, Section 10: "No State shall . . . pass any . . . Law impairing the Obligation of Contracts . . . ."

assistance.

Rather, the burdens this paper addresses are those imposed on Catholic colleges and universities because they engage in activities or have the characteristics of an institution that the federal government can legitimately regulate. For example, a Catholic college must comply with the anti-discrimination provisions of Title VII of the Civil Rights Act of 1964 if it has 15 or more employees.[118] That the college does or does not receive federal financial assistance in some form has no bearing on whether such a institution must comply with Title VII.[119]

When anti-discrimination and other regulatory laws are applied to churches and their affiliated institutions, potential constitutional issues arise. For example, if a woman sued a Catholic bishop and alleged that his refusal to ordain women constituted impermissible gender discrimination under Title VII, that claim would raise constitutional issues of the highest magnitude.[120] Title VII claims against Catholic colleges and universities do not raise concerns of that magnitude. But, as we shall see, constitutional objections have been raised, with varying degrees of success, in suits brought against Catholic colleges under Title VII and other similar regulatory statutes. Those objections range from claims that the regulatory statute in question impermissibly entangles government with religion (an Establishment Clause claim), to contentions that the governmental action interferes with an institution's practice of religion (a Free Exercise Clause claim).[121]

As was true in the public aid context, courts tend to distinguish between Catholic colleges and Catholic parochial schools in the regulatory cases. Because the parochial schools are perceived as being pervasively sectarian in their

---

[118] 42 U.S.C. § 2000e(b).

[119] There are limited exceptions to that statement. For example, Title VI of the Civil Rights Act of 1962, 42 U.S.C. § 2000d, prohibits private institutions with federal contracts from discriminating on the basis of race, color or national origin. Participation in a federal financial assistance program, such as HEFA, would bring a Catholic college under Title VI. But Title VI covers actions also covered by Title VII and, therefore, does not add in any significant way to a Catholic college's regulatory burdens. Anti-discrimination claims asserted against Catholic institutions of higher education under federal law are commonly filed under Title VII.

[120] *See, e.g., Serbian Eastern Orthodox Diocese* v. *Milivojevich*, 426 U.S. 686 (1976) (the Religion Clauses of the First Amendment give churches total freedom to determine internal matters, such as governance, discipline and matters of religious faith); *McClure* v. *Salvation Army*, 460 F.2d 553 (5th Cir. 1972) (the determination of who is qualified to be a minister is wholly within the authority of a church, and Title VII may not be used to second-guess the validity of such decisions).

[121] *See, e.g., E.E.O.C.* v. *The Catholic University of America*, 83 F.3d 455 (D.C. Cir. 1996) (adjudicating a nun's claim that denial of tenure in the Canon Law Department was caused by gender discrimination would violate both the Establishment and Free Exercise Clauses).

operation and closely tied to the Church, attempts to regulate them raise serious concerns about excessive government entanglement with religion and interference with their legitimate religious functions. But, because the courts believe that the secular and religious aspects of the operations of Catholic colleges are separable, they are less concerned that government regulations will interfere with or inhibit the religious aspects of their operations.

Two decided cases involving The Catholic University of America have given that institution considerable autonomy to deal with matters relating to its canonical faculties without civil court intrusion. But, because those cases involved the University's canonical faculties, they have very little relevance to other Catholic colleges and universities.

In the most recent of those cases—*E.E.O.C.* v. *The Catholic University of America*[122]—the University denied tenure to Sister Elizabeth McDonough, a member of the Canon Law Faculty. Sister McDonough and the Equal Employment Opportunity Commission sued the University, alleging that the denial of tenure resulted from gender discrimination in violation of Title VII. The court of appeals characterized the case as presenting "a collision between two interests of the highest order: the Government's interest in eradicating discrimination in employment and the constitutional right of a church to manage its own affairs free from government interference."[123] The court's decision dismissing the Title VII claim turned on its understanding of the mission and purposes of the University's canonical faculties.

The court noted, for example, that those faculties are conducted "according to norms and regulations promulgated by the Holy See."[124] The courses offered in the Canon Law Department are designed "to prepare the student for the professional practice of canon law—in diocesan and religious curias and in ecclesiastical tribunals—for the teaching of canon law, and for scientific canonical research."[125] Over a ten-year period, more than 95% of the students in that Department had been ordained priests or members of religious orders.[126] Moreover, the Vatican retained a veto over all tenure decisions in the Department.[127]

---

[122] 83 F.3d 455 (D.C. Cir. 1996).

[123] 83 F.3d at 460.

[124] 83 F.3d at 464.

[125] *Idem.*

[126] *Idem.*

[127] *Idem.* The concurring judge in the court of appeals disagreed with her colleagues that examining the internal proceedings at the University that denied Sister McDonough tenure would necessarily run afoul of the Religion Clauses of the First Amendment. But she agreed with the disposition of the case because of the veto over tenure decisions reserved to the Holy See: Even if the court were to agree that gender discrimination had been the cause of

Based on these and other facts, the court concluded that "the University's ecclesiastical faculties serve as the instruments established by the Catholic Church in the United States for teaching its doctrines and disciplines."[128] Any judicial second-guessing of decisions made by those faculties would violate both the Establishment and Free Exercise Clauses of the First Amendment, the court ruled.

Another of the University's ecclesiastical faculties—the Department of Theology in the School of Religious Studies—was involved in an earlier and more celebrated Catholic University case: the dismissal of Father Charles E. Curran. The University's action followed a decision by the Prefect of the Sacred Congregation for the Doctrine of the Faith that Father Curran was "not eligible or suitable to teach Catholic Theology." Father Curran, a tenured member of the Department of Theology, brought a breach of contract suit in the Superior Court of the District of Columbia to challenge his dismissal.[129] Among the defenses the University asserted was that the First Amendment prohibited adjudication of Father Curran's claims.

The court's ruling against Father Curran was based on contract law, not constitutional law. However, its opinion examined at length, and rested in substantial part on the canonical status of the Department of Theology, the substantial control that the American bishops retained over the University's Board of Trustees, the role of the Archbishop of Washington as the *ex officio* Chancellor of the University, and the authority of the Holy See over the ecclesiastical faculties. Because of the unique status of the canonical faculties, no other Catholic university could defend a breach of contract suit filed by a dismissed tenured faculty member as successfully as Catholic University did in the *Curran* case.[130] Consequently, the general principles that have emerged from the regulatory cases discussed below apply generally to Catholic institutions of higher education in this country, but not to Catholic University's ecclesiastical faculties.

---

the tenure denial within the University, the Holy See could later overrule any grant of tenure. Such a decision of the Holy See would be beyond the jurisdiction of federal courts to review. 83 F.3d at 470-76.

[128] 83 F.3d at 464.

[129] *Curran* v. *The Catholic University of America*, Civil Action No. 1562-87, D.C. Superior Court. The Superior Court's decision upholding the University's action is not published. Father Curran did not appeal that decision.

[130] A lawsuit against Catholic University in the 1970s, filed by two priests who were members of the law faculty, challenged the lower salary scale that the University used for paying priest members of the faculty. *Granfield* v. *The Catholic University of America*, 530 F.2d 1035 (D.C. Cir. 1976). The Court ruled for the University. The significant aspect of the case was that the priest-plaintiffs argued that, as long as the University discriminated against priests in the salaries it paid, the Establishment Clause barred the University from receiving public funds. The court rejected that claim. It ruled that the salary differential was an insufficient basis to render the University ineligible for public funds under the Establishment Clause.

During the last half of this century, federal laws and regulations that affect colleges and universities have sprouted across the landscape of the independent sector of higher education. Those regulatory intrusions include anti-discrimination laws, environmental laws, restrictions on human and animal research, protection for the privacy of student records and workplace safety requirements. This paper will focus on two areas of federal regulation—faculty unions and anti-discrimination laws—that present special problems in the context of Catholic educational institutions. There will also be a brief discussion of the obligation of Catholic colleges to extend official recognition to student organizations.

Faculty Unions

The Supreme Court's 1979 decision in *N.L.R.B.* v. *Catholic Bishop of Chicago*[131] provides an analytical framework for assessing the permissible scope of unionization—and, indeed, regulatory burdens generally[132]—at most church-related institutions. At issue in that case were the efforts by lay faculty members at Catholic secondary schools in the Archdiocese of Chicago and the Diocese of Fort Wayne-South Bend to form unions under the jurisdiction of the National Labor Relations Board ("Board").

The Board had rejected the schools' challenges to its jurisdiction, noting that it had declined jurisdiction over religiously sponsored organizations "only when they are completely religious, not just religiously associated."[133] The Board concluded that the Catholic secondary schools in Chicago and Fort Wayne were not "completely religious." [134]

After elections supervised by the Board in which the lay faculty members voted for union representation, the schools refused to recognize or bargain with the unions. The unions filed unfair labor charges with the Board, and the Board sustained the charges. The United States Court of Appeals for the Seventh Circuit overturned the Board's ruling, holding that extending Board jurisdiction over Catholic secondary schools was prohibited by the Religion Clauses of the First Amendment. The Supreme Court, by a 5 to 4 vote, agreed with the court of appeals' result but disagreed with how it reached that result.

Chief Justice Burger, writing for the majority, acknowledged that Board

---

[131] 440 U.S. 490 (1979).

[132] Many courts apply the *Catholic Bishop* analysis in anti-discrimination cases, e.g., *DeMarco* v. *Holy Cross High School*, 4 F.3d 166, 169 (2d Cir. 1993); *Geary* v. *Visitation of the Blessed Virgin Mary Parish School*, 7 F.3d 324, 326 (3d Cir. 1993). Both of those cases involved claims by Catholic school teachers under the federal Age Discrimination in Employment Act.

[133] *Roman Catholic Archdiocese of Baltimore*, 216 N.L.R.B. 249 (1975).

[134] 440 U.S. at 494.

jurisdiction over Catholic schools had the potential for creating excessive government entanglement with religion. For example, he noted that an unfair labor charge could be met by the claim that the conduct complained of was undertaken for religious reasons. The Board would then have to assess the good faith of the religious school administrator asserting that defense. The Chief Justice also observed: "It is not only the conclusions that may be reached by the Board which may impinge upon rights guaranteed by the Religion Clauses, but also the very process of inquiry leading to findings and conclusions." [135]

The Chief Justice noted another area of concern. Among the mandatory subjects of collective bargain are the "terms and conditions of employment." Because Catholic schools involve substantial religious activities, any dispute over the "terms and conditions of employment" in such schools would inevitably enmesh the Board in religious issues, the Court said. [136]

The potential for constitutional problems was, therefore, very real if the Board were permitted to exercise jurisdiction over the Catholic schools. For that reason, the Chief Justice shifted his focus to an issue not considered by the court of appeals: Did Congress intend that the Board should have jurisdiction over teachers in church-operated schools? He undertook that inquiry under a long-standing Supreme Court doctrine that acts of Congress should, if at all possible, be construed in a manner that would avoid deciding a constitutional question unnecessarily.[137]

The Chief Justice reviewed the legislative history of the enactment of the National Labor Relations Act in 1935 and its subsequent amendments, and he found "no clear expression of an affirmative intention of Congress that teachers in church-operated schools should be covered by the Act."[138] As a result, the Chief Justice wrote, "we decline to construe the Act in a manner that could in turn call upon the Court to resolve difficult and sensitive questions arising out of the First Amendment Religion Clauses."[139] Consequently, the effort to organize the Catholic secondary schools failed.

Thus, the same Catholic schools that had been denied public aid in *Lemon* v. *Kurtzman* and its progeny[140] escaped the burdens of N.L.R.B. jurisprudence. One is left to wonder, however, at the cost of the victory to the institutional

---

[135] 440 U.S. at 502.

[136] 440 U.S. at 502-04.

[137] 440 U.S. at 500.

[138] 440 U.S. at 504.

[139] 440 U.S. at 507. The dissenting opinion, written by Justice Brennan, strongly disagreed, asserting that the majority's statutory construction "is plainly wrong in light of the Act's language, its legislative history, and this Court's precedents." *Idem* at 508.

[140] Eg., *Meek* v. *Pittenger*, 421 U.S. 349 (1975); *Sloan* v. *Lemon*, 413 U.S. 825 (1973); *Committee for Public Education* v. *Nyquist*, 413 U.S. 756 (1973).

integrity of the Catholic Church in this country. After all, the Church, through papal encyclicals, has long supported the moral right of working people to organize into unions and the moral duty of employers to bargain with unions. [141]

The NLRB did not extend its jurisdiction to nonprofit, educational institutions until 1970. Previously, the Board had concluded that bringing such institutions within the coverage of federal labor laws was not necessarily consistent with the intended reach of those laws. However, in a 1970 case involving Cornell University, the Board noted an increased involvement of schools in interstate commerce and reversed its position. From 1970 forward, the Board asserted jurisdiction over nonprofit private schools with gross annual revenues that met the Board's jurisdictional requirements. [142] Until the *Catholic Bishop of Chicago* case, the Board did not distinguish between secular and religiously affiliated schools.

From a review of reported cases, it appears that only one Catholic university escaped NLRB jurisdiction under the application of the *Catholic Bishop of Chicago* reasoning, and it did so under peculiar circumstances. Central University of Bayamon in Puerto Rico, a Dominican-sponsored institution, refused to bargain with a faculty union, and the NLRB petitioned the United States Court of Appeals for the First Circuit for enforcement of its order that the university bargain collectively. [143] A three-judge panel of that court, by a 2 to 1 vote, granted the Board's petition, concluding that the Board's exercise of jurisdiction over the institution raised no constitutional problems. That court, however, granted the university's petition for rehearing *en banc*. That court split 3 to 3 following the rehearing. The effect of that divided vote was that the Board's order was not enforced and the university could continue to refuse to bargain with the union.

The difference between the two factions on the court of appeals was their disagreement over the proper reach of the *Catholic Bishop of Chicago* ruling. The faction that would have refused enforcement of the Board's bargaining order[144] saw no logic in distinguishing as a matter of law between Catholic colleges and high schools, particularly when the college in question manifested many of the religious characteristics of Catholic secondary schools. The other faction[145] simply

---

[141] Eg., Pope Leo XIII, *Rerum Novarum* (1891), which was strongly reaffirmed by Pope John Paul II in *Laborem Excercens* in 1981, just two years after the Supreme Court's decision in the *Catholic Bishop of Chicago* case.

[142] *N.L.R.B.* v. *Catholic Bishop of Chicago*. 440 U.S. at 497.

[143] *Universidad Central de Bayamon* v. *N.L.R.B.*, 793 F.2d 383 (1st Cir. 1985).

[144] The opinion for that faction was written by Supreme Court Justice Stephen Breyer who was then a member of the First Circuit Court of Appeals.

[145] Interestingly, two of the judges who made up this faction--Judges Frank Coffin and Hugh Bownes--had been members of the three-judge court that had held the Rhode Island salary supplement program unconstitutional in *DiCenso* v. *Robinson, supra*.

relied on the distinctions the Supreme Court had drawn between those two levels of Catholic education in the *Lemon* and *Tilton* decisions.

Because of the even division of the judges in that case, the ruling had no precedential influence on the development of the law in the area of NLRB jurisdiction over Catholic colleges. The religious affiliations of Catholic colleges, for the most part, did not bar the NLRB from asserting jurisdiction over them. Thus, a certain rough balance was achieved. Catholic parochial schools were too religious to receive public aid and too religious to be the objects of NLRB regulation. Catholic colleges, on the other hand, were not too religious to receive public aid and not too religious to be required to bargain with faculty unions. But the NLRB's assertion of jurisdiction over colleges and universities raised some novel questions.

For example, in *N.L.R.B.* v. *St. Francis College*,[146] the college made a limited challenge to the certification of a faculty bargaining unit—the exclusion of Franciscan faculty members from the unit. The Franciscans constituted six of the college's seventy-two full-time faculty members. Because the Franciscans had taken vows of poverty and obedience, the Board had ruled in the certification procedure that they did not share a "community of interest" with the lay faculty members. The vow of poverty, according to the Board, did not give the Franciscans the same interest in a level of income that the lay faculty had. The vow of obedience, according to the Board, could create a conflict of loyalties for the Franciscans in the faculty because their Franciscan superiors occupied key administrative positions.[147]

The exclusion of the Franciscans was challenged in the United States Court of Appeals for the Third Circuit, both as inconsistent with federal statutes governing the composition of unions and as a violation of the First Amendment rights of the excluded Franciscans. The constitutional argument was made principally in a brief *amicus curiae* filed on behalf of the College and University Department of the National Catholic Educational Association. That argument was predicated on the Free Exercise Clause of the First Amendment, which prohibits undue governmental burdens on the exercise of religion: Because the Franciscan faculty members were excluded from the bargaining unit solely on the basis of their vows, the most solemn religious commitment one can make, their right to participate in the faculty union had been denied based on that expression of their

---

[146] 562 F.2d 246 (3d Cir. 1977).

[147] Those rulings were based on a previous Board ruling involving Seton Hill College. 562 F.2d at 250-51. Sisters of the Order of the Sisters of Charity of Seton Hill outnumbered lay faculty at the college by 58 to 34, and the Board viewed the Order as "owning" the college. In two subsequent cases involving D'Youville College and Niagara University, the Board had distinguished the Seton Hill ruling and allowed members of the institutions' sponsoring order to be included in the faculty bargaining unit. *Idem* at 251-52.

religious beliefs.

The court of appeals, while acknowledging the constitutional arguments that had been made, asserted that "only basic principles of unit determinations are involved here. Because we find the exclusion of faculty Franciscans from the faculty bargaining unit to be unreasonable and arbitrary, the [Board's] petition [for enforcement] will be denied."[148] Yet, the court applied the same analysis as that contained in the NCEA *amicus* brief to reach its non-constitutional disposition. For example, it noted that "the vow of obedience . . . pertains to religious matters only, and as such is irrelevant to the employer-employee relationship."[149] That same statement would support a Free Exercise Clause claim.[150] The end result of the case, nevertheless, was to overturn the Board's exclusion of the Franciscans from the faculty union.

Perhaps the most significant of the faculty union cases involved a religious affiliated university—Yeshiva—but did not involve a religious freedom issue. The grounds on which the Supreme Court decided the Yeshiva University case[151] caused faculties at colleges and universities across the country to reassess the whole faculty union movement that had taken hold in the early 1970s.

When the incipient union at Yeshiva filed a representation petition with the NLRB, the University opposed the petition on the ground that all of its faculty members were managerial or supervisory personnel and thus not "employees" within the meaning of the National Labor Relations Act ("Act"). The proposed bargaining unit was composed of all full-time faculty members at 10 of Yeshiva's 13 schools,[152] and included assistant deans, department chairmen and senior professors. Excluded were deans and directors of the various schools.

The record developed before the NLRB showed substantial participation of the faculty in University-wide governance and in establishing academic policies. For example, "the faculty at each school effectively determine its curriculum, grading system, admission and matriculation standards, academic calendars, and course schedules."[153] Faculty power at Yeshiva extended beyond strictly academic

---

[148] 562 F.2d at 248.

[149] 562 F.2d at 253.

[150] In the same way that the Supreme Court would do two years later in the *Catholic Bishop of Chicago* decision, the court of appeals chose to avoid the constitutional issue and decide the case based on its "unreasonable and arbitrary" standard. For the Franciscan faculty members, the result was the same.

[151] *N.L.R.B.* v. *Yeshiva University*, 444 U.S. 672 (1980).

[152] Excluded from the bargaining unit were faculty members at the University's medical school, graduate school of medical sciences and Yeshiva High School. Also excluded were faculty members teaching in any of the University's theological programs. 444 U.S. at 674 n.2.

[153] 444 U.S. at 677.

concerns. At each school, faculty made recommendations about faculty hiring, tenure, sabbaticals, promotion and termination, and "the overwhelming majority of faculty recommendations are implemented." [154]

After the faculty union was certified by the NLRB, the University refused to bargain with it. Following an unfair labor practices hearing, the NLRB rejected the notion that the faculty exercised management authority. It viewed the faculty as professional employees entitled to the protection of the Act. Because "faculty participation in collegial decision making is on a collective rather than individual basis," the Board said, "it is exercised in the faculty's own interest rather than 'in the interest of the employer,' and final authority rests with the board of trustees."[155]

The NLRB again ordered the University to bargain with the union and again the University refused. The NLRB then sought enforcement in the United States Court of Appeals for the Second Circuit, and that court refused to order enforcement of the bargaining order.[156] The appeals court had concluded that the faculty were, "in effect, substantially and pervasively operating the enterprise." [157]

The Supreme Court agreed with the court of appeals by a 5 to 4 vote, with Justice Lewis F. Powell writing for the majority. He began by noting that there was "no evidence that Congress has considered whether a university faculty may organize for collective bargaining under the Act."[158] However, Yeshiva had not contested whether universities were covered by the Act or argued that its faculty could not be considered "professionals" under that Act.[159] Rather, the University's challenge to NLRB jurisdiction was its contention that its faculty members functioned as managers and supervisors and, for that reason, were not "employees" within the meaning of the Act.

Justice Powell noted that "the authority structure of a university does not fit neatly within the statutory scheme we are asked to interpret,"[160] and that "professionals, like other employees, may be exempted from coverage" by the Act's exclusion of "supervisors" and "managerial employees."[161] That exemption, he noted, reflects a concern that "an employer is entitled to the undivided loyalty of its representatives." [162]

---

[154] 444 U.S. at 677.

[155] 444 U.S. at 678.

[156] *N.L.R.B.* v. *Yeshiva University*, 582 F.2d 686 (2d Cir. 1978).

[157] 582 F.2d at 698.

[158] 444 U.S. at 679.

[159] 444 U.S. at 681.

[160] 444 U.S. at 680.

[161] 444 U.S. at 681-82.

[162] 444 U.S. at 682.

The controlling factor for the majority was the scope of authority over the University's academic programs that the Yeshiva faculty exercised.

> Their authority in academic matters is absolute. They decide what courses will be offered, when they will be scheduled, and to whom they will be taught. They debate and determine teaching methods, grading policies, and matriculation standards. They effectively decide which students will be admitted, retained, and graduated. On occasion, their views have determined the size of the student body, the tuition to be charged, and the location of a school. When one considers the function of a university, it is difficult to imagine decisions more managerial than these.[163]

Using an industrial analogy, the majority observed that, within each school, "the faculty determines...the product to be produced, the terms upon which it will be offered, and the customers who will be served."[164] Hence, the Court ruled that the NLRB had certified an improper bargaining unit.

The dissenters, led by Justice Brennan, criticized the majority for acknowledging that the authority structure of a university does not fit the industrial model and then ignoring that critical distinction.[165] Justice Brennan posited that

> ...the bureaucratic foundation of most 'mature' universities is characterized by dual authority systems. The primary decisional network is hierarchical in nature: Authority is lodged in the administration, and a formal chain of command runs from a lay governing board down through university officers to individual faculty members and students. At the same time, there exists a parallel professional network, in which formal mechanisms have been created to bring the expertise of the faculty into the decision making process.[166]

According to the dissenters, the majority went astray by refusing to recognize the existence of the "dual authority system" and the fact that a university is managed only by those in the "primary decisional network," of which the faculty is not a part.

One commentator characterized the Yeshiva University decision as a "road-block" to further faculty unionizing activities on college campuses.[167] While it is probable that there are many colleges and universities where the faculty does not exercise the degree of control over academic policies and practices that the Court ascribed to the Yeshiva faculty, the majority opinion did not indicate which of the

---

[163] 444 U.S. at 686.

[164] 444 U.S. at 686.

[165] 444 U.S. at 694.

[166] 444 U.S. at 696-97.

[167] T.H. Wright, "Faculty and the Law Explosion: Assessing the Impact," *Journal of College and University Law* 12 (1985): 363, 373.

elements of faculty control it found decisive. Perhaps only the "dual authority system" described by dissenters, but ignored by the majority, could have given a clear path to faculty unionizing. However, in the face of the majority's reasoning, faculty unions could be successful only if faculty members were willing to surrender substantial involvement in formulating academic policies and practices. In the face of that Hobson's choice, the ardor for faculty unions cooled.

Compliance with Anti-Discrimination Laws

Title VII of the Civil Rights Act of 1964[168] is the centerpiece of the federal government's efforts, begun in the 1960s, to eradicate discrimination in employment. By its terms, Title VII makes it an unlawful employment practice for employers covered by the Act[169] "to fail or refuse to hire or discharge, or otherwise discriminate against any individual with respect to his compensation, terms, conditions, or privileges of employment, because of such individual's race, color, religion, sex, or national origin."[170] Some state and municipal anti-discrimination laws sweep more broadly by also prohibiting, *inter alia*, discrimination based on sexual orientation and personal appearance.[171] A second federal antidiscrimination statute—the Age Discrimination in Employment Act ("ADEA")[172]—has also figured prominently in cases involving church-affiliated educational institutions.

Title VII has two narrow exceptions that relate specifically to church-affiliated educational institutions. The first allows an institution of higher education to hire persons of a particular religion if the institution "is, in whole or in substantial part, owned, supported, controlled, or managed by a particular religion" or if its curriculum "is directed toward the propagation of a particular religion."[173] This paper will refer to that provision as the "religious employer" exemption. It is important to note that the religious employer exemption applies only to employment decisions based on religion. Entities entitled to that exemption are not shielded from charges of, for example, racial or gender discrimination.

A second exemption allows employment decisions to be made on the basis of religion, gender or national origin if those characteristics are "a *bona fide*

---

[168] 78 *U.S. Statutes* 255, 42 U.S.C. § 2000e.

[169] An employer is covered by the Title VII if employs fifteen or more persons. 42 U.S.C. § 2000e(b).

[170] 42 U.S.C. § 2000e-2(a).

[171] For example, see District of Columbia Code § 1-25; Prince George's County (Maryland) Code § 2-186.

[172] 29 U.S.C. §§ 621 *et seq.*

[173] 42 U.S.C. § 2000e-2(e)(2).

occupational qualification reasonably necessary to the normal operation of the business or enterprise."[174] The omission of race as a legitimate basis for invoking the *bona fide* occupational qualification ("BFOQ") exemption reflects a considered judgment by Congress that racial considerations can never be a legitimate basis for making an employment decision.

As was true in the faculty unionizing cases, courts tend to give more latitude to church-affiliated elementary and secondary schools than to church-affiliated colleges in employment discrimination cases. Indeed, courts in elementary and secondary school cases frequently rely on the Supreme Court's decision in the *Catholic Bishop of Chicago* in their analysis.[175]

In *Little* v. *Wuerl*,[176] for example, a Catholic parish school refused to rehire a divorced, non-Catholic teacher after she remarried without pursuing available canonical processes to obtain validation of her second marriage.[177] While there seemed to be a contract law basis for denying Ms. Little's claim of religious discrimination,[178] the court analyzed at length the constitutional problems that inhered in adjudicating her discrimination claim. It concluded that

> the application of Title VII's prohibition against religious discrimination to the Parish's decision not to rehire Little would raise substantial constitutional questions. We further determine that neither Title VII's plain language, nor its legislative history, demonstrates Congress's affirmative intent that Title VII

---

[174] 42 U.S.C. § 2000e-2(e)(1).

[175] Eg., *Little* v. *Wuerl*, 929 F.2d 944, 946-47 (3d Cir. 1991) (Title VII); *Geary* v. *Visitation of the Blessed Virgin Parish School*, 7 F.3d 324, 326 (3d Cir. 1993) (ADEA).

[176] 929 F.2d 944 (3d Cir. 1991).

[177] The teacher's second husband had been baptized a Catholic but was not a practicing Catholic at the time of the marriage. The court noted that "Catholic canon law 'recognizes' marriages performed by other Christian denominations if the parties are free to marry in the eyes of the Catholic Church (*i.e.*, have not been married before). Catholic canon law also allows non-Catholics to seek annulments of their prior marriages from the Catholic Church on the same terms as Catholics." 929 F.2d at 946.

[178] The contract that Ms. Little signed with the parish school contained a "Cardinal's Clause" that reserved to the school the "right to dismiss a teacher for serious public immorality, public scandal, or public rejection of the official teachings, doctrine or laws of the Roman Catholic Church." In addition, the school's *Handbook of Personnel Policies and Practices* made violation of the Cardinal's Clause a basis for "just cause termination" and gave as an example of such a violation "the entry by a teacher into a marriage that is not recognized by the Catholic Church." 929 F.2d at 945-46. Ms. Little had freely entered into her employment contract and had taught at the school for nine years prior to her dismissal. She had obviously breached her contract, and there would seem to be no reason that the school could not fire her for that reason.

apply here. Therefore, we hold that Little has no Title VII claim against the Parish.[179]

The quoted language is, of course, a precise application of the reasoning of the Supreme Court in the *Catholic Bishop of Chicago* case.

Similarly, in *Powell* v. *Stafford*,[180] a federal district court ruled that a theology teacher in a Catholic high school whose contract was not renewed after being on the faculty for 13 years could not maintain an age discrimination suit against the Archdiocese of Denver. After reviewing the nature of Powell's teaching responsibilities and the religious orientation of the school where he taught, the court ruled that "the relationship between Powell and the Archdiocese is so pervasively religious that it is impossible to engage in an age-discrimination inquiry without impermissible offense" to the Religion Clauses of the First Amendment.[181]

For the most part, the courts have not been that solicitous of claims by church-affiliated colleges and universities that they should not be held accountable under Title VII or the ADEA for their employment decisions. A leading case involved an effort by the Equal Employment Opportunity Commission to enforce a subpoena against Mississippi College as part of an investigation into a charge of discrimination brought under Title VII. [182]

Mississippi College is owned and operated by the Mississippi Baptist Convention, and the Convention considers the College to be integral to its Christian mission. At the time of the EEOC litigation, 95 percent of the faculty and 83 percent of the students were Baptists. All students were required to take two Bible study courses and to attend two chapel meetings a week. Because no woman had been ordained as a minister in a Southern Baptist church in the state, the College hired only men to teach Bible courses.

The discrimination complaint was filed by Dr. Patricia Summers, a part-time assistant professor in the Psychology Department. When a full-time vacancy occurred, she applied for that position. The College hired a man to fill the vacancy, and Dr. Summers filed her gender discrimination suit. The College contended that the man who was hired had the more appropriate training in

---

[179] 929 F.2d at 951.

[180] 959 F. Supp. 1343 (D. Colo. 1994).

[181] 859 F. Supp. at 1349. By contrast, another court found no constitutional barrier to an ADEA suit filed by a math teacher in a Catholic high school. *DeMarco* v. *Holy Cross High School*, 4 F.3d 166 (2d Cir. 1993). The critical fact in that case seemed to be that DeMarco taught a secular subject--mathematics. For example, the court noted that cases the school had relied on in arguing that the constitution barred adjudication of DeMarco's ADEA claim were cases brought by clergy against their religious employer. 4 F.3d at 171-72.

[182] *E.E.O.C.* v. *Mississippi College*, 626 F.2d 477 (5th Cir. 1980).

psychology for the vacancy and Dr. Summers did not. But it also conceded that it took into account that the man who was hired was a practicing Baptist, while Dr. Summers was not.

The EEOC, as part of its investigation into Dr. Summers's claim, issued a subpoena to the College for extensive documentation of its hiring and promotional policies and practices over a two-year period. When the College refused to comply with the subpoena, the EEOC brought an enforcement action in federal district court. That court agreed with the College that permitting the EEOC to pursue its investigation would violate the Religion Clauses of the First Amendment, and that court refused to order compliance with the subpoena. The EEOC then appealed to the United States Court of Appeals for the Fifth Circuit. The College argued on appeal that it should be exempt from Title VII compliance.

First, it contended that it was entitled to the "religious employer" exemption. The court of appeals, relying on one of its previous decisions,[183] noted that organizations qualifying for that exemption were free from Title VII scrutiny of only those employment decisions based on religion. Since Dr. Summers's claim was based on gender discrimination, the College could not invoke the "religious organization" exemption in this case,[184] even if it qualified for that exemption.

Second, the College argued more broadly that the employment relationship between a religious educational institution and its faculty should be totally exempt from Title VII obligations. It relied on the Fifth Circuit's previous decision in *McClure* v. *Salvation Army*[185] to support that argument. The court of appeals rejected that argument, noting that it had restricted the application of that ruling to church-minister relationships.[186] "The College is not a church," the court said. "The College's faculty and staff do not function as ministers. . . . The employment relationship between Mississippi College and its faculty and staff is one intended

---

[183] *McClure* v. *Salvation Army*, 460 F.2d 553 (5th Cir. 1972).

[184] The court of appeals did note that the exemption prevented the EEOC from looking behind a claim of religious preference by an entity entitled to the exemption to determine whether the claim of religious preference was a mere pretext for employment practices based on racial or gender discrimination. 626 F.2d at 484-85.

[185] 460 F.2d 533 (5th Cir. 1972).

[186] 626 F.2d at 485. Other courts have characterized the ruling in *McClure* as establishing a "ministerial exemption" for churches from civil court adjudication of disputes with their ministers. *See, e.g., Minker* v. *Baltimore Ann. Conf. of United Methodist Church,* 894 F.2d 1354 (D.C. Cir. 1990); *Rayburn* v. *General Conf. of 7th Day Adventists,* 772 F.2d 1164 (4th Cir. 1985). The ministerial exemption is part of a broader doctrine of religious autonomy that insulates churches from civil court adjudication of issues relating to the doctrine and faith and internal governance and discipline of those churches. *See, e.g., Serbian Eastern Orthodox Diocese* v. *Milivojevich,* 426 U.S. 696 (1976); *see generally* D. Laycock, "Toward a General Theory of the Religion Clauses: The Case of Church Labor Relations and the Right to Church Autonomy," 81 COLUM. L. REV. 1373 (1981).

by Congress to be regulated by Title VII." [187]

Finally, the College argued that the district court had been correct in ruling that applying Title VII to its employment practices would violate the Religion Clauses of the First Amendment. The court of appeals disagreed, even though it conceded that "the College is a pervasively sectarian institution." It noted that "no religious tenets advocated by the College or the Mississippi Baptist Convention involve discrimination on the basis of race or sex." After a careful analysis, the court of appeals ruled that "the minimum burden imposed upon its religious practices by the application of Title VII and the limited nature of the resulting relationship between the federal government and the College" did not offend the Religion Clauses of the First Amendment. [188]

The Fifth Circuit Court of Appeals revisited the issue of potential constitutional limits on Title VII a year later in a case involving the Southwestern Baptist Theological Seminary.[189] In that case, the EEOC sued the Seminary to compel its compliance with the reporting requirements of Title VII.[190] The district court believed that applying Title VII requirements to any part of the Seminary's relationship with any of its employees would violate the Religion Clauses of the First Amendment, and it refused to compel the Seminary to comply with Title VII reporting requirements. The court of appeals did not fully agree.

The court of appeals considered its *McClure* decision to be the controlling authority. It had no trouble concluding that the Seminary satisfied the first requisite for applying *McClure*'s ministerial exemption, namely that it be considered a "church": "Since the Seminary is principally supported and wholly controlled by the [Southern Baptist] Convention for the avowed purpose of training ministers to serve the Baptist denomination, it too is entitled to the status of a 'church.'"[191]

However, whether all the employees of the Seminary could be considered "ministers" within the *McClure* test was "a more difficult question." The court noted that the Seminary's employees fell into three categories: faculty, administrative staff, and support staff. It readily conferred ministerial status on the faculty whom it characterized as "intermediaries between the Convention and the future ministers of many local Baptist churches."[192] It also readily concluded that the support staff did not have ministerial status, even though some were ordained, because "the tasks they perform...are not of an ecclesiastical or religious

---

[187] 626 F.2d at 485.

[188] 626 F.2d at 487-89.

[189] *E.E.O.C.* v. *Southwestern Baptist Theological Seminary*, 651 F.2d 277 (5th Cir. 1981).

[190] 42 U.S.C. § 2000e-8(c), and 29 C.F.R. § 1602.50 (1980).

[191] 651 F.2d at 283.

[192] 651 F.2d at 283.

nature."[193] Finally, the court divided the administrative staff. Those administrators, such as the president, executive vice president, chaplain and deans, who had ministerial roles or who supervised the faculty were given the ministerial exemption. But those whose functions related to finance, maintenance and other non-academic matters were denied the exemption.[194] Thus, the court ruled that members of the support staff and designated members of the administrative staff could be subjected to Title VII jurisdiction.

If a Baptist college characterized as "pervasively sectarian" could not escape Title VII oversight, one would expect that Catholic colleges would not be successful in defeating Title VII claims because of their church affiliation. For the most part, court decisions support that expectation.

For example, in *Soriano* v. *Xavier University Corp.*,[195] the federal court ruled that there was no First Amendment prohibition against an employee bringing an age discrimination suit against Xavier University of Ohio. The United States Court of Appeals for the Fourth Circuit reached the same conclusion in a Title VII and ADEA suit against Mount Saint Mary's College,[196] one of the Maryland Catholic colleges that survived the Establishment Clause challenge to its eligibility for public aid in *Roemer* v. *Board of Public Works*.

However, two cases decided a year apart by the United States Court of Appeals for the Seventh Circuit gave two Jesuit universities, Loyola University of Chicago and Marquette University, some freedom for using religious considerations in hiring. In the first of those cases, *Pime* v. *Loyola University*,[197] that court allowed Loyola the BFOQ exemption in filling three vacancies in its Philosophy Department.

Loyola had 31 tenure-track positions in its Philosophy Department and, until the 1978-1979 academic year, seven of those positions had been held by Jesuits. In the fall of 1978, one of the Jesuits had resigned and two others intended to retire at the end of that academic year. At a departmental meeting in October 1978, the chairman identified two needs that would have to be met in filling those vacancies. The first was maintaining a sufficient Jesuit "presence" in the department. The second was to replace the subject matter expertise that would be lost by the departures. For those reasons, the department established as its goal hiring three young Jesuits with the necessary subject matter expertise to fill the vacancies.

Pime, a Jewish doctoral student who had been a part-time lecturer in the

---

[193] 651 F.2d at 284.

[194] 651 F.2d at 284-85.

[195] 687 F. Supp. 1188 (S.D. Ohio 1988).

[196] *Ritter* v. *Mount Saint Mary's College*, 814 F.2d 986, 988 n.1 (4th Cir. 1987).

[197] 803 F.2d 351 (7th Cir. 1986).

department since 1976, expected to receive his Ph.D. in June 1979. When he asked whether he would be considered for one of the vacancies, he was told that the decision to fill the vacancies with Jesuits would foreclose such consideration. As a result, he filed a Title VII suit alleging religious discrimination. While the court of appeals found "no hint of invidious action against Pime on account of his religion," it assumed that, "because Pime's faith would prevent him from being a Jesuit, he has a claim of discrimination on account of his religion." [198]

In considering Loyola's BFOQ defense, the court identified the BFOQ in the case as "membership in a religious order of a particular faith." The court also found that "[t]here is evidence of the relationship of the [Jesuit] order to Loyola, and that Jesuit 'presence' is important to the successful operation of the university."[199]

The court did note that two requisites for allowing a BFOQ exemption seemed to be absent from the case. First, there had been no showing that, applying objective criteria, Jesuit training gave a person superior academic qualifications to teach particular courses. Second, in other BFOQ cases, courts considered only the qualifications for a particular job at issue and not a pre-determined quota. Nevertheless, the court allowed Loyola the BFOQ exemption for the three vacancies. "[I]t seems to us," the court said, "that here the evidence supports the more general proposition that having a Jesuit presence in the Philosophy faculty is 'reasonably necessary to the normal operation of the enterprise,' and that fixing the number at seven out of 31 is a reasonable determination." [200]

In a concurring opinion, Judge Richard A. Posner, now the Chief Judge of the Seventh Circuit Court of Appeals, agreed with the result, but on a narrower ground. He disagreed that Pime had been refused a tenure-track position because he was Jewish. While acknowledging that Pime's religion prevented him from being a Jesuit, he noted that "only a tiny percentage of Catholics are Jesuits." Catholics who were not Jesuits were also precluded from the vacancies in the Philosophy Department because of the preference for Jesuits. "[I]t would be odd indeed to accuse Loyola of discriminating against Catholics because it wanted to reserve some positions in its philosophy department for Jesuits, thus excluding most Catholics from consideration."[201] For Judge Posner, therefore, Pime was denied a tenure-track position not because he was Jewish but because he was not a Jesuit, which is also true of many Catholics.

Judge Posner's rationale seems more compelling than that of his two colleagues. Loyola had not stated it was reserving the vacancies for Jesuits

---

[198] 803 F.2d at 353.

[199] 803 F.2d at 354.

[200] 803 F.2d at 354.

[201] 803 F.2d at 354.

because it believed they had better academic training or credentials to fill the vacancies. After all, the emphasis in the BFOQ exemption is on *qualifications.*

The second Seventh Circuit case was *Maguire* v. *Marquette University,*[202] Dr. Maguire had a Ph.D. in Religious Studies from The Catholic University of America, and she had applied for and several times had been denied an associate professorship in Marquette's Theology Department. She claimed she was denied the position solely because she was a woman and sued on a claim of gender discrimination under Title VII.

The court examined at length Marquette's relationship to the Society of Jesus and the importance to the University of a Jesuit presence in its Department of Theology. "The Jesuit perspective permeates the course offerings in theology," the court observed and then quoted from an affidavit submitted by the Jesuit chairman of that department:

> [T]here is a legitimate presumption that the value system of the Roman Catholic tradition permeates the entire offering of the Department of Theology and all students are given an opportunity to deepen their understanding of this tradition as it is perceived and presented by the Society of Jesus.[203]

The court also noted that the University had reserved the right to give preference to Jesuits in its hiring practices, a preference that was most strongly felt by the Department of Theology, where half of the members were Jesuits and only one was a woman.

The trial court had dismissed Dr. Maguire's claim because it believed that Marquette fell within the "religious employer" exemption of Title VII. The court of appeals decided that it did not have to reach that difficult analytical question because it ruled that Dr. Maguire "has simply failed to make out a valid claim of sex discrimination under Title VII." [204]

The court of appeals noted that the University's primary defense was that Dr. Maguire's credentials were not competitive with those of other applications. But the University also contended that, even if her credentials were considered competitive, she would not have been hired because her publicly stated views on abortion were at war with Roman Catholic teachings on that sensitive subject. The court noted, for example, that four Jesuit faculty members had written letters to the chairman of the Department of Theology recommending that Dr. Maguire not be hired specifically because of her position on the abortion question.[205] Dr. Maguire had placed those letters into evidence.

---

[202] 814 F.2d 1213 (7th Cir. 1987).

[203] 814 F.2d at 1215.

[204] 814 F.2d at 1216.

[205] 814 F.2d at 1217.

Thus, the court noted, "by the plaintiff's own admission and proof ...her sex was not the motivating or substantial factor behind the employment decision.... Given the plaintiff's controversial beliefs regarding abortion, Marquette would have reached the same decision even if she were a man."[206] For that reason, Dr. Maguire's gender discrimination claim under Title VII failed as a matter of law.

That one court of appeals would render two such favorable decisions to Jesuit universities within a year seems fortuitous. Perhaps the judges of that court had some unstated affinity for Jesuit universities when those two cases were decided. There are no reported cases that have used the Loyola and Marquette decisions as building blocks to develop a more benign approach to Title VII claims against Catholic colleges. This paper will suggest below how those two decisions might be used to allow Catholic colleges flexibility in using religious preferences in hiring.

For the most part, however, the upshot of the anti-discrimination litigation of the 1970s and 1980s was to leave Catholic colleges and universities virtually indistinguishable from their secular counterparts in the independent sector of higher education in terms of compliance with Title VII and other federal non-discrimination laws. That result should not have been surprising, given the general portrait the Supreme Court drew of Catholic colleges in the *Tilton* and *Roemer* decisions. Indeed, if Mississippi College was unable to avoid Title VII compliance despite being labeled a "pervasively sectarian" institution, it would have been too much to expect that Catholic colleges could escape general federal oversight under Title VII and like laws.

No court has allowed a Catholic college or university to claim the "religious employer" exemption under Title VII. Loyola University had invoked that exemption in the *Pime* case, and Judge Posner examined in his concurring opinion whether that institution might qualify for that exemption. He believed that Loyola would have fit into the exemption at its founding, since it was then "owned" by the Society of Jesus. However, at the time of the *Pime* litigation, it was incorporated "not as a religious corporation but as an ordinary nonprofit corporation, and financial contributions from the Jesuit order provide only one-third of one percent of the university's income."[207] Those facts related to one part of the conditions for the "religious employer" exemption: that the entity claiming the exemption be "in whole or substantial part, owned, supported, controlled or managed by a particular religious corporation, association or society." [208]

Judge Posner then examined the facts related to a second condition for the exemption: whether Loyola's curriculum "is directed toward the propagation of a

---

[206] 814 F.2d at 1218 (internal citation and quotation marks omitted).

[207] 803 F.2d at 357.

[208] 42 U.S.C. § 2000e-2(e)(2).

particular religion."[209] He noted that, while the University required all students to take three courses in theology, none of those courses had to be in Catholic theology. He also stressed that the University did not operate a seminary and that it offered its students a full range of secular courses. As a result, he concluded that Loyola was "no longer a religious or sectarian school in the narrow sense"[210] and that it did not qualify for Title VII's "religious employer" exemption. Judge Posner's reasoning would put the "religious employer" exemption of Title VII off-limits to Catholic colleges generally.

But the question remains: Is there anything in the Loyola and Marquette decisions that might offer Catholic colleges some latitude under the anti-discrimination laws to use their Catholicity affirmatively in the hiring process?[211] How, for example, would the admonition in the Apostolic Constitution, *Ex Code Ecclesiae*, that non-Catholics should not constitute a majority of the faculty at Catholic colleges[212] fare in the courts if it were implemented by a Catholic college and challenged by a non-Catholic who was denied a faculty position for which he was qualified?

In the *Maguire* case, the court of appeals noted that the Theology Department at Marquette had a preference for hiring Jesuits because they would present the value system of the Roman Catholic tradition "as it is perceived and presented by the Society of Jesus."[213] While Dr. Maguire was not denied a position on Marquette's theology faculty because of that Jesuit preference,[214] the

---

[209] 42 U.S.C. § 2000e-2(e)(2).

[210] 803 F.2d at 351.

[211] I emphasize the "hiring" process because it is a virtual certainty that the courts would not tolerate firing existing non-Catholic faculty members solely to achieve a majority Catholic faculty. The very fact that non-Catholics hold faculty positions at a Catholic college establishes that they are qualified to hold such positions. Terminating would be solely on religious grounds. The language used by the court in the *Pime* case is instructive: "There is no hint of invidious action against Pime on account of his religion." 803 F.2d at 353. I suggest that firing existing non-Catholic faculty members to achieve a Catholic majority would be viewed by a court as "invidious action . . . on account of . . . religion."

[212] "In order not to endanger the Catholic identity of the university or institute of higher studies, the number of non-Catholic teachers should not be allowed to constitute a majority within the institution, which is and must remain Catholic." John Paul II, *Ex corde ecclesiae*, General Norms, Art. 4, § 4.

[213] 814 F.2d at 1215.

[214] As noted above, Marquette had rejected Dr. Maguire's applications because of her unacceptable position on abortion. That explanation for the university's action was not based on the classifications prohibited by Title VII: race, gender, religion and national origin. Any applicant, Catholic or not, can be rejected for the same reason that Dr. Maguire was rejected without violating anti-discrimination laws. Consequently, Catholic colleges can implement another provision of *Ex corde ecclesiae* without fear of adverse legal consequences. That provision states: "Those university teachers and administrators who belong to other churches,

court's suggestion that such a preference was legitimate and the analysis in the *Pime* case indicate that Catholic colleges have some flexibility to use religious considerations in hiring. The preference suggestion in *Maguire* would permit Catholic colleges, for example, to hire otherwise qualified practicing Catholics to teach Catholic theology courses on the premise that those who have experienced the Church's traditions and liturgy are better qualified to teach such courses. Indeed, Judge Posner, in his concurring opinion in *Pime*, suggested that Loyola University could reserve a slot for a rabbi to teach Jewish theology without offending Title VII.

The BFOQ reasoning of the majority in *Pime* and the reasoning employed by Judge Posner in his concurring opinion offer grounds for extending the use of religious considerations in hiring beyond the theology department. Clearly, for example, a Catholic college would fall within the BFOQ exemption by insisting it will hire only an ordained Catholic priest to be its director of campus ministry and to staff that office principally with priests, sisters and Catholic lay persons.

As noted above, the majority in *Pime* appeared to stretch the concept of a bona fide occupational qualification to a breaking point in applying it to the seven tenured slots in Loyola's philosophy department. The majority seemed to acknowledge as much by stressing that reserving only seven out of thirty-one slots in that department seemed reasonable. However, if a college can demonstrate that the members of a particular religious order, by virtue of their particular training and experience, are better qualified to teach in a particular area, the BFOQ exemption could legitimately apply to such hiring decisions. For example, a college might decide to emphasize Thomistic or Scholastic philosophy and consider Jesuits the best qualified to teach such courses. Or another institution may decide that members of the School Sisters of Notre Dame have an important perspective to convey in a department of education.

This sort of preference rationale is, of course, not open-ended. There are a limited number of subject areas or academic disciplines that have legitimate "Catholic" perspectives. Nevertheless, where such a perspective legitimately exists, Catholic colleges can, if they choose, use religious considerations in making hiring decisions.

Moreover, Judge Posner's reasoning in *Pime*—preferring Jesuits for positions at a Jesuit institution is not "religious" discrimination since many Catholics are not Jesuits—offers other opportunities. For example, most Jesuit colleges and universities require that their presidents be a Jesuit, and prefer to fill other key academic and administrative positions with Jesuits. Judge Posner's reasoning would insulate such preferences from Title VII attack. By extension,

---

ecclesial communities, or religions as well as those who profess no religious belief, and also students, are to recognize and respect the distinctive Catholic identity of the university." General Norms, Art. 4, § 4.

other Catholic colleges and universities that identify with the traditions of their sponsoring religious orders can have hiring preferences for members of the order, as long as the importance of the order's traditions to the institutions' operations is clearly articulated.

Another reason—economic—can justify hiring preferences for members of religious orders. The Supreme Court in the *Roemer* case was not troubled by hiring preferences at two colleges for religious because, through the device of "contributed services," such preferences were economically beneficial to the institutions. A preference that is economically motivated, by definition, does not constitute religious discrimination.

It should be apparent, however, that these various rationales for hiring Catholics and members of religious orders will not, in combination, produce a majority Catholic faculty. There are simply not enough qualified members of sponsoring religious orders to fill a majority of faculty positions at the typical Catholic college. Consequently, under current civil law, it is not possible to construct a majority Catholic faculty at a Catholic college without risking serious Title VII problems. But those various rationales, if accepted by other courts, would permit many Catholic colleges to maintain a sufficient Catholic presence in its faculty and administration to make them distinctive within the independent sector of higher education in this country. [215]

The Status of Student Organizations

The obligation of Catholic colleges to grant official status to student organizations became the subject of civil court adjudication in the 1980s. Two gay student organizations[216] sued Georgetown University after it refused to grant them "official recognition," a status routinely granted to other student organizations. Georgetown denied that status to the gay student groups because they advocated and promoted the gay "lifestyle" as a legitimate alternative to committed heterosexual marriage, an advocacy position on an important moral issue conflicting with Catholic teachings.

Both organizations brought suit against Georgetown in the District of

---

[215] A word of caution is necessary. The *Maguire* and *Pime* cases were decided by the United States Court of Appeals for the Seventh Circuit, one of 13 federal circuits. A decision by one federal circuit court of appeals has no binding effect on other circuits. A decision in one circuit can be used for its persuasive effect in a case in another circuit. However, the *Mississippi College* and *Southwestern Baptist Seminary* cases were decided by the United States Court of Appeals for the Fifth Circuit, and those decisions seem to be less hospitable to church-related colleges seeking to avoid a less rigid application of Title VII.

[216] The organizations were the Gay Rights Coalition at the University's Law Center and the Gay People of Georgetown, an undergraduate organization at the University's main campus.

Columbia Superior Court,[217] alleging that the University's denial of official recognition constituted impermissible sexual orientation discrimination in violation of the District of Columbia's Human Rights Act.[218] The University denied that it violated the Act because it based its decision on the ideas the organizations advocated rather than on sexual orientation of the groups' members.[219] In the alternative, Georgetown argued that if its actions were considered to be in violation of the Act, those actions were protected by the Free Exercise Clause of the First Amendment.

The evidentiary hearing in the case lasted more than one week. The witnesses who testified at the trial included Georgetown's President, Rev. Timothy S. Healy, S.J., the various University administrators involved in the decision to deny the organizations official recognition, and members of the two organizations. Both sides offered expert testimony by Catholic moral theologians. The expert witness for Georgetown was Rev. Richard J. McCormick, S.J., perhaps the preeminent moral theologian in the United States. The gay organizations presented Professor Daniel Maguire of Marquette University as their expert.[220] The trial judge eventually[221] ruled that the "recognition" the gay groups sought would amount to the University's endorsement of the position those groups

---

[217] *Gay Rights Coalition* v. *Georgetown University*, reported at 536 A.2d 1 (D.C. App. 1987). The case became known in the Washington media as the "Georgetown Gay Rights" case.

[218] D.C. Code § 1-25.

[219] Unlike public universities that are subject to the restraints of the Free Speech Clause of the First Amendment, private educational institutions can, if they choose, discriminate against student organizations on the basis of the ideas or viewpoints they express. In his testimony at the trial of the Georgetown gay rights case, the University's then president, Rev. Timothy S. Healy, S. J., explained that the main campus gay group would have been denied official recognition even if its organizers had been married heterosexuals. By contrast, he also testified, he would have had no difficulty extending official recognition to an organization, such as the Georgetown University Chess Club, even if were organized by and all its members were homosexuals. His concern, consequently, was with the ideas espoused by an organization and not the sexual orientation of its members.

[220] Professor Maguire, a former priest, was the husband of Dr. Marjorie Reilly Maguire, the theologian who filed the Title VII suit against Marquette when it refused to hire her because of her views on abortion. Her husband's testimony at the Georgetown trial was also outside of mainstream Catholic teachings. He testified, for example, that there were three authentic teaching offices in the Catholic Church--the Ordinary Magisterium, the magisterium of the theologians, and the magisterium of the people. All three bodies, Dr. Maguire asserted, had equal standing within the Church.

[221] Many months elapsed between the trial and the issuance of the opinion by the trial judge. In fact, the trial judge issued her ruling only after lawyers for the gay organizations filed a *mandamus* petition with the District of Columbia Court of Appeals, asking that court to order the trial judge to issue a ruling.

took on the moral legitimacy of the homosexual lifestyle, a position contrary to Roman Catholic teachings. For that reason, the trial court agreed that Georgetown's refusal to grant official recognition to the gay organizations was protected by the Free Exercise Clause.

On appeal, the District of Columbia Court of Appeals, through a three-judge panel, initially voted 2 to 1 to reverse the trial court. However, the full court, consisting of seven judges, agreed to rehear the appeal *en banc*. After further briefing and argument, the full court issued a dispositive ruling. All seven judges wrote opinions that totaled 78 printed pages.[222] By a 4 to 3 vote, the court reached what can be described only as a compromise result.

First, the majority accepted Georgetown's contention, and the trial court's finding, that "official recognition" of the student gay groups would amount to endorsing their views on the appropriateness of homosexual conduct.[223] The majority ruled that "[t]he Human Rights Act does not require one private actor to 'endorse' another. Georgetown's denial of 'University Recognition' to the student groups did not violate the statute."[224] Relying on the *Catholic Bishop of Chicago* case and other authorities, the majority noted that a statute "should be read, if it can be, so as to avoid difficult and sensitive constitutional questions."[225] Adhering to that principle of statutory construction, the majority observed that "[t]o read into the Human Rights Act a requirement that one private actor must 'endorse' another would render the statute unconstitutional." [226]

The majority noted, however, that the Human Rights Act did require that educational institutions make certain tangible benefits, including access to facilities and services, available to all students without discrimination. Pointing to some University correspondence that the court believed reflected a discriminatory animus against gay students,[227] the majority ruled that Georgetown had violated the Human Rights Act by not extending to the student gay groups the same tangible benefits enjoyed by other student groups that did not qualify for "official

---

[222] *Gay Rights Coalition* v. *Georgetown University*, 536 A.2d 1 (1987). The case attracted considerable attention in the local media and among groups supporting gay and lesbian rights. A total of nine *amicus curiae* briefs were filed, and six supported the gay student organizations. Among those supporting the student groups in the various *amicus* briefs were the Women's Legal Defense Fund, the Center for Constitutional Rights, the National Women's Political Caucus, the Lambda Legal Defense & Educational Fund, the American Civil Liberties Union, the District of Columbia Bar, the Wisconsin Governor's Council on Lesbian and Gay Issues, and the City of Seattle, Washington.

[223] 536 A.2d at 17-19.

[224] 536 A.2d at 21.

[225] 536 AS.2d at 16.

[226] 536 A.2d at 21.

[227] 536 A.2d at 28-29.

recognition." [228]

The significance of the *en banc* decision was the court's ruling on the endorsement issue. The majority of the court accepted that the proposition that forcing Georgetown to recognize officially, and thereby endorse, the student gay groups would force the University to compromise its deeply held religious convictions and thereby violate the Free Exercise Clause of the First Amendment. But there was also a suggestion that such a forced endorsement might, more broadly, violate the Free Speech Clause of the First Amendment by forcing Georgetown "to embrace a repugnant philosophy." [229]

The Supreme Court subsequently adopted that latter theory in a case that bore a resemblance to the Georgetown gay rights case. In *Hurley* v. *Irish-American Gay Group*,[230] a group of gay, lesbian and bisexual descendants of Irish immigrants sought permission from the organizers of Boston's St. Patrick's Day parade to march in the parade to express their pride in their Irish heritage as openly gay, lesbian and bisexual individuals. The South Boston Allied War Veterans Council, which was authorized by the city to organize and conduct the parade, refused the group permission to participate. The group then sued under a Massachusetts anti-discrimination law, claiming sexual orientation discrimination. The Supreme Court unanimously rejected that claim.

The parade organizers, in the state courts, had justified the exclusion of the gay group on First Amendment grounds. The state courts, however, ruled that a parade did not have any expressive content and, therefore, no First Amendment

---

[228] That ruling is one of the more puzzling aspects of the appellate court's ruling. Throughout the prolonged litigation, the student gay groups made it clear that their sole purpose in suing was to obtain "official recognition" and nothing less. For that reason, the parties did not develop a record on what tangible benefits were available to students groups that failed to achieve official recognition and which of those benefits, if any, had been denied the student gay groups. The appellate court attributed the opaqueness of the record on that and other issues to an "all or nothing" litigation strategy adopted by both sides. *See, e.g.,* 536 A.2d at 31. But some recorded facts did exist on the tangible benefits issue, For example, Georgetown evidence showed that the main campus student gay group had a campus post office box in its own name, a desk and telephone in a student activities, and use of University facilities to hold meetings and other group-sponsored events. However, the University's arguments on appeal did not emphasize those aspects of the record because the *only* issue the students wanted to have adjudicated was the denial of official recognition. The only appropriate course for an appellate court to follow after ruling that the denial of tangible benefits for discriminatory reasons would violate the statute would have been to remand the case for further trial court proceedings. That the court of appeals did not follow that procedure suggests four of its judges believed the student groups should prevail on some point. That compromised but unjustified ruling was expensive for Georgetown. Because that ruling put the University in violation of the Human Rights Act, it was forced to pay substantial attorney fees to the lawyers for the student gay groups.

[229] 536 A.2d at 22-26.

[230] 115 S.Ct. 2338 (1995).

protection. The Supreme Court quickly disposed of that spurious contention. Real parades, the Court observed,

> ...are public dramas of social relations, and in them performers define who can be a social actor and what subjects and ideas are available for communication and consideration. . . . Hence, we use the word 'parade' to indicate marchers who are making some sort of collective point, not just to each other but to bystanders along the way. . . . Parades are thus a form of expression, not just motion, and the inherent expressiveness of marching to make a point explains our cases involving protest marches.[231]

Indeed, the Court further observed, the very reason why the gay group wanted to participate in the parade was to express the idea that there are gay, lesbian and bisexual descendants among Irish immigrants.

The Court then asserted that the state court's application of Massachusetts's anti-discrimination law to require the gay group's participation in the parade had the effect of requiring the parade organizers to alter the expressive content of the event. Such a court order violated fundamental constitutional precepts. "[T]his use of State power violates the fundamental rule of protection under the First Amendment, that a speaker has the autonomy to choose the content of his own message. . . . [The state] may not compel affirmance of a belief with which the speaker disagrees." [232]

The *Hurley* reasoning would have sustained Georgetown's refusal to grant official recognition, and necessarily endorsement, of the student gays groups and the message they wished to disseminate in Georgetown's name. But the significance of the *Hurley* decision is that it extends that constitutional protection beyond religiously affiliated colleges and to all independent institutions of higher education. The *Hurley* decision permits all independent colleges and universities to disclaim and refuse to lend their names to student organizations that promote a message that the institutions consider to be antithetical to their higher education missions.

---

[231] 115 S.Ct. at 2345.

[232] 115 S.Ct. at 2347.

Retrospective on the Issue of Regulatory Burdens

Unlike the earlier discussion of the "benefits" Catholic colleges derived from public aid programs, there are fewer unifying principles in the "burdens" area. In addition, with the exception of the issue of recognition of student organizations, the developments in the "burdens" area over the period covered are less conclusive.

The issue of faculty unions at Catholic colleges is in eclipse because of the *Yeshiva* decision. Whether that narrow 5 to 4 ruling will survive future scrutiny if faculty unionizing takes hold again on college campuses is problematic. However, one would expect the faculty union movement to take hold again only if faculties are satisfied that they can reconcile the benefits they perceive will flow from collective bargaining with the loss, to some degree, of their influence over the development and implementation of academic policies.

Fewer uncertainties exist in the area of compliance with anti-discrimination laws, although not all questions in that area that concern Catholic colleges have been resolved definitively. As a general matter, the employment polices and practices of Catholic colleges and universities can legitimately be held up to scrutiny under Title VII and similar federal anti-discrimination laws. The burden of compliance with such laws is two-fold.

First, an institution must maintain adequate records to show compliance with such laws. When those laws were new, that burden seemed considerable. By now, however, most colleges have institutionalized compliance in an affirmative action office or official, and the burdens have been subsumed into a routine.

Second, the very fact of the anti-discrimination laws presents the risk of the considerable expense and internal disruption that can come with a lawsuit by a disgruntled applicant or employee. The burden is substantially the same whether the lawsuit is meritorious or frivolous. Nevertheless, that burden is simply a fact of life for a corporate citizen of the United States at the end of the 20th century.

Viewed from a Catholic perspective, those burdens should be less troubling for Catholic colleges. After all, anti-discrimination laws embody social justice teachings that the Catholic Church has long espoused. Those at Mississippi College who pressed the legal battle to avoid Title VII oversight could not have been pleased that the court of appeals had to remind them that "no religious tenets advocated by the College or the Mississippi Baptist Convention involve discrimination on the basis of race or gender."[233] For Catholic colleges, compliance with anti-discrimination laws involves little more than observing an article of faith.

Moreover, the decisions in the Marquette and Loyola cases, allowing a preference for Catholics and members of religious orders in some administrative

---

[233] 626 F.2d at 488.

and teaching positions, preserve one method by which such institutions seek to maintain their distinctive identity within the independent sector of higher education in this country. The challenge for the future is to persuade other courts of the correctness of those rulings by the Seventh Circuit Court of Appeals.

2

Changing Conceptions of Catholic Theology/Religious Studies

1965-1995

Patrick W. Carey
Marquette University

This essay focuses upon changes in the discipline of theology/religious studies, particularly the changing conceptions of its nature and aims in Catholic colleges and universities. I argue here that by the middle of the 1970s the nature and aims of the college discipline (whether conceived of as theology or religious studies) were fairly firmly established.[1] The discipline was conceived of as the academic study of religion with a host of internal methodologies and disciplinary specializations. Its aim was not to foster faith or confessional agendas (as was a general aim of college theology prior to the 1960s) but to examine and understand the universal religious dimension of human existence, whether evident in world religions or specific Christian denominations or secular enterprises. From 1965 to 1975, moreover, many drew sharp distinctions between theology and religious studies. By the late 1970s and early 1980s, however, some began to question the disciplinary developments of the 1960s and to call for a redefinition of both theology and religious studies that emphasized their continuities rather than their discontinuities. Some, too, called attention to what was called the fragmentation within the discipline of theology and

---

[1] There are problems in defining the disciplines of "theology" and "religious studies," as will be evident later. In this paper I will repeatedly refer to the college "discipline" when I am referring to the generic study of religion, whether conceived of as theology or as religious studies.

advocated a reform that focused upon the underlying and internal unity of the specializations within the discipline. By the 1990s, a number of departments were beginning to reexamine the discipline and the curriculum that reflected an elective specialization that had little internal coherence or intelligibility. The movement in the last thirty years, therefore, can be described as an ongoing movement from disciplinary specialization, diversification, and secularization to one of disciplinary reintegration.

This interpretive thesis has its limits. First of all it is based primarily upon the changing conceptions of the nature and purpose of the discipline that were published in national journals from about 1965 to 1995; it has not been tested by what actually was taking place in the multiple departments of theology and religious studies in diverse Catholic colleges and universities. The essay focuses upon the conception of aims and not upon the actual curricular implementation of those changing aims. At the present time we do not have many historical studies of departmental changes in specific schools.[2] The essay is divided into three major sections: first, a brief overview of the state of the discipline between the late 1950s and the end of the Second Vatican Council; second, an examination of the discussions on the aims of the discipline and the institutional changes that took place between about 1965 and 1975; and third, a brief summary of some rethinking of the discipline from the late 1970s to the middle of the 1990s.

Theology as Integrating Factor: 1957-1965

In an earlier essay on the evolution of theology as a discipline within the Catholic college[3] I demonstrated that American Catholic professors of theology

---

[2] Two exceptions are William C. McFadden's "'Catechism at 4 for All the Schools': Religious Instruction at Georgetown," in *Georgetown at Two Hundred: Faculty Reflections on the University's Future*, ed. William C. McFadden (Washington, D.C.: Georgetown University Press, 1990), 143-68; and my "Theology at Marquette. A History," privately published pamphlet, revised edition, 1996.

[3] "College Theology in Historical Perspective," in *American Catholic Traditions: Resources for Renewal*, eds. William Portier and Sandra Yocum Mize (New York: Orbis Press, 1997), 242-71. This paper was originally given as the keynote address at the annual meeting of the College Theology Society, June 1, 1996. It is important to emphasize that the discipline of college theology or religion within the Catholic college or university has been evolving and changing throughout the entire twentieth century. Although some dramatic changes took place within the discipline after the Second Vatican Council, the experience of change itself was not entirely the result of the Second Vatican Council as some commentators have suggested. The changes within the discipline in Catholic colleges, moreover, were not unique; the discipline in non-Catholic private and secular colleges and universities had been in a process of transformation since the end of World War II. On this, see *Theological Education in the Evangelical Tradition*, eds. R. Albert Mohler, Jr. and D. G. Hart (Grand Rapids, MI: Baker Books, 1996) and *Models for Christian Higher Education: Strategies for*

during the late 1950s were divided among themselves on the aims of college theology; some emphasized the acquisition of religious truth, others the promotion of religious practice or the moral good, and still others the encouragement of Catholic Action in the modern world. No matter how divided theologians were, however, they were united in believing that theology had an integrating role to play in the overall college curriculum. Theology could be the integrating factor in the college curriculum because it pointed to God as the ultimate source and destiny of every human good, truth, and beauty. Theology was the discipline for helping students realize that all other disciplines ultimately served God's creative and redemptive purposes.

Catholic approaches to the study of religion during the 1950s must be seen within the context of the rapid rise of the study of religion in secular and other private colleges and universities because the developments that were taking place outside of Catholic institutions would eventually have an influence upon the discipline within them. Between the end of the Second World War and 1965 the study of religion became increasingly significant as part of the nation's education at secular as well as at private colleges. The number of undergraduate courses in religion increased dramatically, forcing a corresponding emphasis on the graduate study of religion at a number of universities to prepare teachers for the emerging field of study.[4] As early as 1947, in fact, members of Ph.D. granting university seminaries and religion departments established the Council on Graduate Studies in Religion to provide a national voice and direction for the emerging discipline and for the training of future teachers of the discipline. Since the study of religion had traditionally been the prerogative of theological seminaries, the origin of the study of religion and theology in other settings (e.g., colleges and universities) was significantly dependent (as it was in the 1950s) upon theological seminaries and divinity schools which prepared teachers for positions in colleges. During the late 1950s and early 1960s, as the new field was emerging particularly in public education, a major national discussion emerged on the nature of the discipline, with an attempt to make people aware of its academic respectability.

One of the major problems the discipline faced, particularly in public education, was skepticism about its viability as an academic discipline. As Richard Schlatter indicated in 1963:

A considerable body of American scholars are of the opinion that religious studies are no part of the humanities, no part of the liberal arts, not an

---

Survival and Success in the Twenty-First Century, eds. Richard T. Hughes and William B. Adrian (Grand Rapids, MI: W. B. Eerdmans Pub. Co., 1997).

[4] On this, see Claude Welch, *Graduate Education in Religion: A Critical Appraisal* (Missoula, Montana: University of Montana Press, 1971).

objective scholarly discipline. These scholars think of traditional religious scholarship as a professional study preparatory to the tasks of indoctrination and conversion and want it relegated to the seminaries of the various denominations.[5]

The apologetical task of defending the discipline's academic respectability, therefore, became a dominant preoccupation in the early 1960s and throughout much of the subsequent period. In part, this meant separating the academic study of religion from traditional notions of theology. Even though theological seminaries continued during the 1960s to supply the professors, influence the content of the field, and provide most of the responsible published scholarship, still there emerged a view that the field of the study of religion needed to be separated from its theological tutelage and emerge, as Clyde Holbrook contended, as a "Humanistic Field." Thus, as the study of religion developed in the 1960s, the discussion of its nature and method was limited, as least in public education, to a discussion of its viability independent of traditional theology, in order to present the discipline as academically respectable and as a discipline that did not foster a particular faith.[6] The discipline itself, therefore, was being defined apologetically to meet the standards of scholarship established by a skeptical academy.

1963 marked the year of two important events relative to the discipline. In that year the United States Supreme Court in *Abington Township School District vs. Schempp* decided that the academic approach to the study of religion and the Bible in public institutions was a legitimate part of general cultural education and not a violation of the separation of church and state. That decision reinforced the movement for the study of religion in public institutions and fostered the emphasis upon the academic as objective, neutral, and descriptive.

That same year the Association of Biblical Instructors, primarily Protestant religion teachers in college programs, reorganized themselves and formed what they called the American Academy of Religion (AAR) as a national clearinghouse to support and re-think the aims of the discipline.

These disciplinary developments on the national level provided the social context for changes in the discipline in Catholic colleges and universities, but not because they had a direct bearing upon internal Catholic discussions during the period. Rather, they provided the cultural ambiance and the standards and objectives that would eventually have an impact upon Catholic developments.

The discipline in Catholic colleges and universities was gradually changing in the late 1950s and early 1960s, but the discussion of the aims of the

---

[5] "Foreword," in Clyde A. Holbrook, *Religion, A Humanistic Field* (Englewood Cliffs, NJ: Prentice-Hall, 1963), ix-x.

[6] *Ibid.*, xii.

discipline during these years was consistent with previous internal Catholic discussions more than with the new national discussions on the nature and aims of the study of religion. Nonetheless, in the midst of the internal Catholic debates on the aims of college theology or religion (a discussion that had been going on since 1939), there emerged a new focus for college theology that was analogous to the post-World War II movements in the discipline outside of Catholic colleges.

In the late 1950s, under the leadership of Gerard Sloyan at the Catholic University of America and Bernard Cooke, S.J., at Marquette University, the discipline moved away from its traditional pastoral and exclusively doctrinal aims. What emerged at these institutions was an emphasis upon the descriptive and historical-critical approach to the study of the Bible and Christianity as an aim of the discipline. What this demanded, moreover, was a high level of specialization in the discipline and a greater degree of elective choice in the curriculum to provide courses for professors who had specialized in different aspects of the discipline (Scripture, systematics, ethics, history, etc.). The integrating core of these developments was, as Bernard Cooke, S.J., noted, the historical development of revelation and Christianity itself. Historical consciousness provided the integrating core of the discipline and the curriculum.

Another major new development in the discipline prior to the Council was the establishment of Ph.D. graduate programs in theology and religious studies in a few Catholic universities. Although the Catholic University of America established a graduate program in theology in 1889, it had very little effect upon the college discipline and was almost exclusively directed to the education of clergy. Its program of study, moreover, was primarily the neo-scholastic theology of the manuals. St. Mary's College in South Bend, Indiana, also established a Ph.D. program for women and women religious in 1944 which was successful in supplying religion and theology teachers for a number of women's Catholic colleges. That program was also heavily oriented to neo-scholastic theology and, for a variety of reasons, ceased to exist by 1966.[7] New Ph.D. graduate programs were organized in the 1960s: at Notre Dame (1961, but that program did not graduate any Ph.D. students until the 1970s), Marquette (1963), Fordham (1967), St. Louis (1969), Boston College (1971), Duquesne (1982), Loyola Chicago (1991). In the late 1960s and early 1970s, moreover, the Dominican, Jesuit, and Franciscan theologates joined the Graduate Theological Union in Berkeley, California, an institution previously formed by six Protestant

---

[7] On St. Mary's program, see Sandra Yocum Mize's "In the Court of the 'Queen of Sciences,'" *Records of the American Catholic Historical Society of Philadelphia* 107 (Fall-Winter, 1996): 1-18. Two other doctoral programs had been organized at the Dominican House of Studies (S.T.D., 1941) in Washington, D.C. and at Aquinas Institute (Ph.D., 1952) in Dubuque, Iowa, but I know little about these two programs.

seminaries, and began accepting Ph.D. students (in cooperation with the University of California at Berkeley) and Th.D. students. This and other similar ecumenical programs trained numerous Catholics, lay as well as clerical. Other secular and private universities with long-standing doctoral programs in theology and/or religious studies also accepted and trained numerous Catholics as teachers of college theology and religious studies. These new Catholic and ecumenical programs sought to respond to a need that had been discussed since the 1920s, namely the need to provide substantive doctoral education for lay as well as clerical students who would be prepared to teach theology in Catholic colleges and universities. It was certainly clear during the post-World War II college enrollment surge that colleges would not be able, as in the past, to rely exclusively upon clergy as a source of theological education for college students.

The new Catholic graduate programs self-consciously departed from the old seminary approach to theological education and focused upon the historical and critical dimensions of the discipline, providing students with a genetic approach to the history of the Christian tradition. These new programs, however, would not produce their first graduates until after the Second Vatican Council had concluded and thereafter they would be a major source for the professorate in Catholic colleges and universities. Of the forty-six new Ph.Ds. graduated from Catholic institutions between 1965 and 1969, about half were lay men and women.[8] Gradually thereafter theology programs would become increasingly lay, significantly changing their focus. But those changes did not have much impact until the 1970s when lay professors in theology from the new Catholic programs, the ecumenical theological unions, and the established doctoral programs in secular and other private universities, began to outnumber clergy and women religious.

The Second Vatican Council also provided a legitimation for change within the discipline even though in itself it was not responsible for the climate of change that was going on in the discipline. It did, however, legitimate those pioneers in the discipline who had been calling for some fundamental reorientations in the period prior to the Council.

---

[8] Between 1965 and 1969, the Catholic University graduated twenty Ph.Ds., Marquette seventeen, Aquinas Institute four, and Fordham five. On this see Claude Welch, 235.

Theology as an Academic Discipline: 1965 to 1975

The most dramatic changes in the discipline of college theology took place from 1965 to 1975, a decade of optimistic hopefulness, radical changes, and turmoil in all American institutions. Changes in the discipline reflected responses to internal needs of Catholic colleges and to external definitions of the standards of the discipline in the national academy.

By the end of the Second Vatican Council it was clear to many theologians that a fundamental shift had taken place at the Council in the very conception of theology. The neo-scholastic or dogmatic approach to theology, which had dominated so much of the pre-Vatican II church, had been displaced to some extent by a new kind of theological scholarship that had itself significantly influenced theological developments at the Council. At the annual meeting of the College Theology Society in 1972 Bernard J. F. Lonergan, one of the major theological leaders within post-conciliar theology, characterized the situation as a "Revolution in Catholic Theology."[9] For him this meant that the twentieth century emergence of linguistic, exegetical, and historical scholarship and research had simply eliminated the "old style dogmatic theologian."[10] The new techniques of research and the development of what Lonergan in other places called "functional specialties" had made the dogmatic and metaphysical approaches of the past obsolete. The empirical, rather than the normative, notion of culture and a modern understanding of a person's historicity and subjectivity, moreover, helped to bring about a revolutionary turn to the subject and to history in Catholic theology during the twentieth century–a movement that was clearly evident in the documents of the Second Vatican Council. The upshot of this revolution in scholarship and perspective was a theological realization that the "cognitive meaning of Christianity is continually realized in ever changing situations."[11] The twentieth century theological research and scholarship that helped to shape the Council, moreover, was influenced by modern developments in science and philosophy, which helped to dethrone the speculative intellect– and for Lonergan these tendencies in modern thought were not to be altogether deplored.[12] The result of this revolution in theology, he believed, was a lot less emphasis upon metaphysics in theology and more emphasis upon history, hermeneutics, and cognitional theories that had a tendency to meet the

---

[9] The address was published in *A World More Human A Church More Christian*, ed. George Devine (New York: Alba House, 1973), 129-35.

[10] *Ibid.*, 129.

[11] *Ibid.*, 131.

[12] *Ibid.*, 134.

conceptual frameworks of modern science and philosophy and at the same time to restore earlier pre-scholastic forms of Christian theology.

Lonergan's description of modernization and specialization in theology indicated a transformation that had taken place in the field by the early 1970s, but his positive view of the change was not universally accepted. William E. Murnion, commenting on Lonergan's paper, asserted the older line of thinking when he said that the impact of modernization was not an emancipation from dogmatic theology as much as it was a slippery slope to secularization--a movement away from all theology. What it has led to, he asserted, was the displacement of theology by religious studies (a field of study that operated without the presupposition of the existence of God). Austin B. Vaughan also reacted to Lonergan's paper as an excessively optimistic view of theology's future. He saw the modern developments as analogous to the "decay of the fourteenth century" with its emphasis on nominalism, subjectivism, and an all embracing criticism.[13]

Although there were occasional negative reactions, like those of Murnion and Vaughan, to the newer developments in the discipline, it was clear by 1965 that the direction of the discipline in Catholic as well as in public colleges and universities was toward what was called the academic study of religion. Precisely what the academic study of religion meant was a topic of considerable national discussion. Professional institutions (e.g. the American Academy of Religion, the Commission on Religion in Higher Education of the Association of American Colleges, the Council on the Study of Religion, the Danforth Foundation, the Society for Religion in Higher Education, the Religious Education Association, etc.) as well as individuals defined "academic" as an empirical, comparative, descriptive, objective, neutral approach to the study of religion as a universal human phenomenon. Catholic departments of theology or religion were not uninfluenced by these national developments. Not only did they want to be considered respectable academic disciplines within their own Catholic colleges but they wanted to win a place for their understanding of the discipline in the national academy.

Within Catholic institutions of higher learning the discussion of the *raison d'etre* of the discipline moved in two different directions by the late 1960s, but both directions were influenced by the movement toward the academic study of religion. Some departments, which had formerly been called theology, changed their names to religious studies, indicating that they were no longer offering a purely confessional [i.e., Catholic] approach to the study of religion. Other departments retained their designation as theology but broadened their understanding of the nature of theological studies.

---

[13] Both commentaries are printed in Devine, 137-44.

Whether departments considered themselves religious studies or theology departments, most Catholic departments moved away from what they perceived to be the pastoral and spiritual functions that were generally associated with the aims of instruction in the recent past. Both religious studies and theology departments considered themselves rigorously academic, and that meant that they separated the study of religion (as a universal phenomenon of human life that was evident in particular religious traditions) from the spiritual formation of the student.

These developments within the discipline were clearly evident in 1967 when the Society of Catholic College Teachers of Sacred Doctrine changed its name to the College Theology Society. The name change reflected the desire in the discipline to be perceived as ecumenical and non-confessional. That same year the newly named society endorsed "Religion as an Academic Discipline," a statement of the Commission on Religion in Higher Education of the Association of American Colleges. At the national level the discipline was clearly moving in the direction of standards set by non-confessional external agencies. Pastoral or spiritual concerns for students' religious lives became an obsolete relic of a now defunct system of theological education.

The movement to divorce spirituality from the academic study of religion was further reinforced in the late 1960s and early 1970s by the establishment of campus ministry departments. Campus ministries became the Catholic institutionalization of the separation of spiritual formation from intellectual development. Although there were other reasons for the establishment of campus ministry programs (e.g., the need to release clergy who were religion teachers from the burdens of spiritual and pastoral duties so that they could focus their energies on academic responsibilities, the lack of enough clergy in the colleges to take care of the spiritual needs of students, the professionalization of religious life on the college campuses, etc.), the most significant indirect effect of the movement was the secularization of the college discipline. Religious studies and theology departments, like other disciplines in the colleges, were applying Vatican II's newly won emphasis upon autonomy to their own disciplines.[14]

---

[14] On the general influence of Vatican II's conception of autonomy, see Philip Gleason, *Contending with Modernity: Catholic Higher Education in the Twentieth Century* (New York: Oxford University Press, 1995), 308, 314-20. On assessments of the relationship between autonomy and secularity, see Kenneth J. Schmitz, "The New Freedom and the Integrity of the Profane," in *Proceedings of the Society of Catholic College Teachers of Sacred Doctrine* (Weston, MA: The Society, 1965), 13-38; Rabbi Eugene B. Borowitz, "Confronting Secularity," in *The Paradox of Religious Secularity*, ed. Katharine T. Hargrove (Englewood Cliffs, NJ: Prentice-Hall, Inc, 1968), 3-15; Leslie Dewart, "Autonomy: The Key Word in Secularism," *ibid.*, 177-96.

The emphasis upon the academic study of religion also fit in well with another movement within the discipline in the late 1960s and early 1970s—i.e., the movement to re-examine whether or not theology/religious studies courses should be a universal curricular requirement for graduation. The hard-won battle in the 1920s and 1930s to establish theology courses as a universal requirement for graduation in Catholic colleges was being challenged in two very different ways. In some colleges, like Webster College in St. Louis, the graduation requirement was dropped completely. Advocates of the elimination of the requirement argued that a theology course, because it was confessional in nature, should be an elective (examination of one's faith could not be a requirement in college education). Non-Catholic students, moreover, had never been required to take theology courses in Catholic colleges because of the confessional nature of those courses. Therefore, it was argued, in the interests of equity and religious liberty, Catholic students also should not be required to take such courses. Furthermore, if theology or religious studies courses were electives, students would take more interest in them.

A second approach, and perhaps the majority one, was to make religious studies or theological courses universal requirements (i.e., for non-Catholic as well as Catholic students) for graduation. The rationale for this movement was based upon an understanding of the purely academic nature of the discipline, whether the discipline was considered religious studies or theological studies. Neither religious studies nor theological studies were inherently sectarian, so the argument went; they were academic disciplines and therefore should be required of non-Catholics as well as Catholic students. Religion, moreover, was a universal human phenomenon and was worth studying in itself. A Catholic college or university, in particular, ought to make the requirement universal as a part of its mission to educate the whole person, by including an understanding of the religious dimensions of human life and culture.

The movement to make religion courses a universal requirement for graduation raised three significant and interrelated questions. How, if one abandoned the Catholic confessional nature of the discipline, could one organize the discipline for college students? How could one call what was being done in the academic study of religion theology? How could one call what was being done in the discipline Catholic? These were questions that arose simultaneously with the new requirements for graduation and they continued to arise periodically within the discipline from the late 1960s to the 1990s.

There were a variety of responses to these questions, but we have space to look at only a couple which seem to be representative of what was taking place in the curricular developments in the late 1960s and early 1970s. Christopher Mooney, S.J., chairman of Fordham's Theology Department, responded to the above questions at a 1969 Jesuit Education Association workshop at St. Regis

College in Denver. His paper, "The Role of Theology in the Education of Undergraduates," was quoted repeatedly in subsequent years and seems to have had a major impact on curricular developments in Jesuit colleges and universities.[15] Mooney suggested that theology courses at the undergraduate level ought to become universal requirements for graduation and that in order to accommodate all students, non-Catholic as well as Catholic, the undergraduate curriculum should be organized with a single introductory course. This course would focus upon the academic study of religion as a universal phenomenon in human experience and culture, and a series of elective courses thereafter—some of which could be confessional in nature—which would not be required of every student. He stipulated, furthermore, that no specific course in Catholic theology should be required of any Catholic student. The proposal was an attempt to create a link between religious studies, which examined "the ultimate values of mankind phenomenologically, as these have appeared and continue to appear in human life and history," and theology, which is "the study of ultimate religious values insofar as they have been embodied in a given tradition, whether Christian or non-Christian, and involve a commitment of faith." [16]

Mooney's call for revision of the undergraduate program was based upon two fundamental ideas: (1) that religious experience was a universal phenomenon that any educated person ought to know something about; (2) that students ought to have the maximum amount of latitude in selecting religion courses in the curriculum. He was well aware, moreover, that his proposal departed from any attempt to provide an integrated theological curriculum at the undergraduate level. He justified this departure by arguing that in the discipline of theology itself in recent years there had been a "fragmentation in the theological thinking which should naturally reflect itself in a certain fragmentation of the theological curriculum." Catholic theologians today, he maintained, think less in terms of synthesis than hypotheses and less "about the possession of truth than about its quest." [17]

Mooney's proposal, which was adopted in many schools, was a deliberate abandonment of the idea that theology courses should, as in the past, indoctrinate students or attempt to pass on the content of the Catholic tradition. Mooney also suspected that someone might raise the question of what was particularly Catholic about his proposal. Since the Second Vatican Council, he responded, the Catholic Church has been oriented outward rather than inward. For him, to be Catholic meant "to be open" and ecumenical. Variety in the curriculum,

---

[15] The paper was published in *Catholic Colleges and the Secular Mystique* (St. Louis, MO: B. Herder, 1970), 88-103.

[16] *Ibid.*, 95.

[17] *Ibid.*, 97-98.

moreover, should reflect the church's intense contemporary interest in the variety of religious experiences of all human beings. The proposal, furthermore, was distinctively Catholic in its "availability to all students." [18]

Mooney's proposal reflected the national discussion on the academic study of religion that had been going on feverishly for twenty years, the changes in the church and theology since the Second Vatican Council, attempts to meet the needs of all students within the Catholic college, and attempts to meet the particular needs of Catholic students in the college. In Mooney's judgment Catholic college students had a strong faith commitment which they had received in their Catholic high schools. What they needed from their colleges was the freedom to choose for themselves what in the religious traditions they wished to study. And that study should introduce them to a critical and self-reflective analysis of religion, a form of inquiry that was consistent with the critical studies to which they were introduced in other college disciplines.

Others, like William Sullivan, S.J., a professor at Marquette University, argued along analogous lines for making theology a universal requirement. He, too, proposed that the undergraduate curriculum be reconstructed to meet the needs of all students and to combine the dual aims of religious studies and theological studies. He believed that religion departments should offer two kinds of courses: those that were academically neutral, i.e., purely historical and descriptive; and those that were academically theological, i.e., descriptive, historical, and phenomenological but from a perspective of faith seeking understanding. To be academic for him and for many Catholic theologians did not necessarily mean neutrality. Confessional truth claims could be rationally examined and explored from the perspective of a community of faith especially in the Catholic tradition where reason and faith were not perceived in opposition to one another.[19]

These proposals for the revision of undergraduate programs in theology tried to do two things: (1) serve the needs of a diverse student population, non-Catholic as well as Catholic; and (2) combine the aims of religious studies and theological studies.

By the mid 1970s most of the substantial reforms in the college discipline were in place and most departments had a curriculum in place that reflected the aims of the academic study of religion, whether departments considered themselves religious studies or theology departments. What this meant in

---

[18] *Ibid.*, 96-97.

[19] Sullivan argued his case in three articles: "Theology for Undergraduates," *America* 121.16 (November 15, 1969): 463-66; "Theology Should Be Required of All," *New Dimensions in Religious Experience*, ed. George Devine (Staten Island, NY: Alba House, 1971), 301-13; "The Catholic University and the Academic Study of Religion," *Council on the Study of Religion Bulletin* 2.5 (December 1971): 2-9.

curricular practice was that courses in theology/religious studies were primarily elective courses, even in those schools that required some theology/religious studies courses for graduation. The curriculum reflected a lively diversity and in the course of time a proliferation of elective courses. This meant that a student could take a course in Native American religions, one in Buddhism, and/or one in the Bible without taking any sequence of courses that showed some signs of progressive advancement in a discipline. In some Catholic colleges this approach made prefect sense because those colleges had abandoned the universal requirement and departments of religious studies/theology had to develop exotic or special interest courses that appeal to students' interests—without concern for the integrity of a discipline.

The benefits of the elective approach in the curriculum were many. The curriculum reflected variety, students' interests, and faculty specializations (in many universities the undergraduate programs reflected the specializations that were evident in the graduate program).

The developments within the discipline also produced a curriculum that eventually made little sense to anyone, lacked disciplinary definition, lacked integration, brought about a confusion of internal departmental aims, and had a difficult time explaining to those in other disciplines precisely what it was that theology (or religious studies) did as a discipline and how it in any unique way contributed to the overall mission of higher education. The problem became not just one of the Catholic identity of the discipline, but one of defining the discipline. The discipline itself had developed into a great variety of "functional specialties" and ideological and cultural perspectives, and by the early 1970s the curricular offerings reflected an elective approach consistent with various specialties but one that lacked curricular coherence. Few during the 1970s, as far as I am aware, drew much attention to this growing fragmentation of the discipline; those who did, like Mooney, approved this direction because they were trying desperately to avoid the pitfalls of indoctrination and of a confessional straitjacket that they believed had been the faults of the previous system of theological education.

From Fragmentation to Integration: 1976 to the 1990s

In the second half of the 1970s, two separate but interrelated new developments occurred within the discipline. On the one hand, some began to question the conventional definitions of religious studies and theology, and to redefine the two disciplines by emphasizing the continuities, rather than discontinuities, between them. On the other hand, some began to focus on the deleterious effects of fragmentation within theology and to call for a recovery of the unity of the discipline.

For the most part religious studies had its origins in the theological schools in the United States. During the late 1950s and 1960s, as the discipline was defining itself, it had done so by clearly distinguishing and separating itself from its parent discipline. In the process, in many secular and private schools, it ruled out or pushed to the margins theological study as a part of the discipline. Increasingly religious studies was perceived as emancipated from the tutelage of theology.

In 1977, Schubert M. Ogden, President that year of the American Academy of Religion and professor of theology at Southern Methodist University, gave a Presidential address at the annual meeting of AAR on "Theology and Religious Studies: Their Difference and the Difference it Makes."[20] The address signaled a reexamination and redefinition of the relationship between theology and religious studies. The conventional definition of the differences between the disciplines, he argued, was clearly inadequate to the discipline. The definition of religious studies as descriptive, neutral, phenomenological, and objective and of theology as participatory faith involvement in the subject investigated did not adequately describe the difference nor did such conventional views draw any sufficient attention to the similarities and continuities between the two academic approaches to the study of religion.

Ogden maintained that both religious studies and theology, unlike the study of religion generally (as in psychology of religion, sociology of religion, etc.), investigate religious claims to truth and meaning, and that such a rational investigation is in full compliance with contemporary standards of reflection; theology differs from religious studies in that its particular subject matter is rational reflection upon the meaning and truth of the Christian religion, or the Christian witness of faith.

Ogden's address was indicative of the discussion that was taking place on the national level and in many departments in Catholic colleges and universities in an attempt to define with more precision the nature and methodology of the discipline, a discussion that continues into the present. By 1987, Ogden was still attempting to redefine the approaches by emphasizing the continuity between them. In this effort, he redefined theology, too, making it a critical reflection upon the witness to faith that needs to be rationally justified on grounds other than faith and revelation. Thus Ogden, to avoid the pitfalls of fideism and the

---

[20] *Journal of the American Academy of Religion* 46 (March 1978): 3-17. For an earlier discussion that also redefined the religious studies/theology issue, see Paul G. Wiebe, "The Place of Theology Within Religious Studies," in *The Academic Study of Religion, 1975 Proceedings*, eds. Anne Carr and N. Piediscalzi (Missoula, Montana: Scholars Press, 1975), 17-25.

charges of a lack of critical objectivity, had clearly moved away from a conventional definition of theology which presupposed faith and revelation as the grounds for the discipline.[21]

Ogden's presidential address provoked a number of other reexaminations of the two disciplines in subsequent years.[22] Periodically academicians called for the re-inclusion of theological studies in religious studies programs or for the inclusion of religious studies perspectives in theological programs. [23]

Edward Farley, professor of theology at Vanderbilt Divinity School, like a number of others in the early 1980s followed in Ogden's footsteps in calling for a reexamination of the discipline. In 1981 he issued a call for the reform of theological education in particular. He saw the problem in theological studies itself as one of disciplinary fragmentation and called for a theological solution.[24] In 1983 he reinforced this advocacy with a monograph entitled *Theologia: The Fragmentation and Unity of Theological Education*,[25] arguing historically and theologically that the eighteenth and nineteenth century encyclopedia approach to theology, which continued to inform much of contemporary theological education, had fragmented the material unity of the discipline and made it primarily a professional discipline (i.e., primarily oriented to the preparation of clergy) rather than an essential part of Christian *paideia* and Christian wisdom. Farley's book received some attention in Catholic schools, but his criticisms of the discipline were shared by a number of those in Catholic schools who had experienced the disintegrating effects of an elective curriculum which manifested the fragmentation of the discipline. His book presented the kind of criticisms of the discipline that would continue to be articulated here and there in the field periodically throughout the 1980s and early 1990s.

---

[21] See "The Nature and State of Theological Scholarship and Research," *Theological Education* 24 (Autumn 1987): 120-31. For the persistence of the emphasis upon the scientific study of religion in religious studies programs and a sharp distinction of this study from that of theological studies, see J. Samuel Preus, *Explaining Religion: Criticism and Theory from Bodin to Freud* (New Haven, CT: Yale University Press, 1987) and Terrence W. Tilley's insightful review of Preus's book in "Polemics and Politics in Explaining Religion," *Journal of Religion* 71 (April, 1991): 242-54.

[22] See the bibliography in W. Clark Gilpin, "Basic Issues in Theological Education: A Selected Bibliography, 1980-1988," *Theological Education* 25 (Spring 1989): 115-21; William F. May, "Why Theological and Religious Studies Need Each Other," *Journal of the American Academy of Religion* 52.4 (December 1984): 748-57; Edward Farley, "The Place of Theology in the Study of Religion," *Religious Studies and Theology* 5.3 (September 1985): 9-29.

[23] See William F. May, "Why Theological and Religious Studies Need Each Other."

[24] "The Reform of Theological Education as a Theological Task," *Theological Education* 17 (Spring 1981): 93-117.

[25] (Philadelphia: Fortress Press, 1983).

Not everyone, of course, agreed with Farley's interpretation of the problem. Francis Schüssler Fiorenza argued that the real issue in theological education was not internal theological fragmentation but the societal process of modernization (a process of bureaucratization and specialization that had developed a special form of rationality). Rather than decrying the fragmentation, Fiorenza believed it was better to see fragmentation itself as a necessity of the modern process of rationalization; if perceived in this way one could more clearly approach the reconstruction of theological education as a hermeneutical and practical task.[26] However one interpreted the problem and solution of contemporary religious studies and theological education, by the mid 1980s many in the American Academy of Religion were calling for a reexamination of the disciplines.

During the late 1970s and early 1980s those in Catholic colleges and universities do not appear to have published any significant manifestos that seriously questioned or reexamined the discipline.[27] One reason for this might be that theology/religious studies departments in many Catholic colleges and universities did not in practice separate theological from religious studies courses and approaches in the curriculum. In most cases, it appears, courses that were descriptive, historical, phenomenological, and objective ran parallel to courses that were theological in content and method. Courses in the doctrine of the Trinity had equal elective space with courses in Buddhism and/or the history of American religious traditions. Whether departments called themselves religious studies (which included theological studies) or theological studies (which

---

[26] "Theory and Practice: Theological Education as a Reconstructive, Hermeneutical, and Practical Task," *Theological Education* 23 (Supplement 1987):113-41; see also his "Theological and Religious Studies: The Contest of Faculties," in *Shifting Boundaries: Contextual Approaches to the Structure of Theological Education*, eds. Barbara G. Wheeler and Edward Farley (Louisville, KY: Westminster, 1991), 119-49, and "Theology in the University," *The Council of Societies for the Study of Religion Bulletin* 22.2 (April 1993): 34-39.

[27] When one examines the annual publications (1976 to 1990) of the College Theology Society, the professional organization of Catholic professors that made itself responsible for defining the aims of the discipline, one soon realizes that disciplinary definition, which was a high profile question in the 1950s and 1960s, had by the mid 1970s faded away as a significant issue. Almost all of the published annual convention papers for those years were on particular theological issues (e.g., critical New Testament scholarship, western spirituality, hermeneutical issues, etc.) rather than on the aims of the discipline. By 1976, if the national conventions of the CTS are any indication, the defining issues of the discipline had been fairly well settled and departments had developed a certain comfort with the elective academic approach to the discipline and the curriculum. Other issues drew more interest: academic freedom (an issue that was on the front burner since the mid 1960s); the relationship of theologians and bishops; the inclusion of more and more perspectival courses; and emphases upon the Catholic identity of the institutions.

included religious studies), they both offered a smorgasbord of courses that had little conceptual or disciplinary relationship to one another.

One Catholic sponsored discussion of the new debate on religious/theological studies which did not, as far as I know, receive much national attention, took place in 1983 at St. Louis University. The Theological Studies department there sponsored a symposium on the relations of theological to religious studies within the undergraduate curriculum.[28] Walter Capps, co-organizer and participant in the symposium, acknowledged that the intellectual climate in the discipline had clearly changed since the early 1960s when the two fields were perceived to be more radically separated than they in fact were. Laurance O'Connell, co-organizer of the conference and chair of Saint Louis' department, argued during the symposium that both fields could be integrated in a basic humanities curriculum where students could focus on the academic study of "the religious dimension of ordinary human experience." O'Connell raised the fundamental question: "In the interests of a richer and broader humanities curriculum, how do we legitimately incorporate both theology and religious studies side by side into a coherent undergraduate program, irrespective of the public or church related identity of our institutions?"[29] That question, as far as I know, did not receive a response in any practical institutional or curricular changes in the Saint Louis department.

By the 1990s a few Catholic scholars began to criticize what had taken place within the discipline over the last thirty years in American Catholic colleges and universities. Until the present (May 1997), however, no one has undertaken an historical-theological examination of the development of the discipline in Catholic institutions.

In 1990 Frank D. Schubert published a sociological study of three Catholic religion programs on the East coast and argued that their curricular developments manifested a gradual secularization of the discipline, or at least a "decatholicizing" of the curriculum.[30] From a sociological perspective he argued that the separation of the undergraduate curriculum into specific disciplinary specialties, a movement in favor of variety and freedom as well as specialization,

---

[28] For a description of this symposium, see Walter H. Capps, "Religious Studies/Theological Studies: The St. Louis Project," *Journal of the American Academy of Religion* 52.4 (December 1984): 727-30; see also Jacob Neusner, "Why Religious Studies in America? Why Now?," *ibid.*, 738-41; and P. Joseph Cahill, "Theological Studies, Where Are You?," *ibid.*, 742-47.

[29] "Religious Studies, Theology, and the Humanities Curriculum," *Journal of the American Academy of Religion* 52.4 (December 1984): 731-37.

[30] *A Sociological Study of Secularization Trends in the American Catholic University: Decatholicizing the Catholic Religious Curriculum* (Lewiston, NY: The Edwin Mellen Press, 1990).

had the unfortunate effect of losing a sense of the coherence of the discipline. Furthermore, by removing theological education from the former concerns for the spiritual life and growth of students, and by explicitly claiming emancipation from all external interference (even ecclesiastical) in the discipline (i.e., a movement toward a kind of disciplinary autonomy), the discipline itself had gradually moved in the direction of what sociologists call secularization. Schubert details, moreover, a gradual but general decline of courses that are specifically related to what he calls the "Catholic sacred order." The general move in the discipline from the late 1950s to the 1990s, Schubert claims, is a proliferation of courses beyond the traditional range of Catholicism and even beyond the range of Christianity—a movement from within a particular Roman Catholic sacred order to a study of all sacred orders. Within this development two things have happened: (1) The courses have lost the integrative quality that a traditional Roman Catholic sacred order had provided; (2) The discipline itself has moved beyond its reliance upon an authoritative sacred order as the ground for its decisions and examination to the authority of the methods or standards and criteria of the discipline. It is not a sacred order that provides the authority for the discipline but the methods of the discipline that provide its standard and authority. Schubert's argument was constructed according to the criteria of twentieth-century sociological analysis (relying on Weber, Durkheim, Parsons, Bellah, Berger, and Luckmann).

During the early 1990s, moreover, a few Catholic theologians began to pay more attention to what had happened to their discipline in the recent past.[31] Although the theologians identified different problems in graduate and undergraduate theological education, they all acknowledged (implicitly or explicitly) the need to reform a discipline that had lost internal coherence, that had excessively separated intellectual training from moral and spiritual formation, and that had accepted some of the secularizing influences that accompanied modern thought patterns. Gerald O'Collins in particular called for a real inclusive and integrative approach to theology that allowed for the intellectual, practical, and contemplative aims of theology "to complement and mutually enrich each other" in any reform of theology.[32] These calls for

---

[31] Robert J. Wister, "The Teaching of Theology 1950-90: The American Catholic Experience," *America* 162.4 (February 3, 1990): 88-93, 106-9; Matthew L. Lamb, "Will There Be Catholic Theology in the United States?" *America* 162.20 (May 26, 1990): 523-5, 531-4; Gerald O'Collins, "Catholic Theology (1965-90)," *America* 162.4 (February 3, 1990): 86-7, 104-5; Thomas F. O'Meara, "Doctoral Programs in Theology at U.S. Catholic Universities," *America* 162.4 (February 3, 1990): 79-84, 101-3; James Tunstead Burtchaell, "The Decline and Fall of the Christian College (I & II)," *First Things* 12 (April, 1991):16-29; 13 (May, 1991):30-38; George P. Schner, *Education for Ministry: Reform and Renewal in Theological Education* (Kansas City, MO: Sheed & Ward, 1993).

[32] O'Collins, 105.

rethinking and reforming the discipline became the subject of a national convention on "Theological Education in the Catholic Tradition," held at Marquette University in 1995. That conference again focused on the difficulties within the discipline at the undergraduate, graduate and seminary levels and suggested some directions for reforming the discipline in the future.[33] Although there were a few departments in Catholic colleges and universities that began to reform their undergraduate and graduate programs in the late 1980s and early 1990s,[34] it is difficult to determine, given the present status of scholarship, how widespread was the awareness of the need for reform in the discipline, and even more difficult to determine how many departments were actually involved in reforming their theology and/or religious studies programs.

The historian, as John C. Murray, S.J., once noted, looks for what is "going forward" in history. What seems to be going forward in the last twenty years in theology/religious studies is a re-examination of the discipline in a direction that continues to value specialization and pluralism, that is wary of the problems of fragmentation, that is seeking new ways to integrate the curriculum and to make the discipline coherent, and that emphasizes anew the need to integrate theology with other disciplines in the university. This ongoing re-examination is by no means universal and does not find, even where it exists, substantive agreement on the direction of reforming the discipline. The discipline is still in a considerable state of flux, searching for a definition of its aims and tasks that can be implemented in a coherent curriculum.

---

[33] For a collection of some of the papers of that conference, see *Theological Education in the Catholic Tradition: Contemporary Challenges*, eds. Patrick W. Carey and Earl C. Muller, S.J. (New York: Crossroad Publishing, 1997).

[34] Although I know of no published record of these reforms, I do know that they have occurred in a few places. Creighton University (Omaha), the University of St. Thomas (St. Paul, Minnesota), and St. Mary's College (Emmittsburg, Maryland)have thoroughly revised their undergraduate programs during the 1990s. There may be many other reformed programs, but I am not aware of them.

3

Protestant Colleges

1960-1990

Richard T. Hughes
Pepperdine University

It is difficult, if not impossible, to make binding generalizations regarding the impact of the 1960s on Protestant higher education in the United States. We can all think of schools that responded to the unsettling tumult of those years by battening down their theological hatches, apparently hoping that if they ignored the moral revolution of that period, it might pass.

At the same time, the profoundly moral content of that period helped to prompt at least some Protestant institutions to take the specific Christian traditions to which they were related with greater seriousness than perhaps they had before, to explore in a more meaningful way the implications of their faith traditions for the task of higher education, and to rethink their specific Christian commitments in the light of the moral ferment swirling around them.

While this kind of response to the 1960s surely did not characterize all Protestant institutions, it did characterize a number whose narratives appear in the volume, *Models for Christian Higher Education*.[1] This essay focuses on three of those institutions. They represent all three of the major wings of the Continental Protestant Reformation–Lutheran, Anabaptist, and Reformed–and

---

[1] Richard T. Hughes and William B. Adrian, eds., *Models for Christian Higher Education: Strategies for Survival and Success in the Twenty-First Century* (Grand Rapids, MI: Eerdmans, 1997). The descriptions of the three institutions in this essay follow closely the descriptions that appear in *Models*.

demonstrate how each of these faith traditions can sustain the task of higher education in a time of moral crisis. The three schools we will consider are Calvin College (Reformed), Fresno Pacific College (Anabaptist/Mennonite), and California Lutheran University (Lutheran). First we will explore the theological worldview that characterizes each of these faith traditions. Second, we will ask how each of our institutions appropriated its respective theological worldview and exploited those resources from the 1960s through the 1990s.

The Reformed Model: Calvin College

Because a variety of scholars connected in one way or another with Calvin College (founded in 1876) have been so articulate over the years regarding the legitimacy of the Reformed model for Christian higher education, Calvin College has emerged as the flagship institution for the Reformed wing of the Protestant tradition in the United States and as one of several flagship institutions for a large number of schools that identify in one way or another with American evangelicalism.

Before we consider the way Calvin College responded to the 1960s, we must first ask about the parameters of a Reformed worldview, and second, we must ask how that worldview sustains higher education in the Reformed context. The answers to these questions are found in the original vision of John Calvin. Simply put, Calvin sought to transform Geneva, Switzerland into a model kingdom of God. To achieve this goal, he sought to place every facet of Genevan life—its religion, its politics, its music, and its art—squarely under the sovereignty of God. Ever since those early days, this same vision has motivated Calvinists to bring all human life and culture under the sovereign sway of God's control. For example, Abraham Kuyper led a neo-Calvinist movement in the Netherlands in the late nineteenth century. Concerned to open the entire sphere of human experience to Christian participation, Kuyper triumphantly announced, "There is not a square inch on the whole plain of human existence over which Christ, who is Lord of all, does not proclaim: 'This is Mine!'" [2]

It is precisely this vision that sustains the life of the mind in many Reformed institutions of higher learning. Reformed educators seek to place the entire curriculum—and every course within the curriculum—under the sovereignty of God. According to this vision, all learning should be Christian in both purpose and orientation. For this reason, Reformed educators employ four fundamental concepts that underscore these objectives.

First, they often argue that all truth is God's truth. By this, they mean to say that God is the author not only of our faith, but also of every facet of the

---

[2] James D. Bratt and Ronald A. Wells, "Piety and Progress: A History of Calvin College," *Models*, 141-162.

world in which we live. If this is true, then there can be no discrepancy between Christian convictions and authentic knowledge regarding other aspects of human life. It is therefore possible to understand every facet of the natural sciences, of the social sciences, and of religion and the humanities in the light of Christian faith without risking intellectual dishonesty.

It is this conviction that breathes life into the second concept employed by Reformed educators: the integration of faith and learning. Because all truth is God's truth, secular learning and Christian faith can and should be integrated into a coherent understanding of reality.

This notion lends meaning to the third concept: the construction of a Christian worldview. According to this notion, Reformed thinkers seek to understand all of reality from a distinctly Christian perspective. Quite clearly, this notion is the linchpin that holds the entire Reformed vision together since in the Reformed system of thought there can be no integration of faith and learning apart from a Christian worldview.

Finally, this triad of ideas—all truth is God's truth, the integration of faith and learning, and a Christian worldview—-sustains another notion that is critical to the Reformed understanding of reality: the notion of secularization. From the Reformed perspective, secularization occurs when even one dimension of human life escapes the sovereignty of God, or when we fail to bring all of reality under the umbrella of a distinctly Christian worldview. Because the possibility of secularization is so real in this context, the notion of a slippery slope is a metaphor that many in this tradition take very seriously. This means that if one hopes to avoid the slippery slope toward secularization, the integration of faith and learning around a Christian perspective becomes absolutely imperative.

So if we ask, "How can the Reformed tradition sustain the life of the mind?" the answer is clear. It does so by carefully placing all reality under the control of a Christian worldview and then by integrating faith and learning around that distinctly Christian perspective.

How, then, did Calvin College respond to the 1960s? Ironically, on the very eve of that tumultuous period, Calvin began making its plans to abandon a neighborhood that by the mid-1970s would become predominantly African American, and to develop instead a much larger campus on the edge of town. Though the college endured charges of "white flight," James Bratt and Ronald Wells, authors of the Calvin College narrative in *Models for Christian Higher Education*, argue that racial considerations played no role in the decision to relocate. Rather, the new site was some twenty times larger than the old Franklin Street site which already had been developed to its fullest capacity and was now simply too small. Nonetheless, Bratt and Wells observe that "just as the inner city heated up and students cried for involvement, just when 1960s passions flamed and students demanded relevance, Calvin students found themselves transplanted to the pastoral isolation of Knollcrest Farm."[3]

Calvin College, therefore, would have to respond to the 1960s in a more substantive way, and that is precisely what it did. In spite of all its claims that it had implemented a distinctly Reformed model for Christian higher education, Calvin College embraced a curriculum from 1921 until the early 1960s that essentially had been "imported *"en bloc* from the University of Michigan—with Bible and theology courses added on." As Bratt and Wells therefore observe, "the reformers of the 1960s could make fundamental changes in radical times by invoking orthodoxy."[4]

When their work was done, the reformers published in 1970 their report which they entitled simply, *Christian Liberal Arts Education.* In this report they sought to build the entire curriculum on a distinctly Reformed foundation. It affirmed the dignity of every discipline, reflecting the Reformed conviction that if Christ was Lord over all the earth, he was Lord over each academic discipline as well. Second, it recommended a large core of general education courses and leaner, more streamlined majors, thereby avoiding fragmentation and affirming instead a holistic view of the universe. Third, the report recommended that every "core course in each discipline and every major as a whole reflect upon their grounds and procedures in light of Christian beliefs and norms." Finally, the report argued that learning was not an end in itself, but rather a means to the Christian transformation of the world.[5] In this context, Calvin College proclaimed its new motto, "Christ transforming culture," though it borrowed this phrase not from John Calvin or Abraham Kuyper, but from H. Richard Niebuhr's classic study, *Christ and Culture.*[6]

At Calvin College even in the 1960s and early 1970s, cultural transformation never had much to do with demonstrations and protests, though a few demonstrations did take place during those years. Rather, the college contributed to cultural transformation through systematic attention to the life of the mind, always couched in the context of a "Christian worldview."

Interestingly if not ironically, Calvin College sought to implement all these reforms at an institution where 90 percent of the students and 100 percent of the faculty belonged to the Christian Reformed Church, and where both custom and contract virtually required faculty to enroll their children in Christian schools. Only two years after the report was released, however, Calvin's enrollment fell on hard times, dropping from 3,575 in 1968 to 3,185 in 1972. In response, the

---

[3] Bratt and Wells, 151.

[4] *Idem.*

[5] Calvin College Curriculum Study Committee, *Christian Liberal Arts Education* (Grand Rapids, MI: Calvin College/Eerdmans, 1970).

[6] Bratt and Wells, 152.

college began to recruit students from evangelical Protestant circles. By 1980, only 72% of Calvin's students belonged to the Christian Reformed Church.

Further, in keeping with its Reformed worldview orientation, Calvin College aspired to resist the fragmentation of knowledge and community that so often accompanies secularization and modernization. In spite of themselves, however, fragmentation reared its head as a spirit of professionalism began to dominate the campus in the 1970s. This trend emerged at several levels. First, allegiance to particular academic disciplines began to compete with allegiance to the larger college on the part of some faculty. Second, in the interest of efficiency in governance, the faculty reorganized itself into a variety of disparate committees, each charged with a specialized assignment. This reorganization had the unintended result of fragmentation. Third, the college introduced a host of new professionally-oriented majors–accounting, social work, criminal justice, recreation, and nursing–that threatened to undermine the liberal arts center of the curriculum. And fourth, the co-curriculum also gave way to professionalism as experts displaced widowed mothers and other "sanctified amateurs" in the various departments of student life.[7]

In 1982, Nicholas Wolterstorff, a principal author of the curricular recommendations of 1970, called on Calvin and similar institutions to move beyond the mere integration of faith and learning, beyond the *rhetoric* of transformation, to a genuine commitment to social transformation. In a speech delivered at the inauguration of Richard Chase as president of Wheaton College, Wolterstorff argued that for Christ's sake, Calvin, Wheaton, and comparable institutions should abandon a curriculum defined by traditional disciplines and embrace instead a curriculum defined by programs in "peace and war, nationalism, poverty, urban ugliness, ecology, crime and punishment."[8] Bratt and Wells note, however, that "Calvin gave the local prophet only the honor of a polite hearing" and demonstrated "little inclination to move much beyond the 'faith and learning' consensus" hammered out in the 1960s.[9] Accordingly, from the 1960s into the 1990s, Calvin College rooted the intersection of faith and learning in traditional Reformed understandings that helped define for faculty a distinctively "Christian worldview."

---

[7] Bratt and Wells, 155-157.

[8] Nicholas Wolterstorff, "The Mission of the Christian College at the End of the 20th Century," *Reformed Journal* 33 (June 1983): 14-8.

[9] Bratt and Wells, 158-9.

The Anabaptist/Mennonite Model: Fresno Pacific College

If we wish to study Protestant institutions that define themselves especially in terms of social/ethical issues like peace, justice, poverty, and nationalism, we must turn to the Anabaptist/Mennonite tradition. In the context of that tradition, Fresno Pacific College, a Mennonite Brethren institution in Fresno, California, offers an instructive history of interaction with the spirit of the 1960s. Before we examine that history, however, we need to explore the uniquely Mennonite perspective that sustains the life of the mind at many Mennonite colleges.

When we turn from the Reformed to the Anabaptist/Mennonite tradition, we quickly discover that we have entered into a frame of reference radically different from the Reformed perspective. The first thing we notice is that Mennonites begin with holistic living, not with cognition; with ethics, not with the intellect. More precisely, Mennonites begin their task by seeking to implement a vision of discipleship that takes its cue from the teachings of Jesus. They take seriously Jesus' words to abandon self in the interest of others, or when he charged his disciples to practice humility, simplicity, and non-violence. Theirs is a radical vision, to be sure, and one that stands almost entirely out of synch with the values of the larger culture.

One who is unaccustomed to the Mennonite frame of reference might well ask what this perspective has to do with the life of the mind. How can unconventional virtues like these possibly sustain the values we associate with the academy? Put another way, how does one move from Christocentric living to critical and pluralistic thinking?

We can answer that question in three ways. First, we must recall that sixteenth-century Anabaptism originated in the very womb of dissent. In a world that prized lockstep uniformity, Anabaptists dared to question the status quo. It matters little that their dissent began with lifestyle commitments, not with high-level theoretical formulations. Regardless of their starting point, sixteenth-century Anabaptists proved time and again their commitment to independent thinking. If a willingness to question conventional wisdom stands at the heart of the academic enterprise, then surely the Anabaptist heritage offers important resources for sustaining the life of the mind.

Second, Mennonites routinely counsel one another to abandon self in the interest of others. For this reason, service to other human beings, especially to the poor, the marginalized, and the oppressed, stands at the heart of the Mennonite witness. If we ask how a service commitment like this can sustain the life of the mind, the answer is not hard to find. It is difficult to abandon self for the sake of others in any meaningful sense unless one is prepared to take seriously those "others," their cultural contexts, and their points of view. This means that Mennonite colleges, precisely because of their service orientation, are prepared to take seriously one of the cardinal virtues of the modern academy: the emphasis on pluralism and diversity.

Finally, because of its historic emphasis on humility, the Mennonite tradition prepares its scholars to embrace one of the cardinal virtues of the academic guild: the willingness to admit that my understandings may be fragmentary and incomplete and that, indeed, I could be wrong.

For all these reasons, the Mennonite commitment to a life of radical discipleship can contribute in substantial ways to a vigorous life of the mind. One can find no more illuminating example of this fact than the case of Fresno Pacific University in the 1960s. Arthur Wiebe, installed as president as the decade began, was granted the opportunity to reshape an old institution through massive hiring of new faculty. Wiebe chose to hire young faculty, often fresh out of graduate school and imbued with the idealism of the 1960s. More than this, however, these young faculty had also embraced the theological reconstruction of the Mennonite tradition, begun by Harold S. Bender who in 1944 delivered his now-legendary presidential address to the American Society of Church History on the theme, "The Anabaptist Vision." There, Bender argued that Anabaptism drew its nourishment from three key ideas: discipleship as the essence of Christianity, the church as a voluntary community that insisted on mutual accountability, and an ethic defined by nonresistance and love. [10]

It was Bender's vision that informed the thinking of so many of the young Mennonite faculty that Wiebe hired at Fresno Pacific College in the 1960s. Further, Bender's "Anabaptist Vision" squared in important ways with the peace and justice concerns of that period. Accordingly, Fresno Pacific College adopted in 1966 a new and thoroughly Anabaptist-oriented mission statement called simply "The Fresno Pacific Idea." According to Paul Toews, author of the Fresno Pacific narrative in *Models for Christian Higher Education*, "working out the meaning of the Idea to this day remains a process of continuous discussion." [11]

While "The Idea" defined the college in seven discreet ways, two of these definitions are especially significant in this context: "Pacific College is a Community" and "Pacific College is a Prophetic College."

The notion of community has long been important in Anabaptist/Mennonite circles. The entire congregation, for example, makes critical determinations regarding theology, practice, admission of new members, and ecclesiastical discipline. With the inception of "The Idea," Fresno Pacific College sought to implement this same community-centered standard in the context of the college. For example, since the early 1960s, the college has

---

[10] Harold S. Bender, "The Anabaptist Vision," *Church History* 13 (March 1944):3-24.

[11] Toews, 230.

refused to employ academic ranks and titles. To lend that posture substance, the college has also embraced for all these years a relatively compressed salary scale.

In order to further implement the communitarian dimensions of "The Idea," the college introduced in 1972 a unique freshman-level course, centered on the biblical text and required of all entering students. While the course relied on biblical studies faculty for its core lectures, faculty from a variety of disciplines moderated discussion sections, thereby fostering community among the faculty. In addition, each faculty person who taught in this class mentored a small group of students gathered into a "collegium," a setting designed to help new students experience a sense of community at Fresno Pacific College. Each student participated in two activities specifically designed to nurture community within his or her collegium: a weekend mountain retreat and a required public service project.[12]

The public service component of this course also reflected the second critical dimension of "The Idea"—its insistence that "Pacific College is a Prophetic College." Indeed, the Fresno Pacific faculty of the 1960s explicitly rejected the Reformed notion of "integration of faith and learning." As Paul Toews explains, "Integration was too closely identified with the Constantinian tradition. Like so much of that tradition it meant absorption of faith into the cultural system." For this reason, the faculty adopted instead the language of "transformation," a language far more in keeping with the Anabaptist/Mennonite witness than was the language of "integration." [13]

For all the idealism "The Idea" generated, it couldn't balance the budget, and by the late 1970s Fresno Pacific College had accumulated a serious fiscal deficit. In order to offset that deficit, the college adopted several strategies that took the school in some bold new directions. In the first place, the college dramatically expanded teacher education programs which, for the first time in the school's history, required large numbers of adjunct faculty with little or no connection to the Mennonite Brethren Church. Likewise, these programs tended to draw students from a general population that possessed little or no awareness of the Mennonite heritage.

Second, Fresno Pacific College, long governed by the United States Conference of Mennonite Brethren Churches, was placed in 1979 under the jurisdiction of the Pacific District Conference of the Mennonite Brethren Church. This change created an entirely new board of trustees, largely unacquainted with the school's dynamic history in the 1960s. This new board sought to make the college more "market responsive," emphasizing efficiency and success.

---

[12] *Ibid.*, 230-231.

[13] Toews, 233.

Third, in this new climate, President Edmund Janzen asked the faculty to review and perhaps even revise "The Idea" statement. In the course of that revision, the prophetic dimension of "The Idea" was deleted entirely. This deletion was due not only to the board's concern with market responsiveness, efficiency, and success, but also to the fact that many in the Mennonite Brethren Church viewed with considerable suspicion anything remotely prophetic. Their feelings are not difficult to understand. Many in the church longed to shed their cultural boundaries and to identify more freely with the broader, more conservative strains of American culture. Those who took this position often identified any prophetic witness with the more liberal political counterculture of the 1960s.

Fourth, recognizing that the Mennonite Brethren Church did not possess the resources required to sustain a growing, vibrant institution like Fresno Pacific College, President Janzen in 1983 issued a statement that specifically called for the college to broaden its institutional base.

In keeping with these trends, the board selected in 1985 two Wheaton College evangelicals to fill the positions of president and academic vice-president. By 1994, Mennonites accounted for only 60 percent of the faculty, only 15 percent of the undergraduate student population, and an even lower percentage of the graduate student population. As Paul Toews writes, "this reach to outside leadership, together with the other developments of the 1975-1985 decade, all suggested the future would be more generically evangelical and less distinctively Anabaptist." [14]

And yet, by 1995, Toews could write that "the curriculum today is formally more 'Anabaptist' than at any other time in the school's history."[15] How could this possibly be? The answer to that question lies in an almost dialectical relationship that, by the 1990s, characterized the intersection between "The Idea" on the one hand, and the pluralism that slowly broadened the base of this school on the other. In the first place, "The Idea" turned out to be enormously formative. As Toews notes,

> Internally the document quickly came to function as a "charter" statement and since 1966 has been at the core of the institution's search for self-understanding. It was a clear statement that what made an institution Mennonite was its ideation rather than the demographics of its student body, faculty, or even board of trustees. . . . With time, every program and sector of the college would have to legitimate itself before the Idea.[16]

---

[14] *Ibid.*, 238.

[15] *Ibid.*, 239.

[16] *Ibid.*, 230.

But in the second place, "The Idea" flourished precisely in the context of the rich diversity that came to dominate Fresno Pacific College in the 1980s. As Toews explains,

> "Broadening the Base" brought a recognition that others who came to more fully participate in the life of Fresno Pacific College also brought along their particularity. In this more intensified dialogue with other American religious groups the Anabaptist-Mennonite tradition could be reaffirmed as one variety of evangelicalism with its own strength and legitimacy. Authentic religious ecumenicism could only be achieved by respecting religious particularity. The survival of the two are interlinked.[17]

When we understand the relationship that exists between "The Idea" and the religious diversity that characterizes Fresno Pacific College today, we are then prepared to understand Toews when he writes,

> The influx of faculty from different backgrounds required a more explicit dialogue as to what constituted that ideation. The conversations carried on in various forums about how the religious tradition can flavor the curriculum have intensified rather than diminished.[18]

This is precisely why Toews finally concludes that "the curriculum today is formally more 'Anabaptist' than at any other time in the school's history."

The Lutheran Model: California Lutheran University

Finally, we turn to the Lutheran model for Christian higher education and how that model shaped California Lutheran University in the 1960s and beyond.

The first resource the Lutheran tradition offers for sustaining Christian higher education is Luther's insistence on human finitude and the sovereignty of God. When Luther argues for God's sovereignty, his point is not that Christians should impose God's sovereignty on an unbelieving world. Rather, when Luther points to God's sovereignty, he always points at the very same time to the finitude of humankind.

In the context of higher education and the life of the mind, this position means that I am not God, that my reason is inevitably impaired, that my knowledge is always fragmentary and incomplete, and that, indeed, I could be wrong. Apart from this conviction, there can be no serious life of the mind and no serious appreciation for diversity, for only when I confess that I might be wrong am I empowered to critically scrutinize my own theories, my own judgments, and my own presuppositions. At this point, Lutheran theology stands

---

[17] *Ibid.*, 241.

[18] *Ibid.*, 239.

shoulder to shoulder with the Anabaptist emphasis on humility.

The second resource the Lutheran tradition offers for sustaining the life of the mind is Luther's notion of paradox, a theme that stands at the heart of Lutheran thought. As we know, Luther gloried in the idea of paradox: the King of the universe born in a manger, God Himself nailed to a Roman cross, *simul justus et peccator*. The notion of paradox is a powerful support for the life of the mind since it resists an "either-or" mentality but affirms instead a "both-and" perspective. Indeed, the notion of paradox encourages us to find the truth in diverse points of view that might otherwise seem contradictory or mutually exclusive.

There is no paradox more conducive to the task of higher education, or more supportive of that enterprise, than Luther's notion of two kingdoms. In his view, the Christian lives in the world and in the Kingdom of God and does so simultaneously. The authentic Lutheran vision, therefore, never calls for Christians to separate from the world or to transform the world so that it conforms to the Kingdom of God. Instead, the Christian must reside in two worlds at one and the same time: the world of nature and the world of grace. The Christian in Luther's view, therefore, is free to take seriously both the world and the Kingdom of God.

This notion has enormous implications for the life of the mind, especially if we think of the life of the mind as one which fosters genuine conversation in which all the voices at the table are taken seriously. In the context of Luther's two kingdoms, there is no need to superimpose on other voices a "Christian worldview." Nor is it important to "integrate faith and learning" around a dominant and controlling Christian perspective. Rather, we seek to bring Christian voices and other voices into conversation, into dialogue, with one another. Luther's notion of the two kingdoms is therefore fully capable of sustaining a commitment to the Christian faith and a serious engagement with other perspectives and worldviews at one and the same time. For this reason, the notion of a slippery slope to secularization scarcely makes sense in a Lutheran context. The point is clear: The Lutheran faith offers colleges and universities rooted in this tradition enormous intellectual resources.

What, then, might we say of California Lutheran University? Founded in 1959 in Thousand Oaks, California, California Lutheran University [hereafter CLU] welcomed its inaugural class of students in the fall of 1961. This school, therefore, lived out its infancy in the turbulent decade of the 1960s. How did it respond? How did it seek to connect the ethical and moral issues of that period with the heritage of the Lutheran faith? And in broader terms, how did it connect faith with learning?

As Margaret Wold and Byron Swanson, authors of the CLU narrative in *Models for Christian Higher Education*,[19] tell us, CLU in its earliest years

---

[19] Byron R. Swanson and Margaret Barth Wold, "Faith and Learning at California

experienced some difficulty connecting with the dynamic and open-ended qualities of the Lutheran faith and the way that faith tradition might sustain diversity, academic freedom, and the life of the mind. For example, CLU for its first two years apparently resisted diversity in the faculty and student body, maintaining both those segments at essentially 100 percent Lutheran.

In 1962, however, the new president Rev. Raymond Olson took steps to open the institution up to the larger intellectual world, implementing a policy that welcomed faculty and students from all religious persuasions. In addition, when "several pastors of . . . supporting parishes . . . demanded that . . . CLU fire members of the philosophy, religion, and history departments who violated the inerrancy of scripture by speaking of 'myths' and historical criticism," Olson "staunchly backed the accused teachers citing Lutheran traditions of open scholarship." [20]

The student unrest that brought many American universities to a standstill was hardly a significant factor at CLU in the early 1960s. But in 1968, in the aftermath of the assassination of Martin Luther King, CLU students and faculty, led by President Olson, marched through the streets of the conservative community of Thousand Oaks, demonstrating the willingness of this small community to engage the issues of that period. Later a second march took place, this time in support of the National Vietnam War Moratorium.

Those events were critical in the life of this fledgling institution. One faculty member recalled that the Kent State Massacre and other significant events of that period "caused the . . . students and faculty to debate more openly than ever before what it meant to be a Lutheran college." [21] To heighten dialogue, the CLU administration brought to campus during those years a host of controversial speakers including Angela Davis, Adam Clayton Powell, Dick Gregory, and Bishop James Pike, though the president insisted that both sides of an especially controversial question must be heard during a given academic year. In these ways, CLU demonstrated its growing commitment to the Lutheran tradition of critical scholarship and, in that context, to dialogue and freedom of thought and expression.

Yet CLU paid a heavy price for that commitment. When Raymond Olson became president of the school in 1962, he inherited a significant indebtedness, and when critics of the school's commitment to engage the issues of the 1960s withdrew their financial support, CLU found its fiscal woes seriously compounded. By 1970, CLU faced potential bankruptcy with an overall indebtedness of $3,600,000. The board at that point considered closing CLU altogether, but Lutherans throughout the United States rallied to save the

---

Lutheran University," *Models*, 97-122.

[20] *Ibid.*, 102; 104.

[21] *Ibid.*, 105.

institution. Their support, coupled with the extremely rigorous fiscal measures which CLU now embraced, enabled California Lutheran University to survive that critical period in its history.

In 1972, the CLU board hired Mark Mathews as the third president of CLU. This choice was significant for several reasons. First, as the chairperson of the department of business administration and economics, Mathews came well equipped to bring long-term fiscal stability to the institution. And second, Mathews was not a Lutheran but a Presbyterian. To facilitate his presidency, therefore, the by-laws of the institution had to be revised, thereby further undermining the parochial qualities that had characterized CLU in its earliest years.

Mathews achieved a significant measure of success in stabilizing CLU's fiscal situation, but he refused to retreat from the tradition of critical scholarship and free and open investigation of serious issues that was becoming a hallmark of CLU. As a case in point, Mathews supported the students when they organized in the early 1970s a campus-wide symposium devoted to critical discussion of social and ethical issues facing the United States and the world at that time. Students who convened in that forum addressed "war in Vietnam, abortion, homosexuality, sexism, poverty, racism, sanctuary for Central American refugees, and the World War II atomic bombing of Nagasaki and Hiroshima." The fact that this symposium was rooted squarely in the Christian character of CLU was reflected in the title the students used to designate this discussion series: "Christian Conversations." The campus pastor at that time described these years as the "'golden age' of integration of faith and learning."[22]

Also during Mathews' tenure, the CLU faculty introduced the Humanities Tutorial Program, a one-year, interdisciplinary course designed for exceptionally gifted students and team-taught by English, history, philosophy, and religion faculty. Students in this course studied the Bible and great Christian thinkers, to be sure. But they also studied foes of the Christian tradition like Nietzsche, Lenin, and Marx, allowing Christian ideas to dialogue with other perspectives and thereby implementing the Lutheran model for Christian higher education in especially meaningful ways.

During these years, the demographics of CLU changed as well. By the 1978-79 academic year, "other Christians" outnumbered Lutherans on the CLU faculty by 49 percent to 45 percent. Jews held three percent of faculty positions, while two percent did not identify with any particular religious tradition.

During the decade of the 1980s, CLU sought to become more ethnically and culturally inclusive. On the one hand, the school launched a variety of successful initiatives designed to attract students from both Asia and Scandinavia, while on the domestic front, CLU sought to recruit students from the sizable Hispanic population in Southern California. In part because of this

---

[22] *Ibid.*, 109.

latter initiative, Roman Catholics outnumbered Lutherans in the CLU student body by 1995. The CLU administration has responded to this situation by inviting Roman Catholic priests to celebrate Mass on campus and faculty from nearby St. John's Seminary to teach courses exploring Roman Catholic thought.

The dilemma facing California Lutheran University today grows directly from the Lutheran model for Christian higher education that places such a premium on diversity, dialogue, and paradox. By 1995 the Lutheran presence on the faculty had eroded to only 35 percent. And by 1994 a student body that once was almost 100 percent Lutheran now included only 24.5 percent Lutheran. The problem was obvious: While California Lutheran University for a number of years had sought to live out of its Lutheran heritage and to implement on that basis the critical tradition of Lutheran higher education, fewer and fewer faculty and students possessed much awareness of how the Lutheran heritage could sustain a school of this sort. Indeed, responses to a faculty survey administered in 1995 suggested that only eight percent of the CLU faculty possessed a strong understanding of the Lutheran tradition.[23] The institution therefore embodied many of the ends consistent with the Lutheran tradition, but increasingly found itself disconnected from the means. For this reason, President Luther Leudtke recently embarked on an effort to educate faculty regarding the Lutheran theological heritage and to help them understand what that tradition can contribute to the task of higher education.

Conclusions

What can we say, then, regarding these three schools–Calvin College, Fresno Pacific College, and California Lutheran University—and the models they represent, in the context of the last three and one-half decades of American life and culture? First, none of these schools allowed the pressures of the 1960s to force them to abandon their distinctive faith traditions. To the contrary, each of these institutions responded to the 1960s by renewing its commitment to the religious heritage upon which the school was founded, and by living out of that tradition in meaningful and deliberate ways. With the dawn of the 1970s, new challenges visited each of these institutions, sometimes in the form of declining enrollments, sometimes in the form of fiscal crises, and sometimes in the form of cultural trends that challenged the theological traditions that held these schools together. In each instance, however, these three institutions have weathered the storms by working in creative and flexible ways with their respective faith traditions, thereby demonstrating the ways in which these three different forms of the Protestant faith helped sustain the task of Christian higher education during these critical years of the American experience.

---

[23] *Ibid.*, 119.

4

American Catholic Higher Education

An Experience of Inculturation

Alice Gallin, O.S.U.
Saint Louis University

A question that has plagued American Catholic colleges and universities for the past thirty years is: "Are these 220 institutions still Catholic?" Many who attempt to answer the question immediately focus on an individual college and its recent history. Yet there needs to be some attempt to generalize about them because these institutions are seen as a distinct sector by American society and by the Catholic community. The meaning of the name we give to institutions and organizations is important since it indicates our understanding of their purpose and activity. The literature that has been produced on this topic falls into two general categories: those who bemoan the secularization of the universities and the loss of their Catholic distinctiveness and those who defend their movement into mainstream higher education in the United States, arguing that without making changes they would not be here today and the church and society would be poorer.[1]

---

[1] The former was clearly articulated by Rev. James Tunstead Burtchaell, C.S.C., in his two articles in *First Things:* "The Decline and Fall of the Christian College," 12 (1991): 16-29, and "The Decline and Fall of the Christian College (II)," 13 (1991): 30-8. There have been several subsequent articles in that same publication. Another negative position about the Catholic identity of colleges is held by the Fellowship of Catholic Scholars and can be found in almost every issue of its *Newsletter* since its founding in 1977. The more positive evaluation is offered in several articles in *Current Issues in Catholic Higher Education* and is assumed in the several responses to Rome regarding the development of the document on Catholic higher education. The latter can be found in Alice Gallin, O.S.U., ed., *American Catholic Higher*

This is a story of interaction and ambiguity,[2] arising in part from the role that universities play in the process of inculturation. The ambiguity has arisen from the changed theological understanding of the church itself, a shift already perceptible in the 1950s and given official recognition in the decisions of Vatican Council II. In recent years Pope John Paul II has utilized this newer self-understanding when he has written and spoken on the mission of the church to evangelize cultures, and emphasized the significant role that he sees for the Catholic University in that process. But such a role is not without ambiguity:

> A Catholic university, as any university, is immersed in human society; as an extension of its service to the church, and always within its proper competence, it is called on to become an ever more effective instrument of cultural progress for individuals as well as for society...[3]

Further, he notes: "Their mission appears increasingly necessary for the encounter of the church with the development of the sciences and with the cultures of our age." [4]

The question thus facing the university that knows itself as Catholic is how to carry out this mission in various world cultures without losing its ability to criticize those elements of the culture which contradict the values of the Gospel of Jesus Christ. One way of doing this would be to remain outside the dominant culture, and in fact that was the path followed by the church in the United States in pre-Vatican II days. The opposition to modernity by church authorities in the early twentieth century and the strong attachment to a Catholic culture in the forties and fifties set Catholics in America apart from their neighbors. Whether this separatism is to be praised as safeguarding the faith or denounced as creating a ghetto mentality, the fact remains that Catholics and their universities were regarded by others as a sub-culture. The positive side of the coin was that their various constituencies had no doubt about their identity as Catholic.[5]

Education: Essential Documents 1967-1990 (Notre Dame, IN: University of Notre Dame Press, 1992).

[2] To understand the historical reasons for such ambiguity one should consult Philip Gleason, *Contending With Modernity: Catholic Higher Education in the Twentieth Century* (New York: Oxford University Press, 1995); Andrew Greeley, *From Backwater to Mainstream: A Profile of Catholic Higher Education* (New York: McGraw-Hill Book Company, 1969); David O'Brien, *From the Heart of the American Church: Catholic Higher Education and American Culture* (Maryknoll, NY: Orbis Books, 1994).

[3] *Ex corde ecclesiae*, #32, in Gallin, *American Catholic Higher Education*, 423.

[4] *Ibid.*, #9

[5] This is well documented in Gleason, *Contending with Modernity*. See also his 1994 Marianist Lecture at the University of Dayton, "What Makes Catholic Identity a Problem?"

Nevertheless, despite that strong sense of identification as "Catholic," the colleges and universities were at the same time absorbing some of the standards and ideals of their secular counterparts. Certain symbols of the dominant culture within which the church and its institutions in the United States operated—freedom of speech and religion, democratic organization, individualism—were increasingly visible on Catholic campuses as the twentieth century wore on.

These values—often considered to be the positive outcome of the Enlightenment—were treasured by Catholic educators in the United States, but were not universally owned by their counterparts in other countries. This became clear in the discussions at a series of international meetings held under the auspices of the International Federation of Catholic Universities (IFCU) beginning in 1965. Repeated attempts to dialogue with one another and with the Roman Congregation for Catholic Education on the basic question, "What makes a university Catholic?" ultimately came up against divergent understandings of these basic American values and how they influenced the relationship between American culture and Catholic ecclesial mission. Given the secular foundation of cultures (i.e. the basic physical, social, and political realities), how could secularization (understood as the absence of God from human discourse and the irrelevance of Christian ideals in the academy) be avoided? Did the American experience have anything to offer as a solution?

In 1989 at their final meeting before John Paul II issued *Ex Corde Ecclesiae,* the delegates at the Third International Congress of Catholic Universities struggled to clarify for one another the legal and educational systems within which they lived and which would need to be taken into account in any statement on the nature and mission of a Catholic university. The IFCU, having been born from a desire of Pius XII to have Catholic universities serve as liaisons to the United Nations, was very conscious of the cultural differences among its members and sought for ways of promoting unity among them so that together they might articulate a common identity. It was only logical that cultural questions would be of great importance to the members. John XXIII, Paul VI and John Paul II all stressed the need for serious study of the social sciences dealing with questions of diverse cultures and challenged Catholic universities to promote such investigations by scholars on their faculties. [6]

At the meeting in 1989 it quickly became evident that one of the values which the Americans prized—free debate essential for participative decision-

---

[6] See especially John XXIII, and *Mater et magistra* (15 May 1961) and *Pacem in terris* (11 April 1963); Paul VI, *Evangelium nuntiandi* (8 Dec. 1975); and John Paul II, *Ex corde ecclesiae.* (15 Aug. 1990). The emphasis with which John Paul II has addressed the issue of the evangelization of cultures is highlighted in his addresses to the people of Poland as described by George Weigel, "John Paul II and the Priority of Culture," *First Things,* 80 (1998): 19-25.

making—was not universally shared. Terminology and rhetoric used in preliminary documents and the process designed for the meeting were simply unacceptable. The Americans were joined by some colleagues from other parts of the world who also thought it important to share their own cultural experiences before developing an agenda for the meeting. In the first few days there were many skirmishes between that group and those who had a more canonical approach to the question of Catholic identity. The opportunity was thus provided for an exchange of histories among the different cultural groups. The American experience is one that needs to be understood by all who discuss the issue of secularization.

The American Experience

The American culture in which our Catholic colleges were founded was one dominated by Protestantism. Colleges evolved from private academies and until the twentieth century were not clearly distinguished from them. Unlike the European universities and those in Asia and South America that were modeled on them, colleges in the United States were focused on the student's moral as well as academic education. Most of them were founded by various Protestant denominations and saw moral education as a top priority. Thus the role of teachers and administrators was to oversee young people *in loco parentis*. Until the establishment of Johns Hopkins University in 1876 there was no fundamental commitment to research as the primary purpose of American higher education. Among Catholic institutions only the Catholic University of America was founded for that reason (1889). One of the distinctive marks of American higher education would be the effort to combine in one institution advanced research and undergraduate education. That would occur in Catholic institutions only by the mid- twentieth century.

Like their colleagues in other church-related institutions, Catholic faculties paid attention not only to classroom instruction but also to the development of student leadership, the nurturing of student newspapers, common residential life and the mentoring of student government. The socialization of the young man or woman, generally in separate institutions, was an important part of education. But by the middle of the twentieth century many of the Protestant church-related institutions had moved away from their church affiliations, and their growth into modern universities led to a neutrality toward religious values.[7] The question

---

[7] George M. Marsden and Bradley J. Longfield, eds., *The Secularization of the Academy* (New York: Oxford University Press, 1992); George M. Marsden, *The Soul of the American University* (New York: Oxford University Press, 1994). The sub-title of the latter is *From Protestant Establishment to Established Nonbelief*, which sums up the story in a few words.

naturally arises: Will a similar fate befall Catholic institutions once they achieve status as research universities? And, if so, what difference would it make? [8]

Unlike the Protestant-founded colleges, the Catholic colleges owed their existence not to a sponsoring church body or judicature but rather to individual communities of men and women religious. While such communities needed the approval of the local bishop to open a college, the responsibility for governing and funding all but about a dozen of these colleges did not lie with the diocese. The bishop was often so overwhelmed by the numbers of immigrant Catholics who needed churches, elementary schools and other pastoral services that he was only too happy to leave higher education in the hands of the religious. As the increasing complexity of American higher education became apparent after World War II, Catholic colleges and universities developed internal structures of governance that assumed a certain degree of autonomy. The need to refer questions to the authorities of the religious community had often created difficulties in decision-making. So as the events of the sixties pushed everyone toward a more participatory type of governance, the colleges responded by creating faculty senates and independent boards of trustees composed of lay persons as well as members of the sponsoring religious community. [9]

The nineteenth century American Catholic experience of lay trusteeism had left a residue of suspicion and mistrust on the part of clerical authorities.[10] But with the new theological understanding of the role of the lay person in the church articulated in the documents of Vatican Council II, such attitudes began to diminish. Higher authorities in religious communities recognized the need for the colleges to adapt to the societal changes in the United States and to update their mode of operating.

---

[8] Burtchaell's work suggests a compelling analogy between Vanderbilt University and a Catholic university. Before accepting the analogy as pre-determining the fate of Catholic colleges, we need to examine the circumstances which led to the gradual erosion of Protestant religious goals in their American colleges. In addition to the work of George Marsden, that of Richard T. Hughes and William B. Adrian is very helpful in relating the various denominational world views to the colleges founded by the different churches and examining some models in detail so as to suggest how some institutions retained their identity while others gradually lost theirs: *Models For Christian Higher Education: Strategies for Survival and Success in the Twenty-First Century* (Grand Rapids, MI: Eerdmans Publishing Co., 1997).

[9] Alice Gallin, *Independence and a New Partnership in Catholic Higher Education* (Notre Dame, IN: University of Notre Dame Press, 1996).

[10] James Hennesey, S.J., *American Catholics: A History of the Roman Catholic Community in the United States* (New York: Oxford University Press, 1981) 94-6. See also "Trusteeism," by Patrick Carey, in Michael Glazier and Thomas J. Shelley, eds., *The Encyclopedia of American Catholic History* (Collegeville, MN: Liturgical Press, 1997), 1396-8.

However, these changes became far more radical than anyone had anticipated. Speaking of American universities in the late 60s, Thomas Bender writes: "...the issues of life-style, war, poverty and race converged, making for a volatile compound that produced riots in cities and divided university campuses."[11] At Catholic colleges, points of tension were highlighted when certain radical speakers were invited to campus under the protection of academic freedom and when honorary degrees were given to individuals not approved by ecclesial authorities.[12] American independence was now being asserted by Catholic universities, and the reaction to it by Roman church authorities was an inability to understand how such institutions could still be Catholic. In 1974 they inquired, "Which ones are still Catholic?" [13]

An answer to this question was given in a document published by the college and university department of the National Catholic Educational Association in 1976.[14] The characteristics enunciated in the document "The Catholic University in the Modern World" were affirmed[15] but were then explained within the context of American law and values. In very direct language the position of Catholic colleges and universities in the United States was expounded: "Any indication of interference in the institution's proper autonomy

---

[11] Thomas Bender, "Politics, Intellect, and the American University, 1945-95," *Daedalus* 126.1 (Winter 1997): 22.

[12] An example of both of these issues can be found at Saint Louis University where an honorary degree given to Hans Kung in 1963 and an invitation to the French philosopher Roger Garudy to speak on campus in 1966 were both strongly protested.

[13] Gabriel Marie Cardinal Garrone, Secretary of the Congregation for Catholic Education to Msgr. John F. Murphy, Executive Director of the National Catholic Educational Association, College and University Dept., Washington, D.C. (October 1974), Archives of the NCEA.

[14] "Relations of American Catholic Colleges and Universities with the Church," in Gallin, *American Catholic Higher Education*, 71-86. This document summarized the history of universities and colleges within America's pluralistic society and pointed to the parameters drawn by state and university associations for acceptance into the academic community and the way in which these criteria affected the relationship of the Catholic institutions to the church. "Relations" was approved by the Bishops and Presidents' committee and later included by reference in the National Conference of Catholic Bishops' letter, *Catholic Higher Education and the Pastoral Mission of the Church: Statement of the National Conference of Bishops* (1981), in Gallin, *American Catholic Higher Education*, 135-51.

[15] Gallin, *American Catholic Higher Education*, 37. The four characteristics deemed to be essential were: 1) a Christian inspiration not only of individuals but of the community as well; 2) a continuing reflection in the light of Christian faith upon the growing treasure of human knowledge; 3) fidelity to the Christian message as it comes to us through the Church; 4) an institutional commitment to the service of Christian thought and education. In *Ex corde ecclesiae* two interesting additions can be noted: in # 2 there is a final phrase, "to which it seeks to contribute by its own research" and in #4 it reads, "service to the people of God and of the human family in their pilgrimage to the transcendent goal which gives meaning to life."

by representatives of the official Church would only assist the attempt to deprive church-related institutions of equal treatment before the law with other institutions."[16] Emphasis was given to cooperative relationships among bishops, trustees and college presidents in maintaining the Catholic identity of the institutions in a way that harmonized with American law and custom. [17]

The concept of academic freedom had not originated in the United States but was a European product, especially in Germany. The earliest universities in Europe had been corporations of teachers or, in some cases, of students which hired and paid the instructors. As time went on, the financial responsibility was assumed by the royal patron or the state government. The professors became employees of the state, civil servants of the most respected variety, and the collection of student fees by the professor was eliminated. But the increased dependence on the state called for a declaration guaranteeing "freedom to teach and freedom to learn," first enunciated at Humboldt University in Berlin, and directed against the Prussian state.

Johns Hopkins University, modeled on the German universities, brought this tradition into the American academy and other American universities soon followed suit. From 1915 on, the American Association of University Professors has been the watchdog of academic freedom, drawing up statements defining and describing its implications and censuring institutions found to be violating its guidelines.

A more distinctly American claim was that of institutional autonomy. This was a concept not articulated in European universities since they were totally dependent on the state for funding, and members of faculties were considered civil servants with accountability to a central Ministry of Education. Since both students and faculties tended to move from one university to another, a concept of autonomy for the particular institution would have had little meaning, although by tradition universities had certain exemptions from local ordinances and some privileges that marked them as special institutions. In the United States, on the other hand, the churches founded and governed the early colleges and asserted their jurisdiction over them as far back as colonial

---

[16] Gallin, *American Catholic Higher Education*, 79.

[17] It is important to recall that in 1966 the decision in the *Horace Mann* case had ruled that two Catholic colleges in Maryland were ineligible for government funds because they were "pervasively sectarian," and that in New York State in 1968 the grants to private higher education known as "Bundy" money could be given only to those colleges that were not under the control of a church. See Charles W. Wilson's essay in this volume; it can also be found in *Current Issues in Catholic Higher Education* 18.1 (1997): 3-67.

times, claiming independence from the state.[18] The state, for its part, saw the colleges as preparing men to be good citizens as well as faithful members of the church, and so was content to leave the task of education to them; thus autonomy was experienced before being defined.

How was this task of education to be accomplished? In practice, it was approached through a classical curriculum rooted in the tradition of European culture and the Christian religion. Closely monitored by church guardians—who came to be known as trustees—the teachers were not subject to direct state control but rather to church officials. When Catholic colleges were founded, they tended to follow the same pattern of governance, only with accountability to the religious community rather than to church officials.

With the Morrill Act in 1862 came a new model of higher education in the United States. By that act the land grant colleges came into existence, constituting a nucleus for what would become a system of public or state-sponsored post-secondary education. From that time forward American higher education has been a wonderfully diverse, sometimes contentious, mixture of private and public universities or, to use other terms, independent and state or community colleges. Pluralism of ownership and control has led to divergent understandings of academic freedom and institutional autonomy. But without a "system" of higher education or a national ministry of education, the colleges and universities have been free to develop in a variety of forms according to the needs of people seeking education and the educational philosophy of the founders. Standards and criteria for measuring achievement became the task of regional and specialized accrediting associations, voluntary in membership but powerful in impact on the institutions.

Nevertheless, today the state has tremendous influence on the way that private institutions operate. This point was well articulated by William M. Shea in his address to the annual meeting of the Association of Catholic Colleges and Universities in 1987:

> In fact, American Catholic higher education is already public. It is chartered by the state; its existence is entrusted to boards which are not ecclesiastical in makeup; for most of this century it has sought and found accreditation from public bodies; it uses no religious test for admission and, in many cases, for hiring; it is the recipient of large amounts of public money; its course requirements in theology are taught according to American academic criteria and not under ecclesiastical supervision; its campus ministers are ministers and not proselytizers; and even when it clearly affirms its Catholic heritage, it does not impose it even upon its Catholic students.

---

[18] This was upheld in the decision in the case of the *Trustees of Dartmouth College v. Woodward*, 17 US (4 Wheat) 518 (1819).

He concluded, "The colleges have been redefining their Catholicism,"[19] and we might add, precisely as American.

The concern that Americans have about mission statements is something difficult to explain to our European and Asian colleagues. However, the diversity among the 3200 colleges and universities in the United States suggests that higher education serves many purposes, thus requiring institutional statements about "mission." The church-related colleges, among them the Catholic ones, see their distinctiveness as essential to the purposes for which they were founded and funded. Nevertheless, their claim to institutional autonomy, while historically aimed at prohibiting state interference, has in many cases been made in relation to the church or community that sponsors them. In 1967 a public statement was issued by leaders of Catholic universities claiming both academic freedom and institutional autonomy as essential characteristics of any university.[20] This "Land O'Lakes" document became central to the debate over the next thirty years between Catholic universities and church authorities in Rome, and in a footnote in the Apostolic Constitution, *Ex corde ecclesiae*, issued in 1990, the "American" definition of these terms was included:

> Institutional autonomy means that the governance of an academic institution is and remains internal to the institution; academic freedom is the guarantee given to those involved in teaching and research that, within their specific specialized branch of knowledge and according to the methods proper to that specific area, they may search for the truth wherever analysis and evidence lead them, and may teach and publish the results of this search, keeping in mind the cited criteria, that is, safeguarding the rights of the individual and of society within the confines of the truth and the common good.[21]

To sum up, the impact of the American experience (as distinct from the European) on Catholic higher education can be seen in the commitment to an education that focuses on the student, on the conviction that advanced research and undergraduate education are complementary and can coexist, that voluntary associations can set standards for academic excellence, and that institutional autonomy and academic freedom are basic to higher education. The Catholic colleges and universities adapted to the criteria proposed by American academic associations. Does that mean that they are now no longer Catholic? Does it mean that they are simply imitators of secular universities? Have they no longer any distinctive mission within American society?

---

[19] William M. Shea, "Beyond Tolerance: Pluralism and Catholic Higher Education," *Current Issues in Catholic Higher Education* 8.2 (1988): 38.

[20] "The Nature of the Contemporary Catholic University," in Gallin, *American Catholic Higher Education*, 7-12.

[21] Gallin, *American Catholic Higher Education*, 434.

Students of the process of inculturation tell us that it consists of two stages: The first is the effort to enter into and understand the culture into which one is moving; the second is to bring about an interaction between that culture and one's own so that the values of both can be promoted.[22] How then would we describe the American culture to which Catholic higher education has increasingly related?

In the introduction to his book, *Religion and Twentieth Century American Intellectual Life*, Michael J. Lacey writes: "Until the last third of the nineteenth century, the life of the mind in the United States was largely dominated by the concerns and controversies, innovations and accommodations, of the Protestant clergy."[23] This monopoly by clerical scholars was due, no doubt, to the church-relatedness of the early colleges, but it was broken in the late nineteenth century by scientists and philosophers committed to the values of the Enlightenment. In the twentieth century many of these colleges developed into universities, and by the 1930s, according to Henry May, they prescribed to a naturalist perspective which,

> ...was a progressive, democratic outlook on history, based in part on a set of · assumptions of Enlightenment vintage, 'lodged in the unconscious where assumptions are hardest to dislodge,' that while reason and democracy were advancing, religion was necessarily in decline.[24]

Thomas Bender brings this evolution up to date. He writes: "It is too easy to overlook how deeply encompassing Christian academic culture was before 1945.... After 1945, American intellectual culture, academic and literary, would be de-Christianized." He claims that even the religious movements that were growing were anti-intellectual, and that the events of the 1960s and 1970s led to culture wars and, in the end, to post-modern deconstructionism.[25] The universities themselves did little or nothing to stop this movement. George Marsden and others have described the loss of the university's "soul."[26] It is the

---

[22] Ary A. Roest Crollius, S.J., "What Is So New About Inculturation?" *Gregorianum* 59.4 (1978): 721-38. For an application of the concept to American Catholic higher education see Philip Gleason, "Adventures in Inculturation: An Historical Perspective on Catholic Higher Education," a lecture given at Marquette University, August 1995. Gleason, however, does not attend very carefully to the first stage–listening to the other culture.

[23] Michael J. Lacey, *Religion and Twentieth Century American Intellectual Life* (New York: Cambridge University Press, 1989), 2.

[24] *Ibid.*, 3.

[25] Bender, 11.

[26] See Marsden and Longfield, *The Secularization of the Academy*; Marsden, *The Soul of the American University*.

fear of a similar fate for Catholic universities that inspires Burtchaell's pessimism:

> If our account of alienation as a repeating process is reliable, then the American Catholic institutions of higher education are nearing the end of a process of formal detachment from accountability to their church, and instead of exerting themselves to oblige that church to be a more credible patron of higher learning, they are qualifying for acceptance by and on the terms of the secular academic culture, and are likely soon to hand over their institutions unencumbered by any compromising accountability to the church.[27]

However, George Marsden cautions us about identifying the word secularization with its negative connotations. I agree with him and add that it is also important for us to agree that "secular" is not simply nor always the opposite of "sacred": In a Christian sacramental view of reality, the secular has a legitimate role and one that is congruent with and not opposed to faith or religion. John Crosby has presented this point of view in his article in *First Things*[28] where he makes the case for a productive relationship between Athens and Jerusalem and not a fundamental conflict between then.

Some critics use the word "secularization" to describe the loss of control by the church over the general campus climate, covering everything from the choice of honorary degree recipients to the granting of parietal visitation in the residence halls. The secularity of American culture is sometimes a scapegoat for the lack of coherence in disciplines like philosophy and theology whereas the real culprit may be a loss of nerve on the part of administrators and faculty who lack confidence in their ability to present clear and compelling argument for their own faith and values.[29]

Because the 700 currently identified church-related institutions are becoming less visibly related to their churches and more akin to secular universities and colleges there is a need for leaders who will give direction and not just let the institutions drift. We can, no doubt, learn from those universities that were founded by church communities and later opted to sever that relationship. Was it necessary for them to do that in order to become recognized

---

[27] Burtchaell, II: 38.

[28] John F. Crosby, "Education and the Mind Redeemed," *First Things* 18 (December 1991): 23-28.

[29] A particularly helpful critique of the state of philosophical studies is found in Jude P. Dougherty, Desmond Fitzgerald, Thomas Langan, and Kenneth Schmitz, "The Secularization of Western Culture and the Catholic College and University," *Current Issues in Catholic Higher Education* 2.1 (Summer 1981): 7-23. An interesting observation made by the authors is that "...it is less secularization the college has to fear than its own failure to think through both the positive potential of the new civilization and the question of what Christianity has to offer." Fifteen years later this comment is still worth pondering.

as American universities? If so, is such a step still necessary for those in the last decade of the twentieth century who wish to attain status within the secular academy?

A Comparison

In studying the process by which colleges have moved away from their traditional mode of church-relatedness I perceive five similarities between the Protestant-founded and Catholic-founded colleges, and five differences. Let me begin with my understanding of the processes by which church-related colleges and universities have struggled to keep a balance between their religious roots and their membership in American secular society, and then offer a critique of their decisions. It may be that more is going on here than a simple shift from the city of God to the city of man and we may need to analyze more closely the concept of inculturation as a possible explanation for what has happened. I will deal with mainline colleges and universities and not with those who present themselves unambiguously as alternatives to secular higher education. [30]

Similarities:

1. Both mainline Protestant and Roman Catholic colleges announced their founding purposes in terms of moral development of youth, preparation of leaders for their church, and commitment to a classical liberal arts curriculum as the foundation of all good education.

2. Since the colleges were linked to the churches, they changed as the churches themselves changed. In our own times we have seen the effect that the changed self-understanding of the Roman Catholic church, as it was articulated by the second Vatican Council, has had on Catholic institutions. In the midst of our many debates with church authorities about the Catholicity of our colleges, one president remarked: "When the bishops tell us what it means to be Catholic today, we'll tell them what it means to be a Catholic university." Another example can be found in the Lutheran community. In the past decade there has been a merger of two churches—the Lutheran Church in America and the American Lutheran Church—into the new Evangelical Lutheran Church in America. Since Lutheran colleges are related in a variety of ways to church synods and/or to local congregations, the status of their current relationship to

---

[30] I think here of Steubenville University or Christendom College, and of those faith-related institutions that work together as the Christian College Coalition. See Mary Jo Weaver, "Introduction: Who Are the Conservative Catholics?", Mary Jo Weaver and R. Scott Appleby, eds., *Being Right: Conservative Catholics in America* (Bloomington, IN: Indiana University Press, 1995).

the church is only slowly evolving. At its best, the relationship of church and college is a dynamic one, requiring constant reflection and dialogue.

3. The leadership in the colleges that consciously made changes in the church-relatedness of their structures were men and women who were strongly committed to their churches. The Protestant ministers and the Catholic priests and sisters who presided over the colleges did not intend to undercut the mission or minimize the importance of their religious traditions. They made changes in curriculum and residential life which they thought necessary to equip the students for life in a secular society. They widened the spectrum of religious preference among faculty, administrators, and trustees in order to enhance the education being given in their colleges and universities as well as to meet government non-discrimination laws. While they themselves remained role models in their commitment to common worship and Christian behavior, times changed and new leadership emerged. Where careful selection of leaders for these colleges has not occurred, there are now unintended consequences to be dealt with if these colleges wish to remain identified with particular religious traditions.

4. The American principle of separation of church and state has affected both Protestant and Catholic colleges. The former group emerged from communities that were themselves Protestant, and so the colleges were seen as one more institution within society working for the common good. In this spirit they were admired and supported by public funds as well as by the churches, and in some ways were accountable to both authorities. James Smylie has written of them: "These colleges may not be labeled easily as state colleges, church colleges, or private colleges, since the commonwealth, the church, and private persons played a part in sponsoring and supporting them."[31] The Catholic colleges were founded as an alternative system of higher education, and were not an outgrowth of the civic community. The principle of separation of church and state, as it was gradually interpreted by the courts, affected many of their decisions once they tried to enter the mainstream of American higher education.

5. There has been a continuing struggle between an affirmation of pluralism as a social value and a commitment on the part of a college or university to a single faith community. How open to the value systems of others outside the faith community can an institution be without losing its own identity? This has been indeed a constant question for all church-related institutions, whether Protestant or Catholic.

---

[31] James H. Smylie, "Roads to Our Present," in Robert Rue Parsonage, ed., *Church Related Higher Education: Perceptions and Perspectives* (Valley Forge, PA: Judson Press, 1978), 139.

Differences:

I want to suggest five differences in the way the Catholic and Protestant institutions have moved to a less visibly religious character.

1. The move away from a clear relationship with a church occurred at different points in time. For the mainline Protestant colleges the process occurred in the late nineteenth and early twentieth centuries whereas the comparable question for Catholic colleges arose only after the 1950s. As Marsden and others make clear, the original American colleges were Protestant in origin, in curriculum, and in models of community moral behavior, and were sponsored by a civic community that was itself Protestant. Hence he suggests that we might more properly think of the secularization of those institutions as a disestablishment of religion,[32] a process that the civic community had gone through early in the nineteenth century but which only slowly penetrated the social structures of American life. To this observation we can add that this political and social development coincided with an epistemological revolution which produced a new faith, that is, a faith in the scientific method as the only valid path to truth. In that environment a self-conscious denominational education appeared to be an anachronism. To the leaders of American higher education at the time it seemed wise to separate the intellectual goals of the university from the spiritual and moral development that had previously been so important in church-related education.

Unlike those founded by Protestants, the Catholic colleges began not as an integral part of early American society but as an alternative system of higher education, needed because Catholic teachers and students were not usually welcomed in the major institutions and also because the bishops understandably feared for the sons and daughters of the immigrants whose home-country culture had been more supportive of their faith.[33] The task of the Catholic colleges until the mid-twentieth century was quite self-consciously to serve the Catholic population, even though many specified that students of every faith or no faith were welcome to enroll. As late as the 1950s the Catholic colleges saw their mission as one of fortifying Catholic culture, magnifying and developing the tradition which was their heritage. There was a commitment to the importance of studying the doctrines of the Catholic faith and to upholding the standards of Christian moral behavior among both faculty and students. There was also a clear Catholic tradition which linked the love of learning and the desire for God, a tradition that justified universities as places where learning for its own sake was appreciated. The founding of the Catholic University of America in 1889 as

---

[32] Marsden, *The Soul of the American University,* chapter 1.

[33] Philip Gleason, *Keeping the Faith: American Catholicism Past and Present* (Notre Dame, IN: University of Notre Dame Press, 1987), *passim.*

a graduate school gave a clear signal from the hierarchy that advanced research and graduate education were endeavors worthy of extensive commitment.[34] This gave a signal that the task of Catholic higher education was similar, in some respects, to the purposes of what had become secular universities, and that in the twentieth century Catholics would have a place of their own where research could be carried on under Catholic auspices. I suggest that timing was very important, and the ways in which Protestant and Catholic colleges adapted to American secular education are tied in to particular moments in history, diverse social contexts, and substantially different reasons.

2. Secondly, there is a difference in the way that the colleges related to the parent churches. The history of the Protestant institutions, for the most part, is one of a direct relationship with the parent church, whether the local congregation or some kind of judicatory. They were most often seen as primary places for the formation of ministers and other church leaders. They received funding from their church, and their administrators and trustees were often accountable to the church elders or conventions. On the Catholic side, however, there was a different kind of church-relatedness. Here, the founders were, with few exceptions, members of distinct religious communities within the Catholic church—Society of Jesus, Congregation of the Holy Cross, Sisters of Mercy, Religious of the Sacred Heart, etc.—and a community of the sponsoring religious order lived on the campus and provided a core religious presence that touched every aspect of college life. Although there were lay persons on faculties and in lower level administration, the link to the church was the religious community, and the institution was regarded as Catholic precisely because it was an apostolic work of a particular order or society which had canonical status within the church.

The primary responsibility for the overarching role of religion on campus and in the classroom rested with the religious community that ran the college. Prior to Vatican II, the effectiveness of their presence was seldom questioned, although in the late '50s there began to be voices challenging the appropriateness of such clear religious presence in an academic environment. If Catholic colleges and universities wanted to be in the mainstream of American higher education, was it not urgent to move out of a Catholic ghetto and embrace the secular standards of professional organizations and associations? Were the religious habit and the Roman collar not obstacles to true fellowship with colleagues? Lay faculty at many Catholic colleges began questioning the competence of some

---

[34] See C. Joseph Nuesse, *The Catholic University of America: A Centennial History* (Washington, D.C.: The Catholic University of America Press, 1990). The impact of this university on the development of Catholic higher education in this country should not be overlooked. Until after World War II it was the only true university among Catholic institutions, although several Jesuit colleges were well on the way to university stature.

religious who were assigned to administer or teach in the college. By the late 1950s academic freedom was the buzz word, and participation of lay persons in the governance structures at all levels began to be advocated. Since the relation of the college to the church was through the religious community the question which was now addressed by the presidents at their annual meetings in the 1960s and 1970s became, "If the community does not retain control, how will the colleges still be Catholic?"[35] By the mid-sixties a struggle for control of these institutions between the administrators of the colleges and the superiors of the religious communities was developing, and only by great political skill and sincere cooperation for the good of the institution was the situation resolved in most places. [36]

Several important factors can be identified in the transition that followed, a transition marked most dramatically by the shift in the composition of the governing boards of trustees from entirely religious to predominantly lay:

♦ Beginning in the 1960s there was a sharp decline in the number of persons entering the religious communities. With a lessened presence of religious communities on campuses, the visible signs and the language of Catholic culture began to disappear.

♦ In the documents of the Second Vatican Council in the mid-sixties, a new appreciation of the role of the laity was presented, and a call was issued to involve lay persons more significantly in the work of Catholic institutions.

♦ The complexity of the higher education enterprise was hitting home, and it was clear that if Catholic institutions were to demonstrate proficiency in that arena they would need far more expertise and resources than could be found in their individual religious communities.

♦ In 1965 the federal government committed itself to making post-secondary education available to all, and it was important that Catholic colleges and universities share in the funding that followed upon that decision.

♦ Greater attention to the voluntary nature of church membership, long held by Protestant denominations, as well as a pronounced encouragement by Vatican II to promote ecumenical activities now forced administrators of these Catholic colleges to reexamine requirements concerning curriculum and student regulations. They hoped to expand their own horizons, to

---

[35] Many of these discussions occurred at the annual meeting of the College and University Department of the National Catholic Educational Association, and record of them is found in the *College Newsletter*. A complete file is found in the NCEA archives housed at the Catholic University of America.

[36] For an illustration of this, see Paul A. Fitzgerald, *The Governance of Jesuit Colleges in the United States 1920-1970* (Notre Dame, IN: University of Notre Dame Press, 1984).

attract a more diverse student and faculty population, and to play a more significant role in the larger world of academia.

♦ There was a noticeable increase in the number of Catholic university and college administrators holding office in national associations such as Association of American Colleges, American Council on Education, and the Association of Governing Boards (to mention just a few) and a recognition on college campuses of the validity of such groups as the American Association of University Professors and the National Student Association.

♦ As the link with the religious community—the foundation stone and guardian of the church-related character of the college—was weakened, the college took on a life of its own, and that life would henceforth be lived primarily within the American higher education community. The question became: Can institutions do this and still call themselves Catholic?

3. Conflicting points of view within the two academic communities themselves led to the adaptations that were made. In the late nineteenth and early twentieth century the liberal Protestant community and the scholars that belonged to it were converted to a new esteem for science and scientific objectivity as the only worthy norm of scholarship. Decisions regarding curriculum were made in that context and the impact of such decisions was to stifle earlier religious influences in those institutions.

By the time the Catholic colleges were making their adaptations (late 1950s and early 1960s), the dominant concern on their campuses was not so much the demands of scientific objectivity as of academic freedom for the faculties teaching there. Anxious to be included in the wider world of American higher education, administrators of the Catholic colleges had to confront the twin pillars of academic culture—academic freedom and institutional autonomy. Limits imposed by hierarchical authority on content or method of teaching in such disciplines as philosophy, theology and the natural or social sciences were now resisted as inappropriate for a college or university. Lay faculties sought a role in decision-making and often this led to prolonged strife between lay faculty and the religious community.[37] It was obviously a time to rethink the relationship

---

[37] Although the questions of academic freedom and institutional autonomy are central to the tensions regarding church-relatedness I must refrain from entering upon a discussion of that topic in this paper. I refer the reader to Charles E. Curran, *Catholic Higher Education, Theology, and Academic Freedom* (Notre Dame, IN: University of Notre Dame Press, 1990) and James John Annarelli, *Academic Freedom and Catholic Higher Education* (New York: Greenwood Press, 1987). A work that gives the viewpoint of a layman in 1963 is also of interest: Daniel Callahan, *The Mind of the Catholic Layman* (New York: Charles Scribner's Sons, 1963), 99-100.

between the college and the church and to modify the former structures of governance.

Fortunately, a more collegial relationship could find its legitimacy in various teachings of Vatican II, including the plurality of philosophical and theological methods, the freedom and responsibility of individuals, the gifts proper to the laity in the church, and the role of the church itself in the modern world. The challenge which had been issued in 1955 to Catholic higher education by Msgr. John Tracy Ellis concerning the lack of Catholic leadership in American intellectual life now seemed to be underscored by the universal Church's call to recognize the place of the Catholic university in the modern world.[38]

The debates of the 1970s and 1980s bore witness to deep fractures in the Catholic culture of the pre-Vatican days, but they also provided an opportunity to clarify the distinction between faith and culture, a distinction that is critical in understanding the work of the university. Between 1965 and 1990 a dialogue between the Vatican and the Catholic universities around the world often revealed profound disagreements about the adaptations to different cultures that could legitimately be made, and the role that universities should play in mediating Christian faith and religious values to the culture in which they exist.[39] The passionate discussion of such questions indicates that most American Catholic institutions still want to be identified as Catholic, albeit defined in non-juridical terms.

4. It may be that one reason there is still a strong desire to maintain the Catholic identity of the colleges and universities is the very challenge that they have received from the leaders of the church.[40] The authorities within the Catholic community raised serious questions in the 1970s about the direction in which they saw Catholic higher education in this country moving. The challenge to their position pushed educational leaders to a thoughtful reflection on their

---

[38] John Tracy Ellis, "American Catholics and the Intellectual Life," *Thought* 30.118 (1955): 351-88. The Vatican II document most influential in the rethinking of the relationship between the Church and contemporary secular society was "The Church in the Modern World," (*Gaudium et spes*) and it did much to change the way that American Catholic leaders in higher education regarded their task. *Gaudium et spes*, Austin Flannery, OP, ed., *Vatican Council II: The Conciliar and Post-Conciliar Documents* (Collegeville, MN: The Liturgical Press, 1975), 903-1001.

[39] For documentation regarding the dialogue between the universities and the Vatican, cf. Gallin, *American Catholic Higher Education*.

[40] I am not sure of the extent to which Protestant church bodies challenged the colleges as they moved toward the disestablishment of religion; my understanding is that such a challenge would have had to come from the denominational community within the college or from a congregation or synod that was related to it. Was there any role for the National Council of Churches or similar bodies?

institutions' religious identity. Justifying the colleges' Catholicity is a task that many presidents and others have accepted and addressed in the past two decades.[41] They have also made a strong corporate response through the Association of Catholic Colleges and Universities which has existed since 1899 and to which over 90% of all Catholic colleges and universities belong. At the turn of the century, the Protestant colleges did not have the advantage of a challenge and corporate presence of this sort.

5. Another difference in the Catholic and Protestant situations is the role theology and/or religious studies play in the university curriculum. Again, one of the major changes in the mainline Protestant universities of the late 19th century was the decision to place theological studies in divinity schools and seminaries since that was where the church's ministers would be trained. Presumably, the strong tradition of Sunday school and the emphasis on sermons in church services precluded the need for religious education in public schools or in higher education.

The Catholic decision to have their own parochial schools where religion would pervade the entire curriculum was carried over into secondary schools and thence to colleges. As a result Catholic colleges made philosophical and theological disciplines central to their educational design. The level of religion courses prior to the 1960s seldom rose above didactic or apologetic content. But in the late '50s a new organization of teachers of sacred doctrine in colleges, now called the College Theology Society, spearheaded a significant change in the way that theology was taught, and promoted the education of lay persons and non-clerical religious in theological studies.[42] This was a response, in part, to the decision of states and accrediting agencies to recognize credit given for theology courses if they were of a quality equal to the rest of the curriculum. Even though many theology programs still leave much to be desired, it can be said without argument that Catholic colleges and universities have not abandoned them nor transferred them to the divinity schools and seminaries. Much of the serious work being done today in Catholic theology is being done in universities. While there is a renewed interest in the study of religion in secular universities, it does not seem to be in the direction of strengthened Christian theological reflection. [43]

---

[41] See especially *Current Issues in Catholic Higher Education* for the years 1985-1992.

[42] See Rosemary Rodgers, O.P., *A History of the College Theology Society* (Villanova, PA: College Theology Society, 1983).

[43] For a helpful view of this contemporary movement, see D. G. Hart, "American Learning and the Problem of Religious Studies," in Marsden and Longfield, chapter 7.

Catholic Institutions and Cultural Dialogue

Marsden explicitly excluded Catholic colleges and universities from his study because "they had little to do with setting the standards that eventually prevailed in American academic life."[44] Marsden, however, recognizes that the very fact that they were excluded was significant, and in our study of the experience of inculturation of Catholic higher education in the American experience such exclusion is extremely important. History bears witness that Catholic scholars had not made their mark in the circles of academic reputation. In 1955 Rev. John Tracy Ellis berated Catholic institutions of higher learning for not having gone beyond mediocrity. He denounced their emphasis on moral training to the detriment of creative and critical thinking.[45] In the following decade, his words were repeated by many others, and the Catholic academic community took them to heart and engaged in a great deal of self-examination and public discussion about their weaknesses.

The challenge issued by Ellis was intensified in the documents of Vatican Council II, especially in *Gaudium et Spes*. To the Council Fathers, the role of the Catholic university was crucial in the ecclesial mission of responding to the signs of the times. The call to be active in the formation of culture and to assume places of influence in society gave Catholic universities a new agenda. There needed to be a profound commitment to research at the larger universities and ways had to be found to develop a corps of recognized scholars if Catholic universities were to have any influence on American higher education. Active leadership in scholarly associations and publication in refereed journals began to be required as the *sine qua non* for promotion and tenure, and even at non-research colleges and universities the enthusiasm for scholarship was awakened.

However, we have yet to see widespread scholarly contributions in areas of study that arise from our Catholic roots, such as ethics, philosophy, theology, social justice, jurisprudence, history, literature and science. Where universities have developed research capacity it has often been in fields where money was available, such as engineering, hard sciences, business, or medicine, rather than in those areas where our tradition might have something special to offer. The Christian integration of which we boasted in the 1940s and 1950s did not carry over into inter-disciplinary studies but rather seemed to falter just at the time when the possibility of ecumenical dialogue would have enriched the understanding of such integration. Certainly there is great need for research and teaching about the different Christian traditions as well as the religions of other cultures; where could this be more appropriate than at Catholic universities?

---

[44] Marsden, *The Soul of the American University,* vii.

[45] Ellis, 351.

Ecumenical dialogue does not suggest a lessening of Catholic thought but rather an intensification of it, along with a recognition of the reality of pluralism and a welcoming attitude toward different cultures and religions. According to Bruce Douglass, a true pluralism rests on "the critical indwelling of an established tradition."[46] He underscores the fact that "there is a world of difference between openness with and without a defining center."[47] It is a point similar to that made by William Shea when he urged dialogue only when participants stand on firm ground. For such dialogue there is need "...to take responsibility, intellectual and spiritual, for our convictions, and to exercise and argue those convictions with some courage in the political, educational, and the ecclesial arenas." [48]

Because of their strong religious tradition Catholic universities could become communities where such a dialogue would have pride of place. If they did this, they would be making a tremendous contribution to American higher education and would, one can hope, be welcomed in the academic community as institutions offering a distinctive environment rich in possibility for meeting the intellectual needs of contemporary men and women. Having explored the values of the secular academy, they would have reason to reaffirm their Catholic heritage as they move into the twenty-first century.

---

[46] R. Bruce Douglass, "The Academic Revolution and the Idea of a Catholic University," William C. McFadden, ed., *Georgetown at Two Hundred* (Washington, DC: Georgetown University Press, 1990), 52.

[47] Ibid., 54.

[48] Shea, "Beyond Tolerance," 35-42.

5

Saving Truth

Catholic Universities and Their Tradition

James F. Hitchcock
Saint Louis University

The Context: American Higher Education

The crises of the church and the university are parallel, and indeed may ultimately be the same crisis, since both church and university are institutions proclaimedly dedicated to truths which transcend not only the institution itself but all materially circumscribed existence.

The Church's claim is obvious, but the university historically has made similar claims. Until quite recently no university attempted to justify its mission primarily in practical terms, such as training for employment, but rather in terms of its students becoming "broadly educated," being introduced to "the best which has been thought and said," being "taught to think," and numerous other claims which, if sometimes pretentious, nonetheless did describe a certain reality.[1]

Despite its familiar designation as an ivory tower, the university has never existed in isolation from the society around it, nor could it so long as it claims to study truth in its broadest sense. Thus questions about the identity and mission of the university always go beyond the university itself and cannot be resolved solely in terms of educational theory and practice.

---

[1] A recent statement of that ideal is Jaroslav J. Pelikan, *The Idea of a University: A Reexamination* (New Haven, CT.: Yale University Press, 1992).

121

The university, including the secular university, is now a temple of reason in which reason has been dethroned, a process originating in the 1960s with a jumble of movements — some political, some cultural, some merely personal — which tended to substitute passionate assertion for dispassionate discourse and the insistent priority of the new over "a decent respect" for the wisdom of the past. In the 1960s the New Left understood that it was important precisely not to argue its case, since to do so was to concede that "the enemy" might also have a case. The New Left's demands — for "justice" and other things — were presented as an urgent statement of self-evident truths, so that failure to act on those demands was confirmation of moral illegitimacy.[2] The victories of the New Left were achieved by psychological, sometimes physical, force, and when accused of using argument as a mask for power, the "politically correct" replied that such has always been the case, claims to rational argument being themselves the masks of privilege. The sources of this attitude cannot be found in the particular nexus of historical events which occurred in the 1960s because those sources were nothing less than the delayed but inevitable effects of the spirit of modernism. Paradoxically, the universities were simultaneously the chief disseminators of the spirit of modernism for almost a century and bastions of protection from its effects. Generations of students were taught that objective criteria of truth are suspect, doubt is the authentic human attitude, and outside the walls of the academy people live by illusions which intellectuals have exposed. Yet the universities continued to regard their own structures and activities as self-evidently justified, and their own procedures beyond question. This complacency was sustained for a remarkably long time, but it could not be sustained forever. Never in American history was there so much conscious educational experimentation as in the period 1965-75, precisely because all traditional educational assumptions seemed no longer valid.

Both in the 1960s and today, sincere liberals have often been the main targets of radicals, precisely because liberals concede the premises from which the radicals operate, all the while trying to forestall their conclusions. But for over thirty years there has been no lack of people willing to expose this contradiction. Today's campus atmosphere is a laboratory application of the dominant ideas of skeptical modernism.

The dissolution of traditional liberal education, using the term "liberal" in a double sense, has had two almost opposite beneficiaries — the apostles of radical skepticism on the one hand and the often unreflecting practitioners of technical education on the other. Political correctness tends to rule in the "soft" disciplines, while elsewhere in the university programs multiply whose

---

[2] The literature on the campus upheavals of the 1960s is almost endless. For a study contemporaneous with the events themselves see Seymour Martin Lipset and Philip G. Altbach, eds., *Students in Revolt* (Boston, MA: Houghton Mifflin, 1969).

practitioners often seem to have no opinion at all concerning the larger philosophical battles which engage the academy. In times of profound philosophical skepticism, technical competence becomes a conscious substitute for wisdom. Today almost any discipline can justify itself by claiming to posses a distinctive methodology, without having to justify its existence in any other way except that the market values the services of its graduates.

Political correctness itself has brought a new technical complexity to humane studies, as in the literary method called "deconstruction." Feminists, Marxists, and others have convinced the academy that no text can be read in a direct way, that all are masks behind which lurk labyrinthine complexities negotiable only by the initiated. At the same time, however, political correctness puts itself forward as the university's only soul, its only conscience, in that the passion for "diversity" alone inspires moral sensitivity and a concern for the common good.

Many intellectuals are today politically correct by default, in that they sincerely believe education should have a moral center but have no way of determining what it might be. The demands for "diversity" and "sensitivity" succeed because, if claims to know universal truths compel no general acceptance, no one can deny the reality of particular human feelings, and those who present themselves as victims are taken to be stating an undeniable, because subjective, reality.

Christian Higher Education

A major pattern in the history of American higher education has been the disappearance of liberal Protestant colleges and universities. Long before the establishment of state schools, all higher education in America was religious, usually oriented towards the training of clergy. But repeatedly those colleges first freed themselves from what they perceived as narrow denominational orthodoxy, then eventually lost almost all religious character of any kind. Meanwhile newer colleges were being founded to remedy the perceived religious failings of the old, only to have the same pattern eventually recur in the new colleges as well (the essential story of Harvard, Yale, and Princeton, for example).[3]

An irony which has gone almost entirely unnoticed is the fact that practically all the "experimental colleges" started with such fanfare during that time, which were confidently predicted to be the liberating wave of the future,

---

[3] George Marsden, *The Soul of the American University: from Protestant Establishment to Established Unbelief* (New York: Oxford University Press, 1994) and ed. with B. Longfield, *The Secularization of the Academy* (New York: Oxford University Press, 1992).

have failed, while almost the only examples of successful "new colleges" are those under conservative Catholic auspices. [4]

Except for seminaries, there are no educational institutions which can meaningfully be called liberal Protestant because liberal Protestantism concedes to secular thinkers a preeminence in wisdom and thus is not able to make any binding claims of its own which secularists are required to accept, even something as minimal as taking religion seriously as a cultural phenomenon. Hence religion is steadily driven to the margins of even officially religious institutions; the lack of interest in religion on the part of secular educators is taken as a judgment on religion, not on the academy.

As John Henry Newman warned in his seminal work, *The Idea of a University*, universities have a propensity to become rival churches.[5] Thus Newman argued for the necessary inclusion of theology in the curriculum, to insure that other disciplines did not seek to function as pseudo-theologies. In the U.S. this requirement, despite some relatively recent changes, is still ignored in most secular institutions while, even in those institutions which have made a place for it, probably most faculty do not regard it as truly relevant to the institution's educational mission. [6]

Beginning some time after World War II, Catholic intellectuals in the United States began to experience the same tension between religion and the academy which most Protestant schools had undergone earlier. Catholic universities of the 1950s wondered whether they were too parochial and dogmatic, lacked genuine intellect and scholarship, and failed to enforce sufficiently rigorous standards. Whether or not candidly, they increasingly looked to the most prestigious secular institutions for authoritative guidance. [7]

This was before the hurricane which followed the Second Vatican Council, when most of the spiritual and intellectual landmarks which had guided Catholics seemed suddenly to be swept away. The rapid "reform" of the Catholic schools took place within a few brief years, roughly 1965-70, and in an atmosphere of crisis for the Church and the whole of Western society.

---

[4] For example, Thomas Aquinas College in California and Christendom College in Virginia.

[5] *The Idea of a University, Defined and Illustrated,* ed. I. T. Her (Oxford, UK: Clarendon Press, 1976), 33-50.

[6] Marsden, *Soul,* 34-5.

[7] The most famous and influential statement of this was by the church historian (and priest) John Tracy Ellis, "American Catholics and the Intellectual Life," *Thought,* 30 (Autumn, 1955): 351-88. For a general discussion of the crisis see Philip Gleason, *Contending with Modernity: Catholic Higher Education in the Twentieth Century* (New York: Oxford University Press, 1995).

The crisis of the Catholic university is obviously part of the larger crisis of the Church. It is commonplace to say that most Catholics, including most priests, were not prepared for the Council and that the crisis was thus more severe than it needed to have been. But, although the lack of preparation is often attributed to inadequate education, it is doubtful if the Catholic universities themselves, at least in the United States, were much better prepared, either in practical terms such as governance or in terms of their intellectual mission. On the eve of the Council, Catholic liberals were proposing various ways of reforming their system of higher education. In retrospect those proposals appear to have underestimated drastically the kinds of adjustments which would have been necessary if such schools were to attain the respectability enjoyed by the most prominent secular institutions. [8]

For some years after the Council the Catholic universities mainly experienced drift, during which they quickly abandoned many of the things which had been distinctive about them—Thomistic philosophy and theology, for example, and the practice of *in loco parentis* concerning student life—but not in accord with any clear vision of where they should be moving. On the crucial question of faculty, for example, few institutions formulated specific criteria concerning a commitment to the institution's religious mission as a condition for employment, or even determined how faculty should be acquainted with the nature of that mission.

Instead the process of faculty recruitment went on in piecemeal fashion, some departments remaining predominantly Catholic in their membership, others losing most of that identity, with little guidance from the higher administration. During the period 1965-1975 patrons of these institutions were assured in general terms that the institution was making progress in exciting new directions without losing its religious character, but were rarely told how those directions had been chosen or how precisely they related to previous traditions. More or less by default, every development, whether or not planned or expected, was retroactively blessed as contributing to the new "maturity" of the institution.

The claim that Catholic universities before 1965 were immature "ghetto" institutions was in some ways true, but that very claim tended to undermine the reforming impulse in ways seldom noticed. If the Catholic schools had been founded in the United States precisely to protect the faith of an immigrant population from the dangers of the larger culture, what reason did they have for continuing to exist at all once the ghetto walls had been torn down? Would it not be more reasonable for American Catholics simply to abandon their schools and immerse themselves in the cold waters of secular education, as indeed some have done? Despite endless discussion of the transformation of the Catholic schools,

---

[8] For one such proposal see Justus George Lawler, *The Catholic Dimension in Higher Education* (Westminster, MD.: Newman Press, 1959).

there has been remarkably little discussion of how institutions which were by their very nature parochial, in both the technical and the popular sense, could or should be made cosmopolitan.

In the Catholic universities what emerged from a process which was at best unplanned and piecemeal was an attempt at a liberal Catholic synthesis. Under this dispensation the institution continues to claim a religious identity but also proclaims its universal openness to the larger world. Thus, for example, students are required to study theology and philosophy, partly as an educational habit from the past, partly on the grounds that there is such a thing as "religious experience" with which every educated person should be familiar.

As described in one study, during the period 1965 to 1975 the old "sacred order," in which the truth of the Catholic faith had normative standing in the curriculum, was replaced by a tendency to study the Catholic tradition from various relativizing perspectives — ecumenism, or biblical criticism. After about 1975 even that rather attenuated concession to the importance of the Catholic tradition gave way to an emphasis on world religions and on every religion as an equally valid form of human experience.[9] In this dispensation there are some faculty who have knowledge of the religious traditions of the institution, most of whose undergraduates are probably Catholic. But recruitment of such faculty is far from systematic and is usually left to the discretion of individual departments.

The growth of purely secular influences within the institution is justified on grounds of the school's liberality— students need to be brought into contact with living representatives of other traditions. Even more important, the Catholic tradition itself is sometimes taught from a dissenting standpoint, on the grounds that official dogma does not adequately reflect the modern human experience and, finally, because dogmatic claims themselves are simply unsustainable in the modern academy. The standard by which the university measures itself is not that of the larger Church, certainly not that of the hierarchy, but that of an intellectual community so ecumenical that it includes a preponderance of nonbelievers.

Chronic uncertainty as to what the Catholic universities ought to be doing is the direct result of deep and equally unresolved questions over the meaning of the Second Vatican Council itself and its proper interpretation, with each possible interpretation implying sweeping conclusions about almost every aspect of life. However, even debates about the meaning of the Council are only relevant in the eyes of relatively "conservative" educators, since the Council is thereby conceded to be in some ways an authoritative teaching body. Probably a majority of professors in Catholic institutions feel no need to refer to any kind of ecclesiastical source, no matter how "progressive," to justify their activities.

---

[9] Frank D. Schubert, *A Sociological Study of Secularization Trends in the American Catholic University* (Lewiston, ME.: Edwin Mellen Press, 1990), 77-128.

The final logic of the liberal position, whether in its religious or its frankly secular form, is that the path of wisdom is the same for Christians as for nonbelievers, with faith persisting as a subjective experience without claim to credibility beyond personal conviction.

In theory it might be possible to shape a kind of Catholic higher education which could be called liberal in its broad outlook, while at the same time remaining self-consciously Catholic. In the crucial matter of faculty recruitment efforts would be made to attract Catholics, but the governing outlook would be closer to the theology of Hans Kung than to that of Cardinal Joseph Ratzinger. The institution would commit itself to maintaining a sense of Catholic identity, but an identity often in contrast to its past and committed to widening the dialogue with those outside the Catholic tradition, assuming that often they posses a greater wisdom than the Church itself possesses.

Such an approach has long been in effect in most Catholic institutions, but it is doomed to fail for the same reason liberal Protestant higher education failed —ultimately there are no compelling reasons to assert even an attenuated Catholic identity. The logic of the liberal position leads to more and more radical questioning of the inherited faith, to the point where any affirmation of that faith becomes problematical. The liberal religious stance itself comes to seem arbitrary, insofar as it retains fidelity to any part of the tradition at all. Thus in liberal Catholic institutions it is not uncommon for professors in secular disciplines to object to the special status of theology and philosophy in the curriculum, in the sense of required courses and the commitment of the institution to maintaining large departments in those disciplines.

The liberal Catholic relationship to the tradition is problematical in that sooner or later practically every one of that tradition's claims is "demythologized," so that finally it becomes impossible to justify significant attention to it at all, except as a historical phenomenon.

But the theological curriculum is even vulnerable insofar as it rests on the assumption that a palpable "religious experience" is characteristic of humanity and hence deserving of respectful study. Most modern western intellectuals apparently have no such experiences and are inclined to regard the religious traditions of the world as simply different varieties of culturally conditioned illusion. At best religion is conceded subjective value in the personal lives of believers. Consequently there can be no stable liberal Catholic approach to education, because there is no stable liberal Catholicism. The journey begun at the time of the Second Vatican Council has relentlessly led away from everything which is distinctively Catholic.

An instructive example is the attempt, often by passionately committed people, to transform the Catholic universities into bastions of "peace and justice," resting broadly on the doctrines of Liberation Theology. Although most professors might in some general way endorse the concerns of such Liberationism, in practice the attempt to make this the governing spirit of Catholic higher education has also failed, as it was bound to do. For the Church, whether in its "conservative" or its "radical" manifestations, simply lacks the authority to persuade secular-minded faculty to accept any unifying principle, whether of the right or of the left. The very ways of theologizing which made liberation theology possible have also undermined all claims to authority, so that professors of business, for example, can in good conscience reject the claims of Liberationism on the grounds that liberal theology has precisely taught them not to allow religious dogma to "intrude" on the autonomy of their discipline.

In reality the Catholicism of many church-sponsored universities resembles the Protestantism of the Ivy League schools of an earlier generation. There remains a dying breed of self-consciously Catholic older professors in the secular disciplines, along with increasingly marginalized islands of explicit religious commitment in theology departments and campus chaplaincies.

As Catholic educators began reforming their institutions around 1965, they naturally looked to the most prestigious secular institutions for guidance, but often they failed to realize how uncertain was the trumpet there being sounded.

On one level there was confusion as to what precisely the Catholics schools were supposed to take from the secular schools—merely the standards of disciplinary excellence as conventionally understood (a publishing faculty with respectable degrees), or a whole philosophy of education? Often the two were imported together, without any clear awareness of the distinction.

What few Catholic educators realized at the time was that the secular institutions themselves were about to be plunged into a crisis of identity at least as profound and agonizing as that of the Catholic Church. To take only the simplest example, it is not as obvious at the end of the century as it was in 1965 that there is an educational imperative to recruit only faculty with impeccable professional credentials and a rigorously "scientific" approach to their disciplines, without regard to other qualities. Feminists, racial minorities, and others within the academy now say otherwise, and the spirit of academic professionalization is under attack as elitist, narrow, and desiccated.

Catholic educators began emulating the secular academy at the very end of what can be called classical modernism, the heritage of the Enlightenment which had undermined many traditional certitudes but had seemingly arrived at other, more provisional certitudes which made a stable social and cultural order possible. (Two Columbia University professors, Lionel Trilling and Jacques Barzun, might be cited as quintessential exemplars of this classical modernism.[10])

---

[10] As representative of this spirit see Jacques Barzun, *Darwin, Marx, Wagner: Critique of a Heritage* (Garden City, NY: Doubleday, 1958) and Lionel Trilling, *Freud and*

In education the classical modernists believed above all in Liberal Education, a tradition traceable to the medieval universities but now divorced from almost all religious context. Those who could not believe in God did believe in Great Books, Sublime Thoughts, Genius, High Standards, Rigor, Objectivity, and many other things now often ridiculed in the academy. [11]

The academic battles of the period 1965-75 were destroying the foundations of classical modernism by carrying the corrosive spirit of skeptical modernism to its farthest point, questioning everything and treating all survivals of older certitudes as arbitrary and suspect.

Thus the crisis of the secular academy is at least as profound as that of the religious academy, and of the Church itself. Curricular battles are insoluble, except on the basis of the simplest kind of faculty politics (trading for favors), precisely because they go far beyond curriculum and involve basic questions about the nature of reality. (Is there such a thing as objective truth transcending cultural, racial, gender, and ethnic identity? Is the tradition of the West worth preserving?)[12] Even though the university is practically the only place in society where people are given sufficient leisure to pursue such questions, the university as now constituted seems singularly unsuited to answering them.

If liberal academicism can be said to celebrate one ideal, it is that of "dialogue." But that very ideal, in the prevailing liberal sense, has now exhausted itself, in that no realistic person can any longer believe that continued discussion among divergent viewpoints will in time lead to some kind of consensus. In fact the opposite has happened: The more the academy makes itself open to the discussion of diverse viewpoints, the deeper and more bitter the divisions become. In practice the modern university has become a battleground of disciplines in the narrowest sense, departments and programs often ruthlessly competing with each other for material resources, for protected status in the curriculum, and for prestige, philosophical arguments on their own behalf often crafted by people who in fact recognize no imperative except the aggrandizement of themselves and their disciplines.

That situation is virtually dictated by the fact that there is no longer any hierarchy of truths, hence no hierarchy of disciplines, no transcendent criteria by which the claims of the various disciplines can be measured and evaluated. Every claim as to the necessary role of one's own discipline in the curriculum is

---

the Crisis of Our Culture (Boston, MA: Beacon Press, 1955).

[11] A recent attempt to defend the traditional view was Allan Bloom's *The Closing of the American Mind: How Higher Education Has Failed Democracy and Impoverished the Souls of Today's Students* (New York: Simon and Schuster, 1987).

[12] Among numerous discussions of these issues see Charles Taylor, "The Politics of Recognition" in Amy Guttmann, ed., *Multiculturalism: Examining the Politics of Recognition* (Princeton, N.J.: Princeton University Press, 1994).

inevitably met with the charge of mere self-interest which, as far as the situation now goes, is usually justified. Having systematically cultivated habits of skepticism for most of the twentieth century, the academy now finds itself at last in the situation where it cannot offer persuasive arguments for its own mission, nor sort out the conflicting claims of its own members. Thus, in practice the governing philosophy is vocationalism.

Both the university and the church claim a higher wisdom to which they insist the larger public should attend, even though the sources of that wisdom are thought to be very different. Liberal religion has continued to defer to the university even as the spiritual crisis of the university continues to deepen. Unlike some churches, the universities flourish in terms of attracting "customers," but only because of realities at odds with their own exalted claims to wisdom: They are thought to be selling a valuable, indeed indispensable, product to those who aspire to prosper within the ranks of the great middle class.

No Christianity worthy of the name can rest on anything other than a sacred canon, the very use of that term for works of secular literature being an analogy with Scripture. Thus the forces of "deconstruction" hit especially hard at the Catholic tradition, which claims to rest not only on the sacred texts of Scripture but on those of the Fathers, the Scholastics, the ecumenical councils, the popes, and other authorities. For this reason attempts by Catholic institutions to accommodate themselves to the skepticism of the secular academy will be especially lethal to even their residual identities.

Only a few Catholic institutions have publicly faced the obvious question which has been hanging over them for almost thirty years —whether they wish to remain Catholic at all. It is defensible to answer in the negative, as a few institutions have done. Most, however, have continued to use the Catholic name for whatever it is still worth, insisting to the public that they retain a distinctive religious character, even as their internal dynamic steadily undermines that character. Thus the liberal-conservative battle over the nature of Catholic higher education is in large part a battle over the use of the name, since it would be impossible for even a draconian educational dictator to re-Catholicize most of the institutions which now exist.

But the quarrel over the use of the name is more than semantic, and goes beyond the trite issue of "truth in labeling" to a profound disagreement over the nature of the Church itself. The claim of the Church, the Vatican in particular, to exercise some ultimate authority over those institutions calling themselves Catholic rests on the assertion that the name "Catholic" is a universal name which cannot be defined and circumscribed by any merely local community, no matter how learned or wise that community may think itself to be. A self-proclaimed Catholic institution claims to be the representative of a larger community whose identity it accepts. What it means to be Catholic is finally the decision of popes and councils, not of university faculties and boards of trustees.[13]

In titling one of his official statements on education "From the Heart of the Church," John Paul II recalled the historical origins of the universities within the ecclesiastical community. Thereby he implied that whatever tension might seem to exist between faith and reason ought in principle to be resolvable, since throughout most of their history the universities existed in close relation to the Church, the idea of secular universities being relatively recent. Among the criteria of an authentically Catholic university, according to the pope (himself a former university professor), is "Fidelity to the Christian message as it comes to us through the Church." [14]

The battles which have transformed the Catholic universities have mostly been fought by groups within the faculty and administration, with trustees passively acquiescing in the outcome. However, the very governing structures of most such institutions now make eventual secularity almost inevitable, since there is no juridical way in which the larger Church could enforce its own authority.[15]

Beginning in the late 1960s most Catholic institutions moved from being governed by boards of trustees entirely composed of clergy and religious drawn from a single religious community which had corporate responsibility for the institution, to boards a majority of whose members are lay people, including non-Catholics.[16]

But there were unrecognized ambiguities in that transition, since it was never clear what specific advantages these new boards were thought to bring to a distinctively Catholic vision of higher education. In reality the move seems to have been made primarily to broaden each institution's financial base in the community and to give it an image of diversity. Liberal professors are often critical of the fact that university boards of trustees are dominated by businessmen. But that was precisely the situation which the reforms of the late 1960s extended to Catholic institutions as well. When Jesuit colleges, for

---

[13] These claims are made in the two basic documents issued by Pope John Paul II relative to Catholic universities: *Sapientia christiana* ("Christian Wisdom," 1979) (Boston: St. Paul Editions, n.d.) and *Ex corde ecclesiae* ("From the Heart of the Church," 1990) (Falls Church, VA.: Cardinal Newman Society, n.d.).

[14] *Ex corde ecclesiae*, # 6.

[15] See James Jerome Conn, S.J., *Catholic Universities in the United States and Ecclesiastical Authority* (Rome: Editrice Pontificia Universita Gregoriana, 1991).

[16] For a summary of the process see Alice Gallin, O. S. U., *Independence and a New Partnership in Catholic Higher Education* (Notre Dame, Ind.: University of Notre Dame Press, 1996).

example, were governed by entirely Jesuit boards, most of their trustees were professional educators.

The fact that Catholic institutions are now "owned" by ecumenical boards set up precisely to insure that they are not under direct ecclesiastical control,[17] makes it doubtful if it is possible, in a formal legal sense, to speak of Catholic universities at all.

It is no longer meaningful to speak of Catholic universities in the full sense, since it will probably never again be possible for any institution to claim realistically that it has a Catholic medical school, a Catholic business school, or a Catholic engineering school. Certain selected professional areas — medical ethics or constitutional law — require close attention by Catholic institutions in terms of faculty and curriculum. On the whole, however, the Catholic schools will probably find it necessary to concede that professional education is essentially secular and will not be much different in a Catholic institution than in a secular one.

The heart of the battle is thus in the liberal arts — undergraduate education and graduate schools training future professors and scholars. But it is precisely here that the acids of modernism have most completely dissolved the claims to certitude which are necessary for meaningful Catholic education to be even possible, and there is little prospect that Catholic institutions as they now exist will somehow be able to overcome this skepticism sufficiently to achieve a new intellectual synthesis.

The collapse of so much of American Catholic culture after the Council was both a cause and an effect of the crisis of Catholic higher education, and by now the surrounding Catholic culture which was once so important to the mission of the Catholic universities has all but evaporated. Although culture cannot simply be taught but must be learned through living, the present situation places heavy demands on the Catholic universities to attempt to remedy the deficiencies of the culture as far as possible, using explicit instruction to replace the accumulated experience of Catholicism which previous generations of young people imbibed simply by living. In ways they did not have to attempt forty years ago, the universities must now teach what it means to be a Catholic to young people who often have little living sense of its meaning.

Thus a possible alternative way of providing authentically Catholic education in the absence of such a consensus would be the proposal by the English historian Christopher Dawson, made already in the 1950s, that an undergraduate curriculum be built around the study of "Christian culture," approached almost as an alien reality. At the time popular Catholic culture was flourishing, but Dawson noted that even very devout people had the skimpiest

---

[17] *Ibid.*, 10-11, 105-17.

knowledge of their cultural heritage, and he proposed an entire undergraduate curriculum to remedy this.[18]

Practically all of Dawson's extensive writings sought to disclose the fundamental part which religion played in the development of civilization, especially the Catholic religion, and especially in Europe.[19] While Dawson was confessedly a man of faith, he gained respect from secular historians because of the sweep and penetration of his understanding, and the importance he attached to religion as a cultural force could not be denied.

He developed sample curricula which undertook to introduce students, in a systematic and roughly chronological way, to the major elements of Christian culture from biblical times to the present, including theology, philosophy, literature, art, politics, and science, and encompassing Protestant and Eastern Orthodox expressions of that culture.[20] While his proposal naturally concentrated on Europe, he also recognized that there were important embodiments of that culture in other parts of the world, an awareness which has become much stronger since his death.

Besides keeping alive a vital sense of Catholic identity, such a curriculum would have other educational advantages not necessarily related to religion. It would be broad in terms of academic disciplines, while at the same time embodying a principle of unity. It would provide opportunity for studies which were trans-cultural yet held together by that same principle of unity, since Catholicism has incarnated itself in all the cultures of the world. It would offer the opportunity for students to wrestle with great texts, and if properly implemented would be rigorous and demanding. Institutions could claim with complete honesty that they offered an educational experience which was highly distinctive.

As Dawson himself noted, it would not be strictly necessary that such a curriculum be taught by believing Catholics, or that Catholic beliefs be taught as true. It would be sufficient to make students aware of the existence of a great cultural heritage, which might inspire, or at least orient, them in further study.

Students would not be deprived of the opportunity to study modern secular culture but would do so after they had achieved a substantial grounding in their own tradition. They would retain the possibility of rejecting that tradition's claim to being normative, and of embracing various kinds of secular thought. They

---

[18] Christopher Dawson, *The Crisis of Western Education* (New York: Sheed and Ward, 1961).

[19] Among his numerous works on the subject were: *Progress and Religion* (New York: Sheed and Ward, 1929); *Religion and Culture* (New York: Sheed and Ward, 1948); *Religion and the Rise of Western Culture* (London: Sheed and Ward, 1950); and *The Historic Reality of Christian Culture* (New York: Harper and Brothers, 1960).

[20] For a time such a program did exist at St. Mary's College, Notre Dame, Indiana.

could pursue creative dialogue between the tradition and modern culture. But all this would occur only after they had come at least to understand the points of difference between the Catholic tradition and other traditions, the ability to identify such tensions itself being an exercise of great educational value.

The return of advocacy in secular scholarship and teaching, as exemplified in feminist studies and black studies, means that, even by the standards now accepted in secular universities, Catholic universities need not be embarrassed if many of their faculty are confessed believers who teach the Catholic tradition honestly but also regard it as worthy of credibility.

The demand for "pluralism" and "multiculturalism" in the educational world is best met not within each institution, something which leads merely to fragmentation and widening conflict, but on the level of institutional identity itself. Universities of all kinds should struggle harder to define institutional identities for themselves, and the existence of conspicuously Catholic institutions should be hailed precisely as a sign of healthy cultural and educational diversity within the larger society.

But if the claims of divine revelation are taken seriously, the secular academic approach to truth must be recognized as itself a restricted view of reality. The search for truth cannot be adequately contained within the academic framework, nor can established disciplinary methods exclusively govern the search. The very existence of a "Catholic" university, the very existence of a discipline called "theology," implies a recognition of the truth of such revelation, which comes to the universities from without and finally claims to judge the universities themselves.

Paradoxically, such Catholic institutions will not simply be intellectual ghettoes but will offer authoritative guidance to the larger culture. In an age when virtually no one in secular academia can lay claim to real wisdom, even nonbelievers might have reason to be grateful for the existence of educational communities claiming to offer the possibility of saving truth.

6

The Message and the Messenger

The Untold Story of Father Claude Heithaus
and the Integration of Saint Louis University[1]

Paul Shore
Saint Louis University

You have been seriously disobedient; you have manifested contempt for legitimate authority; you have been disloyal to your Superiors, ecclesiastical and religious; you have been a source of grave scandal both to Ours and to externs. These in our estimation are serious offenses...[2]

I must not forget to allude to the farsighted efforts on behalf of civil rights and equality of opportunity for Negroes. The Christian justice of your position has never been in doubt; its timeliness has been authenticated in more recent years.[3]

The subject of both the above quotations is Claude Heithaus, a Jesuit scholar, teacher, journalist, archeologist, and advocate of racial integration. Vehemently and categorically denounced by his Provincial, his university President, and others within his religious order for his efforts to bring about the integration of Saint Louis University, Heithaus lived long enough to earn the approbation of the

---

[1] The writer gratefully acknowledges the assistance of Father William B. Faherty, S.J., and Father Mark Daues, S.J., in the preparation of this essay.

[2] Joseph P. Zuercher, S.J., Provincial of the Missouri Province, and four other Jesuits, June 14, 1945.

[3] Pedro Arrupe, S.J., General of the Society of Jesus, August 27, 1970; the Heithaus file, Midwest Jesuit Archives, St . Louis, MO.

Father General of his Society and a respected place in the official history of that university.

In the telling of the history of Saint Louis University, Heithaus has even been elevated to the status of a hero, a crusader who helped bring about a momentous change in the evolution of race relations throughout Missouri and the rest of the United States. While elements of the story of Father Heithaus have been told, many details of the career of this Jesuit have never been published or openly discussed. The following essay attempts a fresh look at the activities of Father Heithaus, both before and after his well known sermon, at the cultural forces that shaped both the reaction of his superiors, and at the way in which his story has been remembered and retold.

Claude Heithaus was born in St. Louis on May 28, 1898, one of eight children. His father, Herman Heithaus, had emigrated from Hanover, Germany, as a teenager three decades earlier and had worked as an artist and engraver. Claude's mother was descended from a well established Catholic Saint Louis family which traced its ancestry back to the early part of the nineteenth century. Claude first encountered Jesuit education at the age of twelve, attended Saint Louis University High School, and like several of his brothers enrolled at Saint Louis University, where he played football and studied classical languages within the traditional Jesuit curriculum. During the First World War Claude served as a second lieutenant in the army but apparently did not see active duty. After the war he entered the Society of Jesus, and after helping found the student newspaper at Saint Louis University, was sent to the University of Detroit, where he served as the acting head of the Department of Classical Languages from 1921 until 1929. On June 21, 1930 he was ordained a priest by the Archbishop of St. Louis, John J. Glennon, a man with whom he was to have several significant encounters later.

Claude Heithaus was one of a very small number of Jesuit priests from the Midwest who were given the opportunity to complete their studies abroad in the years before the Second World War. During the first decades of the twentieth century, few Jesuit teachers of the Missouri Province ventured out of their province to obtain graduate degrees, even at Catholic universities. However, Heithaus' obvious enthusiasm and talent for history, art history, and languages enabled him to be an exception. From 1933 to 1939 he was enrolled as a student of classical art and archeology at University College at the University of London.[4] His studies were by no means limited to the classroom. Heithaus later

---

[4] Heithaus later claimed that he had also attended classes in the 1930s at Oxford and the Sorbonne, although this writer has been unable to find documentation of this. Several Missouri Province Jesuits earned doctorates at non-Catholic institutions, including Johns Hopkins, University of California (Berkeley), Munich, Cambridge, and London. See William B. Faherty, S.J., *Better the Dream: Saint Louis University and Community, 1818-1968* (St. Louis, MO: St. Louis University, 1968), 279.

recalled that during these years he had traveled through all of western Europe, and he came to know Italy better than his native Missouri. Heithaus explored the slums of Naples, scaled the Acropolis, and participated in digs in the deserts of Syria and Lebanon. He stayed with his brother Jesuits in houses throughout the Mediterranean region, but was also proud of his contacts with peasants, shepherds, and others whom he met on his travels. While collecting material for his dissertation, the young Jesuit took thousands of photos of pottery and other artifacts; some of these photos were in color, a process relatively new at the time. Thanks in part to the financial support of his mother, Heithaus was able to assemble a collection of photographs of considerable scholarly value.

Heithaus completed his Ph.D. shortly before the outbreak of World War II and returned to Saint Louis University in 1939. His sojourn abroad had brought him into contact with many of the leading archeological figures of England, who apparently respected and admired his work, although none of it was published. Letters and reminiscences written by Heithaus about this period convey the impression of an intelligent, energetic priest, observant and open to new experiences but subject to the cultural biases of the day, an impatient and frequently outspoken lover of language with a taste for the dramatic. These traits would be evident in the next phase of Heithaus' life.

Heithaus was now assistant professor of archeology and faculty advisor to the student newspaper, *The University News*. After his return, he wrote a short book entitled *The Truth About Saint Louis University* which, despite its potentially provocative title, was essentially a public relations piece about the achievements of the university. Hundreds of artifacts that Heithaus had obtained during his travels became a collection exhibited at the university, one which Heithaus hoped would become the nucleus of a significant university museum.[5] Letters from this period reveal Heithaus' concern about the preservation and display of these artifacts, and his frustration with a university administration that placed little value on the collection. During these years Heithaus also came in contact with many of the outcasts of St. Louis society through his work in local jails. He was committed to the promotion of racial integration at the university. The question of racial equality had been taken up elsewhere in the United States as much as twenty years earlier by Catholic reformers such as John LaFarge, S.J., but had made little headway in the Archdiocese of St. Louis.[6] It must be recalled that during the 1960s the city of Saint Louis, as well as the rest of Missouri, was completely segregated. African-Americans had no access to

---

[5] Unfortunately, this collection was dispersed or thrown away after Heithaus' fall from grace. The writer has been unable to determine whether any elements of this collection are still in existence.

[6] David W. Southern, *John LaFarge and the Limits of Catholic Interracialism 1911-1963* (Baton Rouge, LO: Louisiana State University Press, 1996).

institutions of higher education, aside from those "Negro Colleges" that had been established.[7] Several Jesuit administrators, including the Very Reverend Father Peter Brooks, Provincial Superior of the Missouri Province, had initiated some moves to study the question of admitting people of color to the schools of the Province. No public statements on this subject had been made by any Jesuit officials.[8] Saint Louis University itself was located in a neighborhood that at the turn of the century had been solidly middle class and white, but by the beginning of the Second World War was changing to a mix of poor white and black residents. Row houses that had been occupied by Catholic families who aspired to send their sons to the university were transformed during the war years into crowded rooming houses filled with poorer immigrants from the Deep South. Like many universities experiencing the same changes in their neighborhoods, Saint Louis University's initial response was to widen the gulf between itself and the surrounding community, and to withdraw from any effort to recruit students from its immediate neighbors. Yet the intermittent efforts of African-Americans to further their education, and the support of their white allies ultimately compelled the university administration to address, however unwillingly, the question of racial integration. During the fall of 1943 and early 1944, Father Patrick Holloran, president of the university, had quietly explored the question of admitting people of color as regular students.[9] A letter, posing the questions, "Would you look favorably on Saint Louis University's accepting Negro students?" and "Would you be less inclined to send a son or daughter to Saint Louis University if Negro students were admitted?" was sent to a select groups of St. Louisans.[10] According to a pamphlet entitled "The St. Louis Story Retold," this letter was a response to the unsuccessful attempts of a Catholic African American woman who had graduated from St. Elizabeth's parochial school to gain admission to Saint Louis University. This woman was aided in her efforts by two priests from the black St. Malachy's parish, and by another unnamed priest who was almost certainly Heithaus.[11]

Any number of possible issues might have brought the matter of the racial

---

[7] However, an African American who was able to "pass" as a white had apparently been admitted some years before to St. Louis University.

[8] William B. Faherty, S.J., "Breaking the Color Barrier," *Universitas* 13.2 (1987)18-21. See also the minutes of the "Special Committee on the Admission of Negroes to the University," February 2, 1943.

[9] Undated memorandum from Father Holloran.

[10] No responses to this letter are known to have survived. See Faherty, *Better the Dream*, 340. Faherty reports that Board of Trustees minutes from this period are also missing; this writer can confirm that no complete collection of the minutes for the years 1943-44 are available. See also *St. Louis Post-Dispatch*, January 27, 1944.

[11] C. Denny Holland, "The St. Louis Story Retold," March 19, 1961.

integration of the university to a head, but the single event which compelled the university to confront the issue of race discrimination was a sermon preached by Heithaus in the university church to a predominantly female audience on February 11, 1944. Excerpts of the sermon have often been reprinted but important sections have always been omitted.[12] Several of these deserve quotation here:

> The Vicar of Christ upon earth, the great and enlightened Pope Pius XII, made black men bishops of Christ's Church and invested them with all the sublime powers and dignities which the Son of God gave to the Apostles. But some people say it is wrong to have a Negro play the organ in the University Church.... I hate this snobbery against the Negro because it springs from the pride and prejudice which Christ hated. It is the heartless pride of Cromwell and his self-righteous bullies, who proved their superiority over the defenseless white Catholics of Ireland by selling them into slavery with the Negroes of the West Indies. It is the stony prejudice of psalm-singing New England, where Catholics...were despised ....I hang my head in shame when I see that some Catholics, who do not know the history of this country and have forgotten what terrible wrongs were endured by their ancestors in Ireland and Protestant England, have had the full strength of their Catholic convictions diluted by mingling with the descendants of their persecutors.... Do you realize that Communist agitators, specially trained at Moscow, have already made more than a hundred thousand converts among (African Americans) and are pouring out the vials of their wrath upon the Catholic Church, accusing it of being indifferent to the wrongs of the Negro?[13]

Heithaus' sermon, which also noted that Islam did not discriminate against people of color, was followed by a call to those listening to take a pledge against racism. The appeal to Americans of Irish ancestry through references to English and Irish history is especially noteworthy, considering the number of Irish-Americans among the clergy of St. Louis. Heithaus as the advisor to the *University News* no doubt anticipated the controversy the sermon would produce and was able to make sure that the text of the sermon appeared in the school newspaper. He also provided the local press with a detailed announcement regarding his sermon. The next day stories appeared in the St. Louis dailies about the call for integration.

Reaction to Heithaus' sermon was swift. The same day that he delivered his sermon, President Holloran wrote to Heithaus, complaining that the public airing of the topic of racial integration put him in a "decidedly embarrassing position"

---

[12] A brief account of the sermon appears in Paul C. Reinert, S.J., and Paul Shore, *Seasons of Change: Reflections on a Half Century at St. Louis University* (St. Louis: Saint Louis University Press, 1996), 18-20.

[13] *University News*, February 11, 1944.

since the president had declined to make any public statement on the subject.[14] Holloran's own position on the question of admitting non-whites to the university is difficult to assess. In the letters from Holloran to Heithaus in the weeks following the sermon, the president stressed that Heithaus had erred because he had not proceeded through proper channels and had presented his Superior with a *fait accompli* which the Jesuits were not yet ready to respond to formally. There is no evidence that Holloran was personally prejudiced against blacks, but it is equally clear that the university president was in no way motivated to take any steps to accelerate the process of integration. Heithaus, who had known Holloran since the days when they had both played college football, came to view Holloran as a closet racist and later alleged that Holloran had made anti-Semitic comments in private while publicly supporting Jewish faculty and donors. Clear evidence of Holloran's views on race and ethnicity are lacking, however. Implicit in all discussions of racial integration at the university was the terrifying specter of African Americans and whites socializing at dances and other social functions, a prospect which offended some Jesuits and worried others. Immediately after the sermon Holloran reprimanded Heithaus for his actions, pointing out that the sermon was being interpreted as the official position of the university. The president evidently had hopes that the entire issue could be avoided for an indefinite period. He wrote to Heithaus, "This thing is going to blow over unless you by deliberate and direct disobedience resurrect it. When it has blown over, it will be handled and solved quietly and correctly." [15]

This "thing," however, did not blow over. The question of admission of non-white students was debated in the local press, with the African-American newspapers praising Holloran and expressing hope that the university would take decisive action. Responding perhaps to the local publicity, the university made some quiet moves towards modifying its position. Meanwhile, in the weeks that followed the sermon Heithaus received support and praise from many prominent Jesuits, including Daniel Lord, S.J., a noted editor and leader of Catholic sodalities.[16] Likewise the climate of opinion in St. Louis was by no means uniformly behind Heithaus. Although Heithaus later recalled that the student body enthusiastically answered his call for an end to segregation and race prejudice, President Holloran was embarrassed and uncomfortable with the attention given to the topic. A few days after the sermon, on February 14, Heithaus met with both Holloran and Archbishop Glennon. The only known

---

[14] Holloran to Heithaus, February 11, 1944.

[15] Holloran to Heithaus, February 16, 1944.

[16] Cf. Faherty, "Breaking," 19. Heithaus was also criticized later by John LaFarge, who supported his goals, for his lack of tact in the way he raised the issue of racial discrimination. Peter McDonough, *Men Astutely Trained: A History of the Jesuits in the American Century* (New York: The Free Press, 1992), 196.

record of these conversations is found in a letter that Heithaus wrote to Father Zuercher, the Missouri Provincial, some months later. Since he was far from a neutral observer, Heithaus' unconfirmed account of these events may be suspect. However, as a record of what Heithaus believed took place and was willing to report to his superior, this letter is revealing in what it communicates about the tone of the discussions that then surrounded the question of racial integration. [17]

> Heithaus reported that Holloran was deeply distressed at the possibility that white students would leave the university if blacks were admitted: He said (with large tears in his eyes) that he would never forgive himself if he ruined the University by admitting Negroes....I got down on my knees and begged him to give justice to the Negroes, since he alone could do it. He said nothing.

The interview ended with Holloran agreeing to reverse his position if the Archbishop would agree to the change in policy. According to Heithaus, Holloran was in abject terror of the Archbishop, whom he described as "terribly vindictive," but he agreed to call on Glennon, with Heithaus as his companion, that afternoon. Heithaus later recalled that he expected the meeting to focus on what steps, if any, Holloran should take regarding integration. Such was not the case.

At this point the narrative supplied by Heithaus takes on an almost unreal quality. Glennon served as Archbishop of St. Louis for over forty years, was widely revered, and received the cardinal's hat shortly before his death on March 9, 1946.[18] Yet Glennon was known as no friend of racial integration, and at times he played a heavy hand in the internal affairs of the university. A few years earlier, for example, a professor at the medical school, Moyer Fleischer, had been dismissed upon earning the Archbishop's disapproval. [19]

The encounter between Heithaus and the Archbishop ranged in tone from awkward to ugly. According to Heithaus, while Holloran sat with his head in his hands, the Archbishop leveled many charges both at Heithaus personally, and at the African-American community, which were alleged to have been infiltrated by Japanese agents:

> He said with great anger that I was cooperating with the Japs, whose agents were working on the Negroes. I hotly denied this. He ignored me and in a

---

[17] Heithaus to Zuercher, December 18, 1944.

[18] No scholarly biography of Glennon exists; for some details of his career, see Thomas B. Morgan, *Speaking of Cardinals* (New York: G.P. Putnam's Sons, 1946) 206-244.

[19] See Jose M. Sanchez, "Cardinal Glennon and Academic Freedom: the Fleischer Case Revisited," *Gateway Heritage* (Winter 1987-1988) 3-11. Fleischer had supported the visit to St. Louis of a defrocked Irish priest who had launched public attacks against the Church.

voice shaking with emotion painted a picture of the Japs torturing our soldiers and raping our nurses...[20]

According to Heithaus' account, Holloran later told him that he agreed with everything the Archbishop had said, and for a time it appeared that the policy of the university regarding integration would not change. On March 31, one of the deans of the university discussed with President Holloran plans for admitting persons of color to his school, but as late as April 17 a black high school senior seeking admission received a letter from Holloran informing him that the university "has not deemed it wise to change its policy at the present time regarding the admission of Negro students." Nevertheless, only eight days later, on April 25, Holloran announced officially and publicly that five African-American students had already been registered at the university. In his statement he noted,

> It is the evident duty of Catholics to receive Catholic education. This duty... extends to all branches of university training. In the St. Louis area, though there are Catholic grade and high schools for both colored and white students, there does not exist a single institution in which the Catholic Negroes can receive instruction at the university level; nor does it appear that such an institution will come into existence even in the remote future.[21]

Holloran's apparent change of heart was expressed in a way which still held that a separate university or college for Catholic African-Americans would be a preferable solution. Meanwhile Heithaus had been instructed not to discuss the topic publicly. Curiously, local newspapers carried no reports of any statements by the Archbishop regarding the reversal in university policy. At the same time Zaccheus Maher, Assistant of the Society of Jesus for America, reminded Provincial Zuercher that while a Superior might normally forbid a Jesuit to speak on any topic, "we cannot deny to those men the position they take on race."[22] In a letter quoted in a summary of the Heithaus controversy provided to this author, Maher elaborated on his position:

> Fr. Holloran's first approach to the Heithaus problem I regret and he handled certain phases of it surprisingly. He was unfortunate in sending out the questionnaire especially if it contained references to negroes as alleged. When Fr. Holloran states that it is his duty to be guided by others' opinions he gives up his own authority and denies the jurisdiction of higher Superiors. He should have gone alone to the Archbishop. Restrictions imposed on Fr. Heithaus are

---

[20] Heithaus to Zuercher, December 18, 1944.

[21] Quoted in Faherty, *Dream*, 343.

[22] Maher to Zuercher, December 19, 1944.

within the Rector's (Holloran's) rights, but when he forbids his talking to any negro he is imposing an impossible command...[23]

Heithaus obeyed the imposition of silence in the months immediately after his sermon, but he did attempt to defend himself. In a letter of December 18, written to Provincial Zuercher, Heithaus reported what he considered to be prejudiced comments of Holloran.[24] Heithaus, portraying himself as trapped in an environment where moral cowardice predominated, pleaded in the most forceful manner for redress, but was denied any sort of forum for appeal. While the university moved cautiously towards a more tolerant racial policy, the Archbishop, at least in his public pronouncements, remained silent. The avalanche of negative mail from alumni and parents that Holloran had feared did not materialize.

Although reprimanded and chastened, Heithaus soon showed that he was not willing to drop the subject of racial injustice. On October 3, 1944, Heithaus, identified as a "Professor of Languages and Editor of the *University News*, St. Louis Univ.," spoke to the League of Women Voters in an address entitled "An Appeal to American Conscience." In his lecture Heithaus compared white supremacists to Nazis, a comparison that would have produced especially strong reactions in a nation that was just beginning to become aware of the extent of the Holocaust.[25] Provincial Zuercher's reactions to such actions were unambiguous. In a letter to Assistant Maher advising the removal of Heithaus from the university, Zuercher wrote that Heithaus was "forcing the entrance of negroes into St. Louis University and championing their cause in a cold blooded calculating manner."[26] On March 16, 1945 Heithaus published an essay in the *University News* entitled "Why Not Christian Cannibalism?"[27] The article made no direct reference to the problems of racial integration in the United States, focusing instead on a hypothetical situation where Christians would be compelled to accept and even endorse cannibalism because it was the "custom" of the land in which they found themselves. In the context of the racial politics of the city and the university, the article was undoubtedly understood as a commentary to the "go slow" or "don't go at all" policies that had been urged by

---

[23] Undated document entitled "Fr. Heithaus and the Negro Problem." The original of Maher's letter is not available.

[24] Heithaus to Zuercher, December 18, 1944

[25] "An Appeal to American Conscience," Published by the St. Louis Branch National Association for the Advancement of Colored People (November 1944).

[26] Zuercher to Maher, December 29, 1944. These and other letters from Zuercher make it clear that the conflict was never simply a personality clash between Heithaus and Holloran.

[27] *University News*, March 16, 1945, 5.

some high ranking Church officials. The same day Holloran wrote to Father Provincial Zuercher:

> At the University dance in fall of 1944 six negroes attended. There was no trouble but would have been if they had cut in on the whites. No mother or father of St. L.U. students have sent their sons and daughters to dance with negroes....[28]

Evidently even when the path had been cleared for African-Americans to attend classes at the university, social barriers remained. Segregated diners, ballrooms, movie theaters, and other public facilities, all of which surrounded the university campus, would continue to pose difficulties for black and white students alike for many years. Years later, an African-American who had attended the university in the 1960s recalled eating lunch on the sidewalk with her white classmates since she was unable to go into a local café. Neither the university nor the St. Louis Jesuit community were prepared to criticize publicly these forms of discrimination. The cautious integration of the university was all that could be dared or imagined, and even the sincerity of that action was doubted by some black students who felt that they had been admitted to the university only as second class students. Paul C. Reinert, S.J., then Dean of the College of Arts and Sciences and later president of the university, recognized these sentiments and noted them in a letter to Provincial Zuercher.[29] Reinert pointed out that while few black students had planned to attend the university-sponsored Conclave Dance that spring semester, once they learned they were to be restricted from the dance, they felt that they had been admitted to the university under false pretenses. This lack of decisiveness and courage on the part of the university hurt its credibility among elements of the St. Louis black community even before Heithaus himself was banished.

The publication of the "cannibals" article was the last straw for Heithaus' immediate superiors, several of whom had long felt that he had in some way been contaminated during his long period of travels away from St. Louis. Within a month Provincial Zuercher had written to Assistant Maher recommending that Heithaus be urged to leave the Society of Jesus, a recommendation which Maher did not support.[30] Of particular relevance to Maher was the question of whether Heithaus was professed, that is to say, whether he had taken the fourth and final vow of the Society. Since Heithaus had not, it was in Maher's opinion, "not in due order" to dismiss him without certain formalities, which in his case had not been followed. Zuercher nevertheless moved to take severe measures against

---

[28] Cited in "Fr. Heithaus and the Negro Problem," March 16, 1945.

[29] Reinert to Zuercher, March 28, 1945.

[30] Maher to Zuercher, April 10, 1945.

Heithaus. In June Heithaus was informed that he was to be permanently removed from the university, he was to continue not to speak on the topic of race discrimination, and that he was to perform a reading of the Seven Penitential Psalms. Heithaus had by this time probably already received a lengthy letter from Zuercher and four other Jesuits of the Missouri Province detailing his faults, including disobedience, trying to force Holloran's hand in the question of integration, insincere interpretation of an order of holy obedience, and disloyalty to the Archbishop, Holloran, and the faculty of the university.[31] Zuercher and the other signers of the letter also took exception to Heithaus setting himself up as a "champion of the Negro." It was not clear whether the fault in this instance was because Heithaus was unqualified to be such a champion, or whether African-Americans needed no such champion.

The question of academic freedom was not addressed in either the communications from Holloran to Heithaus, nor in the Zuercher letter. This was in part because Heithaus' actions took place outside the classroom and the usual venues of scholarly debate, but most importantly because Catholic universities of the 1940s did not yet feel pressured to follow academic freedom policies adopted in other institutions.[32] The situation was further complicated by the fact that Holloran was not only Heithaus' superior within the university administration, but that he was also, as Rector of the St. Louis Jesuit community, his religious superior. Heithaus' apparent defiance of Holloran's wishes was thus far more than the act of an indiscreet employee; it was a challenge to a sacrosanct authority located within a Counter-reformation tradition of "holy obedience." Likewise Holloran's and Zuercher's responses reveal how completely intertwined the local Jesuit community and the university administration were, not only in practice, but also in the minds of the Jesuits themselves.

The transfer of Heithaus and Fr. George Dunne, another Jesuit active in the push for integration, was officially explained as having nothing to do with "the race question," but an article that quickly appeared in the *St. Louis Post-Dispatch* was headlined "Two on St. Louis U. Faculty Out Over Negro Students."[33] In both the white and the African-American communities, there was a widespread perception, never adequately addressed by the university, that Heithaus had been forced out because of his support for integration. Heithaus himself, although he continued to be an outspoken and active participant first at

---

[31] Joseph P. Zuercher, S.J., William Fitzgerald, S.J., Joseph Gschwind, S.J., William McCabe, S.J., and Daniel H. Connor, S.J., to Heithaus, June 14, 1945.

[32] For the late acceptance of notions of tenure and academic freedom in American Catholic colleges and universities, see William Leahy, S.J., *Adapting to America* (Washington, DC: Georgetown University Press, 1991), 108-112.

[33] *St. Louis Post-Dispatch*, April 20, 1945.

the theologate at St. Mary's, Kansas, later in Wisconsin, and finally again in St. Louis, never spoke openly about the circumstances that resulted in his departure, nor did he ever again take an active role in the continuing debate about racial integration that absorbed the nation in the late 1950s and 60s. Nor was he allowed to continue his work as a classical archeologist and art historian, although he did continue to work to preserve materials related to the early Catholic history of the Midwest. ,

Late in life Father Heithaus received some recognition for his achievements. In addition to the letter from Father General Arrupe cited above, Heithaus also received a high honor from the French government. On May 8, 1976, the Consular General of France awarded Heithaus the "Academic Palms" for his archeological work in the Middle East, an honor bestowed on few American researchers, and all the more unusual since little of Heithaus' research was ever published.[34] The award made no mention, however, of Heithaus' efforts on the part of African-Americans. Claude Heithaus died a few days later on May 12, 1976, and his death was reported in university and provincial publications without much attention to the role he had played in bringing racial integration to the university, and no discussion of the censure he incurred from his superiors. Oral tradition within the St. Louis Jesuit community, however, has kept alive the story of his refusal to remain silent on an issue that in the post Vatican II world is seen as crucial to the educational mission of the Society.

Viewed from fifty years on, the historian's task of understanding the case of Fr. Claude Heithaus has been complicated by the manner in which Saint Louis University has made use of his story. As an urban campus located in a central part of St. Louis, a city with enduring racial problems, Saint Louis University has appropriated the story of its admission of people of color as part of its efforts to refashion its own image as a modern, progressive institution. Diversity and tolerance are accepted as unambiguous goods in the majority of contemporary American academic settings, and therefore the university points with some justifiable pride to its record as the first institution of higher education in a former slave state to admit African Americans. Heithaus' sermon forms an appealing prologue to this story, and has been utilized on many occasions for just this purpose.[35] Yet the account of Heithaus' contribution to the development of Saint Louis University not only pays insufficient attention to the price that the Jesuit paid for his outspoken condemnation of racism, it also avoids the way in which the university itself and the Jesuit community have never formally repented of their actions, nor honored Heithaus in a way commensurate with the contributions that it now acknowledges he made. Nowhere on the Saint Louis

---

[34] Letter from the Consular General de France, May 8, 1976.

[35] Cf. *The St. Louis American*, March 9, 1995, 8.

University campus is there a marker or memorial to Heithaus, although many other faculty are recognized with plaques, and even buildings in their name. Nor is there any endowed chair, scholarship fund or other means of honoring this man, whose name is not familiar to many students and younger faculty. Heithaus' valuable archeological collections, dispersed or destroyed, have been ignored, and little effort has been made to determine if any portion of them survives.

There remains the issue of Heithaus' decision to refuse to accept the judgment of his superiors on the question of the appropriateness of speaking on the "race question," as it was then called. As a Jesuit, Heithaus was expected to be true to his vow of "holy obedience," a mainstay of the Society of Jesus since its founding.[36] Heithaus always maintained that he was not being disobedient in promoting integration, but was in fact being true to the educational mission of the Church.[37] At least at first, his decision to speak out on what he considered to be the sin of racial prejudice was supported by some high ranking Jesuits and by many other American Catholics. At stake were both the interpretation of the vow of obedience, and the issue of acculturation, a policy that the Jesuits have followed since the sixteenth century. From Ignatius' time on, the Society has striven to understand and incorporate elements of the cultures in which it operates. The willingness of some Jesuits to embrace the cultural norms of the communities in which they worked has led the Society into serious trouble more than once.[38]

The culture of St. Louis in the 1940s included institutional segregation, a policy undoubtedly endorsed by the majority of the white population, Catholic and non-Catholic. Yet the problem of adapting to the local culture was not as simple as Heithaus painted it in "Why Not Christian Cannibalism?" Jesuit educators in St. Louis were not missionaries struggling to make meaningful contact with an alien society. Many, if not most of them, were, like Heithaus, natives, intimately familiar with the mores of the community. The value system

---

[36] See John W. O'Malley, *The First Jesuits* (Cambridge: Harvard University Press, 1993), 333ff., for a discussion of the early importance of obedience. Obedience figures prominently in the *Constitutions* of the Society. See Saint Ignatius of Loyola, *The Constitutions of the Society of Jesus*, George E. Ganss, S.J., trans. (St. Louis, MO: The Institute of Jesuit Sources, 1970), 245-249. For the position of the Society in the middle of the twentieth century regarding obedience see documents from the 30th General Congregation, item 45, paragraph 3, in *For Matters of Greater Moment: The First Thirty Jesuit General Congregations*, John W. Padberg, S.J., Martin O'Keefe, S.J., and John L. McCarthy, S.J., eds., and trans. (St. Louis, MO: Institute of Jesuit Sources, 1994), 672.

[37] Heithaus to Zuercher, March 25, 1945.

[38] The most notable instance of this conflict was the "Malabar Rites" controversy of the seventeenth century. See William V. Bangert, S.J., *A History of the Society of Jesus* (St. Louis, MO: The Institute of Jesuit Sources, 1986), 329-334.

that Heithaus found so abhorrent was for many merely a part of the world-view they had held since childhood. Indeed, previous to the Civil War, Jesuits of the Missouri Province themselves had owned slaves. The challenge that Heithaus put before them was much more than a plea to break with immoral societal values, which were in fact their own values. By attacking the issue of racial prejudice Claude Heithaus called attention to the contrast between the universal message of the Gospel and the attitudes and prejudices of a particular time and place.

It is striking that nowhere in the lengthy statement of rebuke issued to Heithaus by his superiors is the question of the universal applicability of the color-blind message of the New Testament addressed. Nor are the color-blind values of Ignatius himself, who made no distinctions among nationalities, acknowledged. Equally striking is the relative lack of overt support Heithaus received within the Jesuit community of St. Louis following his sermon. The difference between the perspective of Assistant Maher and other Catholics throughout the nation and those of the leaders of the Missouri Province is a mirror of the range of perspectives with which racial issues were viewed half a century ago. This is not to say that only in southern and boarder states was racial prejudice evident, but that long-standing institutional and legal segregation helped foster an atmosphere that made the acceptance of people of color at the University more difficult. The silence of Zuercher and others who had opposed Heithaus in the years after black students were admitted suggests how deep seated the resistance to this reform actually was among some members of the Society.

The intertwining of university administration and Jesuit hierarchy adds another dimension to the story. The Heithaus case illustrates an instance where incompatible traditions of educational leadership and Jesuit institutional organization collided at a time when the administration of American higher education was undergoing an important change. By the middle of the twentieth century, academic freedom was well on the way to becoming enshrined as a fundamental principal of American higher education. A series of legal and administrative precedents had established the right of American university faculty to speak freely in a variety of venues. By contrast, the academic values espoused by the Society of Jesus drew heavily from the nineteenth-century reaction to modernism and liberalism. Loyalty, obedience, and acceptance of the hierarchical structure of the Society and the Church were still essential elements of American Jesuit culture in the 1940s. At the same time, the motives of men like Holloran who feared the affects of the integration of the university were conditioned by the sense that American Catholicism was still vulnerable to attacks from without. Today it is difficult to grasp to what degree some Catholics in the 1940s still felt themselves to be victims because of their religious affiliation, and therefore as victims unable or unwilling to address the needs of others who were themselves being victimized. In a dynamic, evolving American society whose boundaries were being pushed further by the exigencies of a world war, these attitudes would be challenged and transformed, although few in 1944 could foresee in what way or to what extent.

Finally, the internal politics of the Missouri Province of the Society may have played an important role in the way in which it responded to Heithaus' challenge. As has been noted, Heithaus was perceived by a few of his fellow Jesuits as having already strayed too far from appropriate work in the Province by traveling abroad for many years and receiving training at a public university in a predominantly non-Catholic country. The culture of both the Province and the university had been overwhelmingly insular previous to the presidency of William Banks Rogers, S.J., which began in 1900, and remained so in significant ways into the 1930s.[39] Even in the 1940s, memories still lingered among older Jesuits (and perhaps alumni as well) of a time when the university did not concern itself much with the outside world and when its student body consisted of a small group of men studying a narrow curriculum far removed from the revolutionary developments going on elsewhere in American higher education. The resistance to Heithaus' call was therefore more than a racist reaction to an appeal for integration; it was at least in part a globally conservative response to the most recent in a series of changes at the university that had included the admission of women to undergraduate study. (Holloran always asserted that he received much criticism from alumni as a result of the Heithaus sermon and the presence of African Americans at dances and other social events. Independent documentation of these claims has not been possible.) Internal fissures among the Jesuits of the Missouri Province themselves are also extremely difficult to document, but there may have been polarization between Jesuits of varying ethnic ancestries within the Province that would have placed Heithaus at a disadvantage. In particular, a division between Jesuits of Irish and those of German descent may have played a role. The looming figure of Archbishop Glennon undoubtedly cast a shadow over the entire affair, but the exact role of the prelate is difficult to ascertain since many of his papers appear to have been lost or destroyed.[40]

As the centenary of Heithaus' birth approaches, the long overdue recognition of his life and accomplishments would be an entirely appropriate undertaking for Saint Louis University and for the Missouri Province. Moreover, the anniversary could also be an occasion for reflection and discussion concerning the responsibility of the university to its community, and even, if

---

[39] See Faherty, *Dream*, 205-211.

[40] Sanchez, "Glennon," 9.

enough individuals are brave enough, an opportunity to engage in a discussion of the dilemmas posed by the potential conflict between vows of obedience and the pangs of conscience. In such a discussion Claude Heithaus need not be made into a martyr, but rather should be understood as an exemplar of a Jesuit stranded between two incompatible belief systems. On the one hand both the religious faith that Heithaus professed and the alleged ideals (if not the practices) of society in which he lived could not support racial discrimination as it was practiced in St. Louis in the 1940s. On the other hand obedience was expected of Heithaus from his superiors, some of whom still felt themselves to be experiencing discrimination because of their own religious and ethnic identity. In the specific instance of Saint Louis University, anti-Catholic violence during the previous century had produced a cautious, inward-looking intellectual climate throughout the second half of the nineteenth century that complemented the conservative social climate described above and survived down to the time of Claude Heithaus. A conversation that examines the multiple layers of the dilemma faced by both Heithaus and his superiors is not only eminently appropriate for a university to undertake, but would also shed light on the Jesuit mission of the university and the relationship of the Society of Jesus to its educational commitment, and to its relationship to the greater world which it seeks to serve.

The questions surrounding the treatment of Claude Heithaus have more than limited historical importance. The silencing and reprimanding of the Jesuit in 1944 can be placed within an historical context which may cause us to refrain from making a hasty judgment against his superiors. Yet there remains the question of the appropriate response of the university community today to the historical facts as they are currently understood. The assessment of Claude Heithaus' contribution articulated by Pedro Arrupe reveals the inherent tension between evolving notions of acceptable behavior as defined by the mores of the time and place, and the claims of eternal truth made by the Church. It is not simply that between the 1940s and the 1970s a shift in society had occurred, causing what was once acceptable now not to be, while what was insubordinate was now seen as righteous. The Jesuit social and educational mission was also undergoing a reappraisal during these years. After a century and a half of possessing an often deserved reputation as supporters of ultramontanism and political conservatism, many Jesuits have emerged once again as challengers to the existing social and political order, drawing on elements of the Gospel and on Ignatian tradition to support their arguments, and occasionally appearing as social critics and reformers. While much of this development can be linked to the reforms of Vatican II, the process was underway within Jesuit educational circles even before the ascension of John XXIII.[41] In such a climate, even without the

---

[41] Cf. Father General John Baptist Jansens, speaking in 1949: "Let (those trained at

added pressure to grant academic freedom to faculty, obedience to human authority today must compete with love of justice as a virtue. Yet social justice was only a secondary motivation for Heithaus, who instead was primarily concerned with obedience to a religious mission as he understood it.

When questions of social justice are raised on Catholic university campuses, it is very seldom in concert with an examination of the meaning and value of obedience in modern higher education. The Heithaus case, with its conflict between institutional expectations and individual initiative, both of which were understood in terms of obedience, thus contains elements that seem remote or medieval to a generation that has grown up since the 1960s. The very word "obedience" frequently acquires a connotation of unappealing subservience or craven lack of integrity. Yet repeatedly, and no doubt sincerely, Heithaus referred to an obedience to the message of the Gospel as he understood it, an obedience that ran counter to the expectations that his superiors held for him. The choice for Heithaus seems to have been between two expressions of obedience, rather than between obedience and rebellion. It is noteworthy that Heithaus' superiors, as far as the surviving records indicate, did not perceive his actions as derived from a sense of obedience, but were only willing to attribute them to willfulness and self importance. How we assess his actions depends on our willingness to accept Heithaus' own justification for his position.

Heithaus himself, along with the pioneering Jesuit parish priest J. P. Markoe, expressed the motives for the integration of the Church and its educational institutions in the following fashion:

> Apart from mass schism and heresy we know of nothing that could be more injurious to unity and vigor of the Mystical Body (of Christ) in the United States than race discrimination. It has divided the American members of the Mystical Body into two groups, built a wall of segregation between them, and filled them with mutual misunderstanding, suspicion, and fear.[42]

Heithaus' central concern was always the furtherance of the message of the Church, not social justice. Yet his goals were, in retrospect, always entirely compa-tible with the goals of those who sought social justice. In obedience to the mission of the Society he sought to increase the number of the faithful, and in St. Louis he endeavored to embrace blacks, particularly if they were Catholic. Like many other reformers and more than a few Jesuits, Heithaus pursued his goals in an uncom-promising and sometimes overwhelming fashion. A letter he once wrote to his provincial, Fr. Zuercher defending his position ran to thirteen

---

Jesuit schools) learn to hunger and thirst after justice, the justice which sees to it that all men receive the due reward of their labors..." in John W. Donohue, S.J., *Jesuit Education* (New York: Fordham University Press, 1963), 209.

[42] Heithaus and Markoe to Zuercher, November 23, 1944.

single spaced pages! Obedience in this context became an aggressive, even virile defense of principle and morality.

The ultimate vindication of Heithaus' position by the Father General of the Society and by history can obscure the important role that these two competing visions of obedience played in the Heithaus case. Further examination and discussion of the positions of both Heithaus and his accusers must focus on varying conceptions of obedience and justice, on the vulnerability that many Jesuits felt in taking on a controversial problem, and on the local culture of St. Louis, which provided the context in which the drama was played out.

Today, Saint Louis University is still located in midtown St. Louis, an oasis of green space and fountains a short distance from poverty stricken neighborhoods. While the university continues to make efforts to reach out to the community around it, it remains predominantly white. The city of St. Louis, despite considerable efforts by both whites and blacks, is still segregated in significant ways and is far from resolving its racial problems. Its citizens are heirs to the injustices and prejudices which motivated Claude Heithaus to speak out. By coming to understand the motivation and the faith of Heithaus in all their facets, we may be better able to address these problems, and thereby do honor to the message and the messenger.

7

The Ethical Eloquence of the Silenced

A Levinasian Reading of Teilhard de Chardin's Silencing

Michael Barber
Saint Louis University

The Strange Phenomenon of Silencing

The question of the Catholic identity of Catholic colleges and universities, that is, how institutions can both embrace ethico-religious commitments and pursue truth impartially through teaching and research, is part of a more encompassing philosophical question of the relationship between ethics and truth. Likewise, the question of the academic freedom to speak and publish one's research within such value-directed Catholic institutions pertains to this broader question. Even institutional Roman Catholicism must deal with how its value commitments relate to the search for truth when it ponders, as it does in *Ex corde ecclesiae*, how it ought to intervene when theologians within Catholic universities teach or publish ideas that seem at odds with official Catholic teaching. This paper will not resolve these intricate questions of Catholic identity, academic freedom, or the proper stance of ecclesial authorities toward seemingly renegade theologians. Rather, it will address an issue underlying all these issues, namely the relationship between ethics and truth, an issue rarely examined in most discussions of these more concrete and practical issues. In this connection, the strange phenomenon of ecclesial silencing can serve as an illuminating starting point for reflection. For it is indeed a strange thing when a brilliant, creative intellectual, passionately dedicated to the enterprise of finding the truth, conforms with an ecclesial ordinance silencing him or her.

One could select as an example any of the great thinkers constrained in varying degrees because of Roman suspicions during the nineteenth and twentieth centuries, prior to the Second Vatican Council: Montalembert, Newman, Rosmini, Lagrange, Duchesne, Blondel, Rousselot, Battifol, Bardy, Bonsirven, Maritain, Chardin, Chenu, Congar, De Lubac, Bouillard, Rahner, and Murray. For the purposes of this paper, I have chosen to reconstruct Teilhard de Chardin's silencing since his abundant correspondence is widely available and thus makes insight into his motivation more possible than in other cases.[1]

Ordained a Jesuit priest in 1911 at the age of thirty, Chardin did military service in World War I, then earned his doctorate in paleontology at the Sorbonne, and held a chair in geology at the Institut Catholique from 1920-1923. In 1925, the Roman curia of the Jesuit order gained possession of a paper of his, never intended for public circulation, in which he embraced the theory of evolution, ruled out the existence of a historical Adam, and interpreted symbolically Adam's Fall. The curia not only removed him from teaching and exiled him to China, but they also personalized their intellectual disagreement by punishing him, as he expressed it, "not only because of my paper, but because of my tendencies 'which cannot be corrected.'" In Peking, he focused on East Asian geology and paleontology and partook in the discovery of the first skull of *Homo Sinanthropus*, before returning to Europe after World War II. In 1948 he traveled to Rome to seek, though in vain, authorization to publish *The Phenomenon of Man*. Until his death in 1955, he was only allowed to publish scientific and technical works, and it deeply grieved him that his theological works on evolution and spirituality, such as *The Divine Milieu* and *The Phenomenon of Man*, were never permitted to go to press. It is somewhat shocking that as late as 1961 Henry de Lubac, S.J., Chardin's close personal friend, never even knew the reasons why these two great works had been censored. De Lubac responded to a series of charges, which may have resembled these never revealed reasons, in a 1962 letter commenting on an anonymous article in *l'Osservatore Romano* that accused Teilhard of embracing evolution uncritically, of believing in a pantheistic culmination of everything in God, of positing a "cosmic" Christ beyond the human and divine Christ, of de-emphasizing the importance of heredity in original sin, and of confusing spirit and matter. Teilhard reacted to the censorship he experienced throughout his lifetime by complaining in letters that he felt himself "at the limit of his rights,"

---

[1] Joseph A. Komonchak, "The Catholic University in the Church," in *Catholic Universities in Church and Society, A Dialogue on Ex Corde Ecclesiae*, ed. John P. Langan, S.J. (Washington, DC: Georgetown University Press, 1993), 50-51. For an historical analysis of John Courtney Murray's silencing, see Joseph A. Komonchak, "The Silencing of John Courtney Murray," in *Christianesimo Nella Storia, Saggi in onore di Giuseppe Alberigo*, eds. A. Melloni et al. (Roma: Il Mulino, 1997), 657-702.

that "it is unfortunate that ... one does not even try to see in Rome what is constructive or worthy of conservation in my effort," that Rome needs to understand "that one does not play with people's ideas as one does with their status," and that he is "absolutely and physically 'suffocated' with the 'Christian world' as represented in ecclesiastical documents and Catholic actions and conceptions." [2]

Before proceeding to examine how Teilhard reconciled his intellectual search for truth with being silenced, one ought to recognize the cultural obstacles making it difficult even to reflect upon such instances of ecclesial silencing. For liberal democratic societies, characterized by a free exchange of ideas, particularly within secular universities in which academic freedom is normative, the institutional behavior of church authority in cases of silencing as well as the compliance of those silenced appears morally offensive, and few would think that such instances of silencing contain anything instructive for modern societies. Indeed, these democratic societies represent the culmination of a long history whose philosophical origins could be traced to Socrates, who in *The Apology* appropriated the courage of the Homeric soldier for philosophers who needed to be brave enough to raise any question regardless of the consequences for themselves. Similarly, Kant issued his clarion call to Enlightenment, which he defined in terms of bravery: *"Sapere Aude!* 'Have courage to use your own understanding!' "that is the motto of enlightenment." To the modern mentality, Catholicism's silencers and silenced might well epitomize a kind of intellectual cowardice. [3]

Catholics themselves, chagrined in the company of their fellow citizens and academic colleagues, might experience shame in reverting to instances of silencing before the Second Vatican Council. Moreover, for many Catholics it is a particularly cruel irony that church authority suppressed some voices that had significant influence at the Second Vatican Council, which in turn vindicated

---

[2] Teilhard de Chardin, Letter of August 11, 1920 to Pére Valensin, in *Lettres Intimes, B Auguste Valensin, Bruno de Solages, Henri de Lubac, André Ravier 1919-1955* (Paris: Aubier-Montaigne, 1974), 68; Letter of June 4, 1933 to Pére Valensin, in *Lettres Intimes*, 246; For details of his difficulties see Mgr. B. de Solages, *Teilhard de Chardin, TJmoignage et étude sur le développement de sa pensée* (Paris: Edouard Privat, 1967), 42-43, 54; Henri de Lubac, S.J., *Teilhard Explained*, trans. Anthony Buono (New York: Paulist Press, 1968), 79-81; Mary Lukas and Ellen Lukas, *Teilhard* (Garden City, New York: Doubleday and Company, Inc., 1977), 72-3. De Lubac's recounting of his defense of Teilhard is in Henri de Lubac, S.J., *At the Service of the Church, Henri de Lubac Reflects on the Circumstances that Occasioned His Writings*, trans. Anne Elizabeth Englund (San Francisco, CA: Ignatius Press, 1993), 324-334.

[3] Immanuel Kant, An Answer to the Question: "What is Enlightenment?" in *Perpetual Peace and other essays on politics, history, and morals*, trans. Ted Humphrey (Indianapolis, IN: Hackett Publishing Company, 1983), 41.

these voices and which has widely transformed practices throughout Roman Catholicism, including the exercise of church authority itself. In addition, the occurrence of Vatican II, which these thinkers helped bring about, produced a climate making it impossible for church authority to sustain the same kind of systematic repression of its critics, as it did prior to the Vatican Council.

Moreover, because of the impetus which the Second Vatican Council has given to the church, urging it to become engaged with the world and to transform socio-economic structures, the piety which those silenced exhibited, accepting without protest the muzzling of ideas they knew to be true, seems strangely out of date. In the preface to a book recounting the deeds of several women who have challenged church authorities since the Vatican Council, the author captures very well the shift in the winds of piety:

> Once upon a time I loved saintly men and women who suffered ignominy in silence. Their going to their graves without vindication appealed mightily to my sense of sainthood. But now, I love courage. I admire those women "there seems to be more of them" and men who take rightful risks in spite of their fears. Such valor seeps under my nerve endings, stretches the ecclesial horizon, and provides hope for the future. The most engaging women I know are those Catholics who stand up to hierarchical oppression, who name the evil done them and others, and who refuse either to be victimized further or to leave their church.[4]

In this citation, the elevation of courage over a timid and emasculated sanctity reflects the impact, which is healthful in many respects, of modernity upon post-Vatican II Catholicism.

In a sense, one might even feel reluctant to bring up the tragic cases of these silenced individuals for fear that church authorities might resort to a facile use of divine providence to justify their behavior since, after all, "all things worked out for good in the end." Ironically, the final result is that these silenced thinkers paid a huge price to usher in a new ecclesial atmosphere that is perhaps less capable than ever of appreciating the price they paid. This paper will attempt to move beyond these many obstacles to appreciation in order to reconstruct how Teilhard de Chardin understood his own being silenced—as a basis for further reflection on the relationship between truth and ethics. One final caution: since I will view Teilhard's silencing and its implications through the prism of the broader *philosophical* relationship between truth and ethics and since I will strive to retrieve Teilhard's example as instructive even for *a-religious* modernity, I will not myself adopt a specific faith stance. Instead, I will construe Teilhard's faith commitment as a kind of ethical commitment—and thus I may

---

[4] Preface, *The Inside Stories, 13 Valiant Women Challenging the Church*, ed. Annie Lally Milhaven (Mystic, CT: Twenty-Third Publications, 1987), xiii.

not understand him fully in his terms.

Teilhard de Chardin: The Motives for Observing Silence

What motivated Teilhard de Chardin to observe the silence imposed upon him? In the first place, it would not be fair to attribute intellectual cowardice to him. In his correspondence prior to being silenced, he describes his own intellectual daring.

> It is practically impossible for me to be involved in some matter without constituting myself "ipso facto" as a center of influence toward the directions which are disquieting. All the same, I would be no more able, while speaking to people as a priest, to present them with a theory of miracles to which I would swear with all my conviction, than I would be able to refrain from spreading, with all the force of my personality (little or great, it does not matter much) my ideas on evolution which, I know, are essentially repugnant to the teaching authority.[5]

Similarly, as if anticipating what was to come, he asserts to "Pre Valensin, 'interiorly I maintain integrally my positions, for I am not able to do otherwise without committing suicide.'" Later, when silence was imposed, Chardin retains this spirit of integrity by refusing to capitulate in his thinking. Just as John Henry Newman in his *Apologia* argued that ecclesial silencing forbade only the *publishing* of thoughts and could not control how one thought since that was a matter of conscience,[6] so Teilhard explains to Valensin, "The delicate side, on the contrary, with my situation with respect to Father General, is that it is doubly impossible for me (psychologically first of all, and then in my conscience) to 'change my ideas' as one tells me to do naively enough." Although cooperating with the silencing and willing to entertain Rome's questions, Chardin makes it explicit that his unwillingness to retract convictions does not spring from some fear of the consequences of recanting, such as, for example, the intellectual repudiation that might follow on such a retraction. Rather, he affirms, "I will place everything in question (although I am unable to do so completely, *not because of fear of the consequences but because of conviction*)." [7]

Since Chardin's integrity in abiding by what he believes to be true, however, does not lead him so far as to disobey the order not to publish, it is necessary to explore the motives prompting his compliance with that command.

---

[5] Letter to Pére Valensin, August 11, 1920, *Lettres Intimes*, 67-68.

[6] John Henry Cardinal Newman, *Apologia Pro Vita Sua, Being a History of His Religious Opinions*, ed. Martin J. Svaglic (Oxford: Clarendon Press, 1967), 231.

[7] *Ibid.*; Letter to Pére Valensin, June 4, 1933, *Lettres Intimes*, 246; Letter to Pére Valensin, July 28, 1925 cited by de Solages, 43-4.

While he rarely expresses the piety motivating his obedience in the self-effacing terms of Yves Congar, who, upon being restricted, opted for "complete resignation to the cross and to reduction to insignificance,"[8] Chardin, like Congar, has a sense that divine providence, working in history, will vindicate his views. He writes to Valensin, "Time and obedience will explicitly make manifest whatever is immortal and essentially Christian among censured ideas." Echoing Newman's belief that later generations might rehabilitate what was silenced, Chardin observes that "in order for ideas to triumph, it is necessary that many of their defenders die obscurely; their anonymous influence makes itself felt." Indeed, this historical/providential motivation seems particularly appropriate for Teilhard the paleontologist, who, ever aware of history's vast scope, writes, "I am deeply convinced that religious thought develops only traditionally, collectively, 'phyletically.'"[9]

In addition to relying on this providential/historical motivation, Teilhard remains loyal to Catholicism and abides by the decree of silencing because he does not want to cut himself off from the Catholic tradition, which serves as a perennial source of theological and human insight. He remarks that "the church has the right to expect our compliance in some things, because in the current that she represents she is the vehicle of more truth than any one of us in his slender individuality." He explains more fully the importance of the Catholic tradition in a letter to Valensin before his conflicts with church authorities:

> I am absolutely persuaded that there is infinitely more truth in the complex, empirical attitude of the church than in all our simplifying philosophies. The practice of the saints, difficult to rationalize as it may be, is the "imposed" real, the concrete truth. It is therefore this practice that ought to mold our attempts at systematization, and it always overflows them. With respect to our speculations, they will remain sterile, for us and for others, if we do not reach the point of transforming them into an example, into living in accordance with them.[10]

These statements about our "slender individuality" within Catholicism do not forbid critical analysis of church teaching, since, as indicated above, Teilhard clearly recognized the importance of forming one's own beliefs in

---

[8] Yves M.J. Congar, O.P., *Dialogue Between Christians, Catholic Contributions to Ecumenism*, trans. Philip Loretz, S.J. (Westminster, Maryland: The Newman Press, 1966), 43.

[9] In a letter to Pére Valensin, August 11, 1920, *Lettres Intimes*, 67; *Apologia pro Vita Sua*, 232; *GenPse*, December 23, 1916, p. 200-201, cited by de Solages, 44; "Christianisme et Ivolution" in *Comme je crois*, 203-204, cited in Henri de Lubac, S.J., *The Eternal Feminine, A Study on the Poem by Teilhard de Chardin*, and *Teilhard and the Problems of Today*, trans. René Hague (New York: Harper & Row, Publishers, 1971), 194-195.

[10] Letter to Pére Valensin, December 29, 1919, *Lettres Intimes*, 45; *The Eternal Feminine*, 193.

conscience and not capitulating to church authority when it asks one to act against conviction. Rather, Chardin recognizes that reasoning about Christian faith arises out of a pre-theoretical context of communal-historical practices that cannot be easily or completely rationalized. By situating his own theological thinking with reference to the lived, traditional setting that precedes and nourishes it, Chardin follows a pattern that many of his philosophical contemporaries adopted in reaction to what they perceived as tendencies toward over rationalization in modernity. Thus, for example, Martin Heidegger undercut Descartes's seemingly eccentric doubts about the existence of the real world by insisting that one begins thinking out of an encompassing, practical, social setting where no such doubts exist. Similarly, Edmund Husserl recognized that logic and science arise out of the lifeworld in which one is immersed and which one never reflectively masters. This lived dimension, prior to theory, to which Heidegger, Husserl, and Teilhard refer, by no means precludes, but rather gives birth to critical reflection. Teilhard's recognition that cognition encompasses both a rational and lived pole explains in part why he did not find contradictory his effort to maintain both the integrity of his own critical thinking and his loyalty to the Catholic tradition.[11]

Teilhard, however, remained loyal to Catholicism not only for the intellectual insights that its pre-theoretical matrix afforded him. That same pre-theoretical matrix included ethical dimensions that played a central role in his decision to comply with the silencing mandate. In 1933, years after his expulsion to China, he writes to Leontine Zanta of his deep insertion within the church, which equips him better for the work of setting the church free. This dream of helping in the church's liberation never leaves him and perhaps explains why years later he would continue to seek authorization to publish *The Phenomenon of Man*, although to no avail. His writings and actions reveal an ethical commitment to the community of Catholicism underpinning his intellectual career, inspiring him to strive to contribute intellectually to the uplifting of that community, and enabling him in the end to accept the suffering of silence for its sake.[12]

At the same time, his intellectual integrity proves that his fidelity to the community had nothing do with the mindless conformism of an automaton

---

[11] In the debate that took place between Hans-Georg Gadamer and Jurgen Habermas some thirty years ago, it is tempting to speculate that Chardin both might have allowed for more critique of traditions than Gadamer and yet might not have concurred with tendencies in the earlier Habermas toward a type of rationalist modernity disengaged from any lived, traditional milieu. As is well known, Habermas' subsequent writings have been more attentive to the lifeworld whose beliefs, when problematized, lead to the search for a discursively established consensus.

[12] Letter to Leontine Zanta, March 20, 1932, in *Letters to Leontine Zanta*, trans. Bernard Wall (New York: Harper & Row, Publishers, 1969), 106-107.

unwilling to question authorities. Although he would not retract the ideas he believed to be true in accord with the Enlightenment's insistence on obedience to one's intellectual conscience, he would accept at least provisionally (as shown by his later petition to publish) an imposed silence, an injustice done against him, as part of the price to be paid for what looked to be a long and slow process of transformation of the community to which he was dedicated. Perhaps because many contemporary intellectuals are often devoid of such ethical attachments to a community, they find it difficult to understand how one could value one's ethical obligations to a community over the dissemination of one's ideas in the marketplace of truth. In terms of the dialectic between ethics and truth, Teilhard would not allow the demands of ethics to override truth if it meant altering well-considered opinions, but he did allow ethics to circumscribe at least momentarily the circulation of his ideas and thus to constrain partially the free flow of thought so dear to the Enlightenment.[13]

In fact, the experience of being silenced revealed to Chardin the preeminence of the desire to serve others in his value scheme. In a prayerful moment, recorded in a diary, when he entertains the possibility that his works might never see the light of day and thus that history and divine providence might not vindicate him, that no recognition or gratitude might ever come his way, his overriding and only remaining motive comes to the fore as he writes, "Jesus, once more I give over to you my effort so that it might not be lost, but that it might serve the World, in passing through you, even if it ought to remain confined finally within myself." In another passage he confesses that "if I pass without having been heard, I have confidence that I will have served." It is as though his being silenced, possibly forever, stripped him of every other possible motivation and left him only with the ability to *re*-dedicate his manuscripts to the purpose that had governed him in producing them in the first place. Thus, it would seem that he reconciled himself to being silenced by conferring on his works an ethical intentionality "for others," that would endure even if his works were to stay mute, inert, and fruitless forever.[14]

Because of such ethical motivations, Chardin also struggled not to respond hurtfully to others and not to become disillusioned after his silencing. He

---

[13] While unwilling to commit an injustice, like Socrates in the *Apology* who would not disobey the daemon whispering to his conscience, Teilhard would not retract what was true, but at the same time, he was willing to suffer an injustice, like Socrates in the *Crito*, who would not break out of prison in spite of his innocence.

[14] C3, February 14, 1917, cited by de Solages, 41; *GenJse*, December 23, 1916, 200-201, cited by de Solages, 44. That Teilhard's loyalty to Catholicism was based on his loyalty to individual Catholics and not just impersonal allegiance to an institution can be seen in a letter to de Lubac describing his relationship with Valensin whose friendship prevented him from "having the impression of being a stranger in one's own religion." *At the Service of the Church*, 321.

localizes the agony of being silenced within this same ethical setting, even as he vents his frustrations to Pere Charles and requests his aid, "You will help me not to do something stupid and, if some injury occurs (as scarcely seems avoidable), to remain on the side of 'love.'" Chardin also expresses a fear of becoming the "tinkling cymbal" (*cymbalum tinniens*) of which St. Paul speaks in 1 Corinthians 13 when Paul reminds his audience that it is possible to understand all mysteries, know everything, achieve prodigiously, and yet be without love. This love, though, is not a matter of sentimentality, but rather ethical *agape*, which, "not resentful", "is ready to excuse, to trust, to hope, and to endure whatever comes."[15]

However much a modernist mentality might dismiss an institution that silences its members and those who would comply with its ordinances, Teilhard de Chardin's example raises issues that modernity itself would do well to ponder. First of all, Teilhard exhibited precisely the kind of intellectual courage, personal integrity, and critical activity that the Enlightenment prizes both before and even *during* his silencing. Furthermore, his compliance with church mandates can be traced, at least in part, to his awareness that intellectual activity is born within a pre-theoretical, socio-historical context, capable of stimulating theoretical insights. It is precisely this kind of setting that modernity itself can at times overlook in its haste to subject traditions to a much needed and legitimate critical examination. To just this possible blindspot in modernity critics of modernity—some of them modernists themselves—have often directed their attention, whether one thinks of Husserl's emphasis on the lifeworld, Heidegger's recovery of Being-in-the-World, or of the various postmodern currents highlighting the limits of rationality. Moreover, Teilhard's scholarship emerged out of a sense of ethical responsibility for others, as his compliance with the decree of silencing so pointedly reveals. This example stands as a kind of prophetic indictment of the contemporary intellectual milieu in which all too frequently the reasoning and theorizing prized by modernity have become unmoored from any ethical anchorage. As a result, intellectual discourse has often deteriorated into a competitive one-upmanship or an ideological defense of power or economic interests, as critics like Marx, Nietzsche, and Nietzsche's postmodern successors have so clearly discerned. Furthermore, Teilhard's virtue can also be instructive for any Catholic piety that, having drunk at modernity's well, would place a premium on courage and the refusal to be victimized. Such piety, while appropriating from modernity valuable insights about autonomy and courage, ought not overlook the communal, historical, and ethical atmosphere within which Teilhard exercised his courage and autonomy. In fact, the previous citation praising women who have challenged the church acknowledges this

---

[15] Letter to Pére Charles, February 3, 1937, cited by de Solages, 54; Letter to Pére De Lubac, February 26, 1933, in *Lettres Intimes*, 242; de Lubac, *The Eternal Feminin*, 195.

atmosphere when it lauds those who, resisting hierarchical oppression and refusing victimization, also refuse to leave their church.

Although Chardin by no means exhibits a naive saintliness or uncritical conformism, he never seems to have entertained the possibility of confronting openly his silencers as a legitimate ethical option on behalf of them and the Catholic people. To be sure, it might have been impossible for him at that time to take such a stand and remain within the church, especially given his religious-clerical status, as it has been possible for many men and women who have resisted church authority in the wake of the Second Vatican Council. Nevertheless, had Chardin decided to do battle with the authorities silencing him, he might have envisioned actions such as confronting the authorities and leaving the church as deeds of love, performed at great cost to himself. He might have further conceived his departure as a final, prophetic, symbolic gesture aimed at shocking Catholicism into self-recognition and undertaken in ethical responsibility for the very church that he would have been abandoning. Of course, he would have had to gauge beforehand whether such a strategy would have been more beneficial for others.

But one might object that if leaving the church would have been as legitimate an option as staying, then any action taken on behalf of others would be justifiable. It is important to understand, though, that this analysis has concentrated on how others oblige one at a pre-theoretical level. Because of such responsibilities for others, one needs to move to a theoretical plane to evaluate which course of action is really for the good of others. On such a theoretical plane, one could also develop and apply first principles of ethics, which enable one to rule out certain actions as immoral. Of course, while engaging in such theoretical discussions, it is quite easy to forget the other, in response to whom one commences such a theoretical inquiry in the first place. Rather than pursuing such a theoretical investigation, this study has attempted to return to the pre-theoretical level, with its cognitive and ethical dimensions, and to explore there the specific motives of Teilhard de Chardin as he coped with being silenced. The unusual—and hopefully more and more unusual—phenomenon of silencing, which on a theoretical plane could be shown to entail an unjust violation of human autonomy, nevertheless reveals, as few other incidents, Teilhard's attitudes and his significance for modernity.

Emmanuel Levinas: The Ethical Context of Truth

To appreciate Teilhard's significance and to situate it with reference to the linkage between truth and ethics, the question that underpins the topics to be touched on in the next section, it is valuable to interpret him from the philosophical perspective of Emmanuel Levinas. Levinas, born in Lithuania in

1906 of Jewish parents, studied Heidegger and Husserl during the 1920s and, after taking French nationality in the 1930s, introduced Husserl's phenomenology into France through his dissertation, *La théorie de l'intuition dans la phénoménologie de Husserl*. After imprisonment during World War II and the loss of part of his family to the Nazi holocaust, Levinas in the post-war years developed his "ethical" phenomenology in *Totalité et infini: essai sur l'extériorité*, in 1961, and *Autrement qu'étre ou au-delà de l'essence*, in 1974.[16]

For Levinas, thinking occurs in a discourse between interlocutors, each of whom is usually focused on the content discussed. But Levinas prefers to concentrate on an often neglected aspect of such discourse: the ethical character of the relationship between the discourse partners. For Levinas, whenever one human being meets another, at the initial moment of the encounter, one experiences such an ethical dimension. One feels oneself summoned to respect the other, and the other invites one to respond in some way. Thus, for example, the other who is hungry pleads for the bread one puts in one's mouth, or the other about to be murdered can command the murderer "you shall not kill," even though this resistance, visible in the victim's eyes, is the resistance that has no resistance—ethical resistance. Less dramatically, one can feel invited to speak to the other or to embark upon a discourse with the other. At the inception of a relationship, as one faces another, before one demands that the other reciprocate, one experiences one's sovereign freedom to do as one pleases circumscribed by the other, who appears not as one's equal, but rather as commanding a response as if from a position above oneself, as if from a Amoral height."[17]

In later writings, Levinas considers how easy it is to overlook this experience of the prescriptive character of the other's face by inviting his reader to examine how the automaticity of one's response often conceals how one has already unreflectively absorbed the other's ethical invitation. Just as the creation responded to God's command to come into being before it even existed, so one takes up the other person's invitation to reply so readily and immediately that a later reflective moment is needed to recognize that the other person's order is given in one's response or that one must have already heard the other's

---

[16] Emmanuel Levinas, *The Levinas Reader*, ed. Sean Hand (Oxford: Blackwell, 1989), 1-2, 301-306.

[17] In investigating the presuppositions of theoretical discourse, Levinas resembles many of his philosophical contemporaries, such as Husserl, who turned to the life-world out of which theory arises, or Heidegger, who brought to light "Being-in-the-World," that is, one's embeddedness in a socio-historical, practical setting that antedates any adoption of a theoretical attitude. Levinas describes the theoretical contents of a discourse as "the said," over against the relationship between interlocutors, "the saying." Emmanuel Levinas, *Otherwise than Being or Beyond Essence*, trans. Alphonso Lingis (The Hague: Martinus Nijhoff, 1981), 5-7, 37, 153-162; *Totality and Infinity, An Essay on Exteriority*, trans. Alphonso Lingis (The Hague: Martinus Nijhoff, 1969), 35-40, 100-101, 199-201.

command insofar as one answers at all. Thus, for instance, when one finds oneself giving change to a beggar on the street or stopping to explain that one has no change or crossing the street to avoid such a beggar, one may stop and reflect that in all these activities one has already in some way felt this destitute other's demand to be taken account of, even when one flees it. Similarly, if one examines one's polite acknowledgment of the person one is surprised to find upon entering a room, one becomes cognizant that this other person has elicited that greeting. Likewise, after carefully preparing an academic critique of a colleague's work, one can legitimately look back upon one's efforts as an act of service due the colleague, evoked by the colleague, with an imperative as much ethical as it was professional.[18]

This mandate from the other, Levinas contends, is there whether it is perceived or not, and Levinas, his family being victims of Nazi oppression, has no illusions about the fact that whole cultures can at times be trained to disregard these ethical dimensions. Even though Levinas's disciplined phenomenological descriptions might not win the assent of unrefined common sense or of some more refined philosophical theory which could itself be blind to the primordial experience to which Levinas points, the failure to win assent is no reason to regard his descriptions as mistaken. Rather, as is the case with every phenomenological description, one presents such[19] descriptions or reformulates them in the hope that one's interlocutor will, upon consulting his or her experience without prejudice, find them valid or supply new evidence supporting an alternative account.

These phenomenological descriptions, disclosing the ethical dimensions of the face-to-face relationship with the other, enable Levinas to approach the relationship between ethics and truth in a fresh light. In whatever discourse truth is pursued, whether in the natural sciences, the social sciences, or theology, the ethical stratum of the face-to-face is implicated since theorizers must have already allowed themselves to be put into question by others, that is, by their theoretical interlocutors, to whom they strive to reply in their very theorizing. Insofar as the very process of theorizing requires one to prescind from centering on oneself, to set aside at least momentarily one's own drives and impulses, and to take up the self-critical "attitude of a being that distrust itself," the traces of the decentering effect of the other can always be found in the theorizer. [19]

For Levinas, the search for truth begins in an ethical moment, in the encounter of the other's face which is the initial discursive moment, the discourse before discourse:

---

[18] *Otherwise than Being*, 74, 150.

[19] *Totality and Infinity*, 82.

Thus I cannot evade by silence the discourse which the epiphany that occurs as a face opens, as Thrasymachus, irritated, tries to do in the first book of the *Republic* (moreover without succeeding) . . . The face opens the primordial discourse whose first word is obligation, which no "interiority" permits avoiding. It is the discourse that obliges the entering into discourse, the commencement of discourse rationalism prays for, a "force" that convinces even the "the people who do not wish to listen" and thus founds the true universality of reason.... preexisting the plane of ontology is the ethical plane.[20]

Since one commonly considers ethics, particularly ethical theory, as a philosophical discipline derivative from metaphysics or philosophical anthropology, Levinas appears revolutionary in showing that all theorizing ultimately arises out of an ethical relationship with an interlocutor to whom one seeks to give an account. In affirming this reversal of paradigms, he insists "Morality is not a branch of philosophy, but first philosophy." [21]

As discourses progress, whole domains of cultural activity—such as science, philosophy, and theology—are built up, systematic theories are constructed, and ethical first principles (at least in philosophy) are elaborated. Furthermore, via such discursive exchanges, cultures develop institutional arrangements to govern the relationships of their members, such as those of politics, law, and economics. Clearly, such institutional settings provide the context for discussions of academic freedom and Catholic identity, and within such structures Church authorities exercise their official functions. In all these cultural enterprises and institutions emerging from discourse, one tends to conceive human relationships as interchangeable and reversible, with A relating to B as B to A, with A and B as equals on the same plane with each other. [22]

On the one hand, such cultural and institutional undertakings are legitimate and ethically necessary for Levinas since they are a means for guaranteeing justice for the other encountered within such cultural and institutional structures. On the other hand, he is also apprehensive since these cultural and institutional enterprises can become oblivious to their underlying ethical dimensions because they "are at every moment on the point of having their center of gravitation in themselves, and weighing on their own account." For instance, the modern understanding of rationality, itself a cultural achievement, runs a risk insofar as it requires that isolated subjects renounce their arbitrary individuality and ascend to universal principles or a universal viewpoint. Thus, for example, Jose de Acosta

---

[20] *Ibid.*, 201.

[21] *Ibid.*, 304.

[22] *Otherwise than Being*, 155-159; *Totality and Infinity*, 28, 35-40, 212-214. Levinas dubs this level at which such cultural and institutional activities are pursued as "the Third" because these activities presuppose the appearance of a third person who introduces modifications into the face-to-face dyadic relationship.

played a role in unleashing the violent potentials of this modern notion of rationality by justifying fifteenth-century Spain's subjugation of indigenous Americans because they clung to their individual barbarian practices, resisted modernization, and rejected "right reason and the common mode of humanity." In order to offset this centripetal tendency of cultural and institutional structures, Levinas recommends returning to the face-to-face relationship in which the other challenges one from a "moral height" that will be more likely to evoke self-critique and accountability than if the other is conceived merely as one's equal. Hence, Levinas argues for his own less perilous account of rationality since "if the face brings the first signification, that is, the very upsurge of the rational," then one is fixed as an independent being in relation to an other and enters a discourse, not to disappear in it, but to agree or to defend one's disagreement.[23]

Levinas's radical reframing of the relationship between truth and ethics, namely, his recovery of the ethical relationship that subtends every discursive pursuit of truth and every cultural and institutional edifice, permits a novel understanding of Teilhard de Chardin's experience of being silenced. For Chardin's experience exemplifies a search for truth that unfolded within the context of ethical responsibility to others. Indeed, one can discern a layer of ethical significance when he speaks of his inability to "change" his ideas because of "conviction" and not because of "fear of the consequences." Although he is not explicit about being obligated to anyone, it is as if he sensed an ethical as well as intellectual responsibility to his scientific/theological interlocutors, whom he would have betrayed had he retracted his well-considered beliefs.

Moreover, it becomes evident that Teilhard sought truth not only in response *to* others (his scientific/theological interlocutors) but also for others

---

[23] *Otherwise than Being,* 16; see also *Totality and Infinity,* 218-219 and Enrique Dussel, *The Invention of the Americas: Eclipse of "the Other" and the Myth of Modernity,* trans. Michael D. Barber (New York: Continuum, 1995), 54. In *Otherwise than Being,* 161, Levinas indicates how the ethical necessity of the level of the Third arises out of the face-to-face: "The extraordinary commitment of the other to the third party calls for control, a search for justice, society and the State, comparison and possession, thought and science, commerce and philosophy, and outside of anarchy, the search for a principle." Levinas is saying in effect, that in the face-to-face relationship, when one sees how much the other is dedicated ethically to the third person, one grasps the need for moving to the level of the Third. One's ethical responsibility to the other and the Third requires just institutional relationships in which the many can live. Moreover, Levinas admits that the "I" may be called upon to be concerned with itself and that the Third provides "incessant correction of the asymmetry of proximity in which the face is looked at." (*Otherwise than Being,* 158, see also 128) How does one reconcile these two levels, the face-to-face and the Third? Levinas seems to be thinking in terms of a dialectic, in which each challenges the limitations of the other level. To see how this dialectic might unfold, see Michael D. Barber, *Equality and Alterity, Phenomenological Investigations of Discrimination* (Atlantic Highlands, NJ: Humanities Press, forthcoming).

(those in the Catholic community). Thus, he conceived his intellectual work as aimed at liberating the community of the church for which he tolerated being silenced, at least until he could petition once again for authorization to publish. Likewise, when he entertained the possibility that his ideas might never reach a public forum, that no notoriety, success, or financial gain might ever be bestowed upon him, he re-dedicated all his works to the purpose that guided their production in the first place, namely his commitment to God and others and to their service. This pre-theoretical ethical commitment to others, like his familiarity with the pre-theoretical cognitive matrix of the Catholic tradition, lay at the base of his contributions to the institutional activity of systematic theology.

By conceiving Teilhard's struggle in Levinasian terms, one might also better situate the virtue of courage that characterizes the philosopher in the tradition of Plato and Kant and that figures importantly in Catholicism insofar as it has absorbed modern influences through Vatican II. For one often conceives courage as embodied in strong individuals, like Socrates in the *Apology*, who defy institutions and authorities that seek to subjugate their subjects and that, of course, deserve the critique and resistance that Kant recommends in his *What is Enlightenment?* However, while modernity, fitted out with such a concept of courage, rightfully emphasizes the powerful subject who resists being bound to unjust institutions, it can underemphasize the importance of being a vulnerable subject who deliberately accepts being bound ethically to others and shoulders burdens for their sake. It is this very vulnerability and bondedness that Levinas highlights and that must complement the strength of spirit and resistance to (unjust) bondage that modernity has rightly upheld. In this regard, it is significant that when one thinks of Teilhard's silencing, the first thing that often comes to mind is a sense of outrage and opposition to the kind of institutional tyranny under which he suffered—often at the expense of an appreciation for the ethical generosity that his life exhibits. The modernist stress on courage and autonomy may be so pervasive that even Catholic authors, impatient because Teilhard did not engage church authorities directly in battle, might look upon his life-story only as an instance of an outdated, passive piety and thus overlook his intellectual integrity and ethical nobility.

Furthermore, Levinas brings into a theoretical synthesis the virtue of courage and ethical bondedness to others near the end of *Totality and Infinity* when he speaks of courageous moral heroes who are so preoccupied over the murder of others that they give little thought to their own death. They "fear murder more than death." One can think of ethical giants such as Martin Luther King, Mahatma Gandhi, or Oscar Romero who manifested the maximal courage and the most assertive subjectivity precisely because they were so preoccupied with the oppression and murder of others that they disdained the bullets of the lurking assassin. While not opposing the institution oppressing him with the same directness and at the cost of his life, as did these three great figures, Teilhard nevertheless showed great courage in following the demands of intellectual integrity and in living up to his ethical commitments to intellectual colleagues and to members of the Catholic faith in spite of the consequences of censoring to himself. It was indeed a kind of bloodless death to which his lived synthesis of courage and ethical responsibility led. [24]

Beginning with the ethical relationship that takes its start from the ethical demand of the other, Levinas also articulates an ideal of human solidarity that is instantiated in Teilhard's life. Levinas notes that it is possible for one to sense an ethical demand emerging from the other and yet refuse responsibility by claiming that one has not done anything harmful to the other that would require one to come to the other's aid. But this claim to innocence, exempting one from responsibility for the other, locates the origin of responsibility in one's self and not the other, as if one might say to the other, "Since *I* have done nothing to you, *I* am not accountable for you." A person evading responsibility in this fashion, Levinas argues, "washes his hands of the faults and misfortunes that do not begin in his own freedom." Like Job and his friends, puzzled by Job's misfortunes, those who exempt themselves from responsibility for others on the basis of their innocence believe that "in a meaningful world one cannot be held to answer when one has not done anything." But it is possible, according to Levinas, that in suffering at the hands of others, "*by* the other," one can give up one's outrage over one's innocent suffering and refrain from making focal the self's desire to reassert itself by claiming "I do not deserve this." Instead, one can remain in responsibility and accept one's sufferings "*for* the other." By so doing, one continues in fidelity to the ethical obligation that commenced with the other and not oneself, or, as Levinas puts it, "The for-the-other keeps all the patience of undergoing imposed by the other." There is indeed something of this ethical grandeur in Teilhard, who, having no illusions about the wrongness of his persecutors, never begged off his responsibility for others because he had done nothing to merit what he suffered. Thus he converted his suffering by the other into a suffering for the other. [25]

Finally, it was mentioned in the introduction that modern societies might not hope for any instruction from those who have accepted ecclesial silencing. But if Teilhard de Chardin's case discloses the ethical obligation to the other, that lies at the base of theory and rationality, which Levinas so well depicts, then perhaps a lesson can be learned. For if the search for truth in modern academia often seems to have deteriorated into a kind of "tournament jousting," to use Karl Otto Apel's expression, this may be because rationality, theory, and

---

[24] *Otherwise than Being*, 244.

[25] *Ibid.*, 121-129.

argumentation have become detached from their ethical roots. Chardin's lived example and Levinas's theory suggest that rationality will be so much the better if it is conceived in terms of service to others and exposure to their questions instead of a quest to conquer all opponents and reduce them to silence. But by thus rendering modernity more self-critical, do not such counterpoints to modernity as Chardin and Levinas really help modernity live up to its own deepest aspirations? [26]

Academic Freedom, Catholic Identity and Ecclesial Authority

One usually considers academic freedom on a cultural-institutional plane in terms elaborated by the Enlightenment, namely, that rational agents possess a universal right to express their thought freely and courageously without interference from arbitrary and tyrannous institutional authorities. But this question needs to be considered from a supplementary perspective, namely, from that of the ethical relationship lying at the origin of cultural and institutional practices, from the level of the face-to-face in which the other, the interlocutor, summons one into an ethical relationship. There, to be sure, academic freedom could hardly mean the freedom to say whatever one wants, arbitrarily or irresponsibly, because face-to-face with one's academic opponent or with the religious tradition with which one might not concur, one is still called to be

---

[26] Karl-Otto Apel, *Diskurs und Verantwortung, Das Problem des Ubergangs zur postkonventionellen Moral (Frankfurt am Main: Suhrkamp, 1988)*, 235-237. William Shea and Alice Gallin, O.S.U., attempt to achieve some kind of synthesis between Catholic higher education and modernity. See William Shea "Catholic Higher Education and the Enlightenment: On Borderlines and Roots," *Horizons* 20.1 (1993): 99-105 and Alice Gallin, O.S.U., Chapters 1 and 2 of her forthcoming history of American Catholic higher education since 1960. Nevertheless, in order to avoid an uncritical appropriation of modernity, Gallin and Shea need Levinas's critique of modernity, especially since this critique brings into focus what the Judeo-Christian tradition can contribute to modernity. Similarly Charles Curran's approach to academic freedom within a Catholic higher education setting, namely that the hierarchy of the church can criticize positions but need not use institutional force to compel compliance with its teaching, also seeks a rapprochement with the Enlightenment. However, Curran's discussion takes place at the level of the Third and could profit from being inserted with a Levinasian setting. The Levinasian ethics of the face protesting against totalization converges with the Kantian view of persons as ends in themselves, justified at a theoretical level, and both would seem opposed to Curran's justification of academic freedom through a kind of utilitarian appeal to the benefits of academic freedom for the Church--a teleological argument that could also be used to justify the deprivation of academic freedom. Curran himself represents an instance of someone who may have lost the institutional struggle to retain his position at Catholic University but whose ethical claim haunts any future use of hierarchical power to ensure doctrinal purity. See Charles E. Curran, *Catholic Higher Education, Theology, and Academic Freedom* (Notre Dame, IN: University of Notre Dame Press, 1990), particularly 117,161,171-174,181.

responsible.

In addition, from a Levinasian view, it would be the academic freedom of the other to which one would be first and foremost attuned, and hence one would conscientiously seek to protect others—and, in predominantly Catholic institutions, particular one's non-Catholic colleagues—from the many subtle and not so subtle obstacles that prevent them from having their say and that effectively isolate and alienate them. Furthermore, for Levinas it is possible to transfer the ethical obligations originating in the other to oneself, conceiving oneself as someone who also deserves not to be repressed by a university administration and who is thus entitled to struggle in defense of one's own academic freedom. However, even such a defense can also be envisioned as other-oriented, that is, as a struggle to protect the rights of anyone else like oneself, who might be endangered in the future within the institution to which one belongs. Such an orientation might well embolden one in the struggle more so than when one's purpose is only self-protection.

Finally, when one has been deprived of academic freedom within an institution, it may be necessary to resort to the coercion of law, since such an institution, founded to guarantee justice for the other, has betrayed its own purpose and fallen into "having its center of gravitation in itself and weighing on its own account." But if one pitches one's analysis of academic freedom solely at that level, the level of legal compulsion, one risks losing sight of the underlying ethical relationship of the face to face. For the face of the victim whose academic freedom has been taken presents a plea for ethical treatment, which indicts repressive authorities even in its ethical forcelessness, which "validates" ethically the recourse to law, and which continually forbids authorities from reducing the question of academic freedom to a mere struggle between self-interested power brokers.

Similarly the Catholic identity of institutions would not be simply a matter of first principles, definitions, or mission statements to which all would be obliged to approximate. Rather, beneath this level of cultural and institutional enterprises, Catholic identity would have to be conceived also in terms of ethical obligations between persons within a complex professional and institutional network. Thus professors, bound professionally and ethically to colleagues within and outside their home institution, would also find themselves responsible to students and parents, who have financed denominational education in order that students be exposed to Catholic values and traditions. At the same time, professors are called to deal respectfully and professionally with students in a classroom, to enhance their critical capacities, and to hold them accountable, just as one must also deal both respectfully and critically with historical texts and traditions, even when one disagrees with them. In such settings, it is a matter of ethical exigency to express one's well-thought out *disagreements* with the other for the other's sake, whether the other be a colleague, administrator, student, or classical author. In brief, the obligations related to Catholic identity have to do with the ethical context out of which every search for truth emerges.

Finally, one can appeal to ethical and theological principles to criticize abuses of ecclesial authority. But if one's critique remains at this level of institutional procedures, then the face of the person silenced which calls church authorities into question might recede from sight. It is precisely from relationship that church authorities distance themselves by acting coercively, without a patient dialogue, without vulnerability to the questions and responses of the other, and without striving to ensure that the other has been heard. By so acting, they have deployed a rationalizing every bit as disconnected from ethical responsibility as the modern forms of rationality that these same church authorities often deplore. Church authorities, as Charles Curran has noted, have every right to specify how church doctrines differ from a theologian's teaching after the careful dialogue that the face of the other invites. However, coercive silencing, such as that inflicted on Teilhard, which reduces a human being to a means for ecclesial purposes, violates autonomy and treats the reading public of the church paternalistically, would not seem justifiable at a theoretical level (by appeal to ethical principles such as the categorical imperative), however much church officials might feel themselves motivated at a pre-theoretical level by a concern for the good of church members. However, rather than approaching the violent uses of church authority with one's own armory of theoretical weaponry—an approach that only solidifies authoritarianism—this paper has sought to remember the ethical nobility of the church's "other" who in their powerlessness submitted to the ordeal of silencing. By this remembering, one recovers their high ethicality, finding in them a model of long-suffering, ethical commitment to others, and in their cases a model of how church authority itself ought to be exercised.[27]

---

[27] *Catholic Higher Education, Theology, and Academic Freedom*, 171-174. Komonchak details how church authorities ought to approach a theologian whose writings might appear questionable, namely, they ought to be careful that there not be a misunderstanding of church teaching on their part that causes the appearance of conflict, that they ought to be patient and avoid hastiness, etc., "The Catholic University in the Church,"44-45. By abandoning a juridical approach toward the theologian whose writing seems questionable in favor of a dialogue, the U.S. bishops in the application document regarding "Ex Corde Ecclesiae" have opted to seek resolution of conflicts in the mode of the face to face rather than via mechanisms at the level of the Third that could detach themselves from the face to face. Cf. "'Ex Corde Ecclesiae': An Application to the United States," *Origins*, vol.26/no.24, November 28, 1996, 383. That document recommends that relationships between university and church authorities be characterized by "mutual trust, close and consistent cooperation and continuing dialogue." The Vatican has remanded it to the Bishops' Committee for correction.

8

Catholic Higher Education in the Public Sphere

Tensions and Possibilities

William Rehg, S. J.
Saint Louis University

Murders in the University

In the early morning of November 16, 1989, six Jesuit priests, their cook and her daughter were assassinated by government soldiers on the grounds of the University of Central America in San Salvador—thereby adding still more victims to the disheartening number of noncombatants brutally murdered in El Salvador's bloody civil war. In this case, however, the evidence also pointed to the suspicion that the Jesuits were targeted precisely because of their work at the UCA. Under the leadership of the principal target, Ignacio Ellacuría, the UCA had assumed—above all through its scholarly research and social outreach—a central role in the *public political life* of El Salvador.[1] Tragic though this event was, it also confirmed the social importance of university work: It said

---

[1] For a historical account of developments from Ellacuría's early days in the Society of Jesus and his influence on the UCA, see Teresa Whitfield, *Paying the Price: Ignacio Ellacuría and the Murdered Jesuits of El Salvador* (Philadelphia: Temple UP, 1995); for Ellacuría's vision of the university, see his "Is a Different Kind of University Possible?" in *Towards a Society that Serves Its People: The Intellectual Contribution of El Salvador's Murdered Jesuits,* trans. Phillip Berryman, ed. John Hassett and Hugh Lacey (Washington, D.C.: Georgetown UP, 1991), 177-207; also Ellacuría, "The Task of a Christian University," and Jon Sobrino, "The University's Christian Inspiration," in *Companions of Jesus: The Jesuit Martyrs of El Salvador,* ed. Jon Sobrino et al., trans. Sally Hanlon (Maryknoll, N.Y.: Orbis, 1990), 147-51 and 152-73, resp.

173

something about the potential of the university that the work of professors could be perceived by their opponents to have such an impact on the public sphere as to evoke this desperate, insane response.

The relatively unique El Salvadoran situation at the time—unique perhaps even for El Salvador—resists generalization to other contexts.[2] All the same, this striking event raises questions for us in the United States. The university work of the six Jesuit martyrs and its distinctive position in the public life of El Salvador was clearly rooted in and shaped by their Catholic faith. This connection between religious belief and university work inspires the leading question of the present essay: Does Catholic higher education in the United States have a distinctive role to play in the public life of the nation?

We find a broader motivation for this question in the call of Vatican II for dialogue between the Church and the modern world.[3] The focus on dialogue has been a consistent theme of Church documents since then, but it recently received a particularly focused reiteration in the document *Ex corde ccclesiae.* In this document addressed specifically to university work, Pope John Paul II links dialogue with the very definition of the Catholic university: "a Catholic university . . . is also a primary and privileged place for a *fruitful dialogue between the Gospel and culture.*"[4] What is more, the Pope also acknowledges the socially critical potential of research in a manner that reinforces the self-understanding of the UCA, thereby sharpening the questions that the UCA experiment raises for us in the United States:

> Included among its research activities, therefore, will be a study of *serious contemporary problems* in areas such as the dignity of human life, the promotion of justice for all, the quality of personal and family life, the protection of nature, the search for peace and political stability, a more just sharing in the world's resources. . . . If need be, a Catholic university must have the courage to speak uncomfortable truths which do not please public opinion, but which are necessary to safeguard the authentic good of society.[5]

---

[2] With the cessation of overt hostilities in El Salvador, the role of the UCA has become more ambiguous, according to Dean Brackley, S.J., a U.S. Jesuit currently working at the UCA; Dean Brackley, S. J., informal talk at Saint Louis University, April 4, 1997.

[3] See especially *Gaudium et spes* in Austin Flannery, O.P., ed., *Vatican Council II: The Conciliar and Post-Conciliar Documents* (Collegeville, MN: The Liturgical Press, 1975) 903-1001.

[4] Pope John Paul II, *Ex corde ecclesiae,* para. 43, in *Origins* 20.17 (4 Oct. 1990): 265-76.

[5] Ibid., para. 32. A number of these points dovetail with Ellacuría's understanding of the university in "Is a Different Kind of University Possible?." in particular the engagement with the national culture, the concern for justice for the oppressed majority, the taking of an uncomfortable--or in Ellacuría's words, an "aggressive"--stance against social irrationality, and so forth.

Finally, the question also arises, at least for Jesuit universities and colleges, in the documents of the Thirty-Fourth General Congregation of the Society of Jesus. GC 34 connects the general call for dialogue with inculturation, the promotion of justice, and interreligious dialogue. The Congregation goes on to link the university work of teaching, research, and outreach (or "extension") with the promotion of justice. [6]

However, we can respond to these challenges adequately only in the light of the concrete circumstances of our American context. In particular, if we in the United States are to take up these challenges to Catholic higher education today, then two aspects of our context require examination: The history of the question itself in Catholic education and the democratic character of the public sphere in the United States. In fact, this question is a familiar one for twentieth-century Catholic intellectuals. Today, however, we can bring a range of new perspectives and concerns to its asking. Specifically, we can address the question anew in light of recent developments in democratic theory. New analyses of public deliberation and civil society offer a means of reframing the question of the identity of Catholic higher education in more extroverted terms—terms consonant with the call for a dialogue with the modern world and critical assessment of public life.

After briefly recalling the earlier version of the question and the shift that came with the 1960s, I review the relevant developments in democratic theory, that is, the new attention to the role of civil society and the public sphere in democratic governance. I then sketch some roles that higher education in general has played in this context. We can then ask whether Catholic higher education has a specific contribution to make to this complex political reality. Here the idea of Catholicism as a public religion offers a suggestive lead.

Precursors

Catholic intellectuals and educators have long worried about their role in American life.[7] The question found perhaps its most timely expression with John Tracy Ellis.[8] But note that Ellis put the question in terms that were at once rather

---

[6] See *Documents of the Thirty-Fourth General Congregation of the Society of Jesus* (Saint Louis, MO: Institute of Jesuit Sources, 1995), esp. the Decrees on Mission (Decrees 2-5) and Decree 17 ("Jesuits and University Life"), esp. para. 413.

[7] For the history up to Vatican II, see Philip Gleason, *Contending with Modernity* (New York: Oxford, 1995); see also Philip Gleason, "The New Americanism in Catholic Historiography," *U. S. Catholic Historian* 11.3 (1993): 1-18; and William R. Leahy, S.J., *Adapting to America: Catholics, Jesuits, and Higher Education in the Twentieth Century* (Washington, D.C: Georgetown UP, 1991).

[8] John Tracy Ellis, *American Catholics and the Intellectual Life* (Chicago: The Heritage Foundation, Inc., 1956).

broad—how much have Catholics contributed to the intellectual life of the United States? —and scholastically narrow—his standards of contribution were, beyond an intellectual seriousness in lifestyle, typical academic measures of scholarly success.[9] This can be partly understood in light of Catholic educators' concern with *culture* as the primary field in which the Catholic contribution should appear. By fostering an intensely "Christian culture" at its colleges and universities, a renascent Catholicism would revive a modern American culture dispirited by materialism and Enlightenment skepticism.[10] The focus was on a specific ethos, albeit an ethos with political implications: Medieval Catholic scholasticism, it was argued, supplied the higher-law basis for the American political tradition.[11] This link with the medieval natural law tradition played a key role in John Courtney Murray's search for a public consensus that would undercut denominational differences and integrate Catholicism and American democracy.[12]

The 1960s permanently altered this earlier landscape. The institutional and economic pressures to enter into the mainstream of higher education joined forces with the opening to modernity initiated at Vatican II, and Catholic higher education could never be the same.[13] More importantly, the Catholic identity of the institution could never be so easily assumed as it once was, guaranteed through the juridical links and religious commitment of its teachers and administrators. With separate incorporation under independent boards of trustees, with the growing role of lay faculty and administrators and decreasing presence of members of the founding religious community, the Catholic identity of the school would have to be secured from the ground up, as it were. In the last decade, the identity question has been gaining increasing attention at Catholic colleges and universities.

---

[9] See Ellis, *American Catholics,* 14-26 for rather vague references to "intellectual prestige" (15); "intellectual tone" (22); an intellectual lifestyle (25-26). For the indices of scholarly success, see pp. 40ff. Ellis's charge of mediocrity has recently been reiterated by Leahy, *Adapting to America,* 135-47.

[10] See Gleason, *Contending with Modernity,* part 2.

[11] Gleason, *Contending with Modernity,* 125-30.

[12] See John Courtney Murray, *We Hold These Truths: Catholic Reflections on the American Proposition* (Kansas City, MO: Sheed and Ward, 1960; 1988), esp. part 1. For an attempt to carry on Murrar's project today, see George Weigel, *Catholicism and the Renewal of American Democracy* (New York: Paulist Press, 1989).

[13] See Alice Gallin, *Independence and a New Partnership in Catholic Higher Education* (Notre Dame, IN: University of Notre Dame Press, 1996). I am also indebted for the sketch that follows to Alice Gallin, "The Catholic University in the Modern World," ms. 1997. Compare also David J. O'Brien, *From the Heart of the American Church: Catholic Higher Education and American Culture* (Maryknoll, NY: Orbis, 1994), chaps. 1-4.

Working Hypotheses

Questions of identity harbor a number of pitfalls, not least of which is an overly introverted focus on internal policing, boundary maintenance, and even separatism. An extroverted formulation of the identity question thus offers important correctives. My *first working hypothesis* is this: If Catholic higher education has a specific contribution to make to American life, then its identity takes it outward and not just inward. This not only helps avoid the dangers of unchecked introversion, it also accords with the Church's own emphasis on evangelization and dialogue as part of the task of the university.[14] My *second working hypothesis* identifies one particular area of American life in which we might search for this specific contribution: the political life of the nation. The underlying connections that support this second hypothesis are quite straightforward and may even sound naive: In a democracy the citizens exercise at least some measure of political control, and thus it matters that citizens be informed and reflective in how they exercise that control. As centers of reflection involved in the education of young citizens, universities and colleges have at least an indirect role in democracy. This idea has deep roots in Western educational thought, although its most intense recent expression—the student activism of the 1960s—has long since flared out. The excesses and failures of the sixties, however, should not blind us to the real dangers that can arise when scholars deny the political responsibility of higher education; here the German university system of the Weimar period stands as a stark reminder.[15]

In the next section, I hope to show how recent democratic theory provides a more realistic, less naive understanding of the above links between informed reflection and democracy. Once we have a more sophisticated account of the democratic process in hand, the second hypothesis allows us to tackle the leading question of this essay: What does Catholic higher education, precisely as Catholic, offer to democracy? This question will occupy us in the last section of the paper.

Democracy and the Public Sphere

In recent years, democratic theory has been increasingly fascinated by models of "deliberative democracy." In contrast to earlier approaches that were skeptical of a common good and viewed politics as a strategic competition of pre-political

---

[14] See, for example, *Ex corde ecclesiae*, paras. 15-20, 48-49.

[15] See Alice Gallin, *Midwives to Nazism: University Professors in Weimar Germany, 1925-1933* (Macon, GA.: Mercer UP, 1986); also Jürgen Habermas, "The Idea of the University: Learning Processes," *The New Conservatism: Cultural Criticism and the Historians' Debate*, ed. and trans. Sherry Weber Nicholsen (Cambridge, MA: MIT Press, 1989), 100-27.

interests for power, deliberative models stress the importance of public discussion as a process in which citizens strive to reach substantive agreement on justice and common goals.[16] Deliberative democratic theory thus picks up older ideals of citizenship, public reason, and rational discussion and attempts to refurbish them for contemporary societies. To be more precise, deliberative democracy links the legitimacy of government with both rational deliberation and democratic participation. Thus, deliberative democratic theories are committed to some version of the claim that laws are legitimate insofar as the citizens subject to them have also, through their participation in public deliberation, authored those very laws. This claim can take stronger or weaker forms. In light of contemporary realities, the claim is often weakened by lowering the requirement of actual participation; even if citizens are not directly involved in ordinary legislation, they should at least approve of—or they should "reasonably be expected to endorse"—the constitutionally defined procedures through which their democratically elected representatives make ordinary law and exercise power.[17] Whether participation is thus attenuated or not, however, deliberative theorists must show how such claims for public reason still speak to us today, all the complexity and pluralism of contemporary societies notwithstanding.

To meet this challenge, deliberative theory combines normative and empirical investigations. Normatively, it must show how the democratic process ought to be arranged and implemented if citizens are to have confidence that political outcomes are reasonable—or at least not so unreasonable as to raise doubts about their legitimacy. Empirically, deliberative theory must show that the normative model can be, or indeed sometimes is, approximated under realizable social conditions.[18] Much hangs here on the model of reason with which one begins: Setting the standard too high only insures a pessimistic conclusion, whereas too low a standard could foster an uncritical satisfaction with the status quo. This rather tricky task of defining public reason is somewhat ameliorated by a procedural approach; the deliberative model need not fully specify a substantive standard of public reason ahead of time because it conceives reason procedurally, as built into the very process of public discourse and debate.

In other words, if the Constitution is an ongoing project in which the very standards of reason are open to discussion, then the reasonableness and

---

[16] For a range of views and introduction to further literature, see James Bohman and William Rehg, eds., *Deliberative Democracy* (Cambridge, MA: MIT Press, 1997).

[17] See John Rawls, *Political Liberalism* (New York: Columbia University Press, 1993) 137, see also lecture 6 generally ("The Idea of Public Reason"). For a stronger version, see Jürgen Habermas, *Between Facts and Norms: Contributions to a Discourse Theory of Law and Democracy,* trans. William Rehg (Cambridge, MA: MIT Press, 1996).

[18] For one of the most sophisticated attempts at this project to date, see Habermas, *Between Facts and Norms;* the normative and empirical are also brought together by James Bohman, *Public Deliberation* (Cambridge, MA: MIT Press, 1996).

legitimacy of a given law or political decision is dynamic, always relative to the current level of development of the polity's understanding of itself as a constitutional association.[19] The amendability of the Constitution is perhaps the most concrete proof of this open-endedness.[20] But one can also point to more elusive conceptual shifts, which may or may not be bound up with amendments. For example, at an early stage the capacity to reason on political issues may be attributed to a rather restricted subset of the population, say a cultural elite. But this context does not define what should count as reason at a later stage, after the earlier assumptions are questioned and citizen participation broadens. A further example is provided by shifting definitions of "private" versus "public" —a distinction that crucially determines what arguments citizens may or may not make in public discussion. If public reason is conceived in dynamic terms, as open to ongoing discussion and contest, then one should expect that earlier versions of the public/private distinction can be reasonably questioned and replaced.[21]

Conceiving public reason as an ongoing task, as discursive and dynamic, does not get the deliberative theorist completely off the hook, however. An open-ended, procedural account of constitutional democracy is still a standard of public reason that must give an account of itself. Specifically, one must show how the laws that finally issue from the machinery of government should reflect the process of public deliberation. This, in fact, is a rather daunting task. Theoretically, it requires a differentiated conception of political deliberation and lawmaking; practically, it requires the institutional innovation necessary to make government responsive to citizen input.

The theoretical task requires one to distinguish, on the one hand, the formal institutions of government that have power to make law and binding decisions, and, on the other hand, the informal arenas of public discussion and opinion formation—the public sphere.[22] One might ask whether a unitary public

---

[19] See *We Hold These Truths*, chap. 7, also 99: "the consensus [that underlies the United States Constitution] . . . . is never finished, complete, and perfect, beyond need or possibility of further development."

[20] On the history of amendments, see Richard B. Bernstein and Jerome Agel, *Amending America: If We Love the Constitution So Much, Why Do We Keep Trying to Change It?* (New York: Times Books, 1993).

[21] The private/public distinction has been a flash point for much of feminist political theory; see, for example, Susan Moller Okin, *Justice, Gender, and the Family* (New York: Basic Books, Inc, 1989), chap. 6; also Iris Marion Young, *Justice and the Politics of Difference* (Princeton, NJ: Princeton University Press, 1990), chap. 4.

[22] See Habermas, *Between Facts and Norms*, chap. 8; also Craig Calhoun, ed., *Habermas and the Public Sphere* (Cambridge, MA: MIT Press, 1992). For a social history of the rise of the bourgeois public sphere in the seventeenth century and its subsequent commercialization, see Jürgen Habermas, *The Structural Transformation of the Public Sphere: An Inquiry into a Category of Bourgeois Society,* trans. Thomas Burger and

sphere even exists.[23] As we shall see, the various informal publics that make up "the" public sphere cannot be completely fragmented if this normative model of deliberation is to get off the ground. In any case, the theoretical challenge is to state the conditions of reasonable public discussion and explain how such discussion should have a positive effect on formal decision-making mechanisms. For example, if we assume a context in which voting forms the link between the formal and informal arenas, then at least two questions arise. First, what does it mean to say that citizens have become informed and reasonable through public discussion? Second, what gives us confidence that their voting decisions— whether directly for a law or referendum, or indirectly through their representatives—translate the results of reasonable discussion into a reasonable political outcome?

The answers one gives to such questions will, again, be dynamic and very much a matter of the particular circumstances of a given society and its possibilities. But deliberative democratic theory has little hope of providing a realistic answer if it does not shift to a level that is structural and, to some extent, aggregative. That is, if a reasonable "public opinion" is to emerge through discussion in the informal public sphere, then it must do so in virtue of the "discursive structures" of communication and the (partly aggregative) effects of those structures. With the term "discursive structures" Habermas refers to the conditions and forms of political communication through which public deliberation occurs. I am concerned here with the structures that make up the informal public sphere. For example, insofar as the basic rights of communication and association, such as the right to freedom of expression guaranteed by the First Amendment, constitute the public sphere to begin with, they provide an important set of such "structures."[24] In addition to such basic legal guarantees, we can formulate four broad, more or less realizable, functional requirements for a democratic public sphere.[25]

First, the public sphere must be receptive to broadly relevant problems as they are perceived by citizens in their everyday life. If the public sphere is out of touch with the problems that actually confront the polity, then there is little chance that legal solutions based on public deliberation will emerge. Even if

---

Frederick Lawrence (Cambridge:, MA MIT Press, 1989).

[23] For a critique of Habermas's model, see Klaus Eder, "Politics and Culture: On the Sociocultural Analysis of Political Participation," in *Cultural-Political Interventions in the Unfinished Project of Enlightenment*, ed. Axel Honneth et al, trans. Barbara Fultner (Cambridge, MA: MIT Press, 1992), 95-120.

[24] Habermas, *Between Facts and Norms*, 374.

[25] Habermas, *Between Facts and Norms*, 359-87. For a defense of Habermas's account of the public sphere in relation to two alternative models, see Seyla Benhabib, "Models of Public Space: *Hannah Arendt, the Liberal Tradition and Jürgen Habermas*," *Situating the Self: Gender, Community and Postmodernism in Contemporary Ethics* (New York: Routledge, 1992), 89-120.

experts and bureaucrats perceive and attempt to address this or that relevant social problem, without broad public discussion and input it is all too likely that the experts' solution will overlook important dimensions of the problem as experienced by citizens. What is worse, the solution will more likely reflect the interests of powerful social actors, such as large corporations, rather than those of citizens. Second, in order to be receptive to social problems, the public sphere must be rooted in a robust civil society and an open, pluralist culture. As used in this context, "civil society"—as distinct from both the commercial and governmental spheres—refers to the various informal voluntary associations that provide individuals with sympathetic audiences before which they can articulate their experiences, needs, and identities.[26] In civil society the problems that the legal-political system must eventually solve are first detected and articulated by those who experience them most acutely—acutely enough to form associations such as Mothers Against Drunk Driving, or to coalesce into social movements such as the civil rights movement.

The first two conditions, when adequately realized, primarily ensure that everyone is potentially included in public discourses, i.e., that persons affected by the relevant issues have some initial avenues for voicing their concerns and suggestions. The next two conditions govern the quality of deliberation itself, that is, the quality of arguments and reasonableness of the participants. The third condition holds that the various informal publics generated by these different associations must be at least partly open to one another, so that an exchange of arguments and viewpoints can occur in the public sphere: "boundaries inside the universal public sphere as defined by its reference to the political system remain permeable in principle."[27] This condition implies that civil society by itself is insufficient for deliberative democracy without a unifying public sphere. A rich associational life does not promote deliberation without an overarching public sphere which unites these "partial societies" and avoids Madison's "mischief of factions." Only in this way can arguments be challenged by counter-arguments and transform citizens' views. Fourth and finally, the public sphere must be relatively free of serious distortions and blockages in communication. At the very least, this means that in critical moments it must be possible for the public sphere to mobilize and place issues on the agenda. It also means that the mass media, which play a central role in the dissemination of arguments and information, cannot simply be controlled, restricted, or distorted by powerful social interests.

To the extent that a public sphere approximates these conditions, we have some grounds to look for a public reason that emerges from a multi-layered,

---

[26] See Nancy Fraser, "Rethinking the Public Sphere: A Contribution to the Critique of Actually Existing Democracy," Calhoun, ed., *Habermas and the Public Sphere*, 121-28. On this concept of civil society, see especially Jean Cohen and Andrew Arato, *Civil Society and Political Theory* (Cambridge, MA: MIT Press, 1992).

[27] Habermas, *Between Facts and Norms,* 374.

socially diffuse mix of public communication. This is not without some empirical support.[28] However, my aim here is not to settle the various difficulties with this proposal. Rather, I want to indicate how we might rethink ideals of public reason and political autonomy in a manner adequate to large-scale, complex societies. With this background in mind, we can now ask what contribution higher education, and Catholic higher education in particular, might make to a robust public sphere.

Higher Education and the Public Sphere

One can point to a number of paths of influence exercised by the university and its members on society.[29] Here I want to focus on the university's potential contribution to the political public sphere. This particular avenue of influence seems to fit in rather nicely with the self-understanding of the university as a protected space for critical reflection. Here "political views may be developed, expressed, and criticized. Indeed, it is the university's duty to society to maximize political debate within its walls—as a guarantee of its moral seriousness and to provide society with ideas it might otherwise never consider."[30] As an incubator for new ideas and criticisms of current assumptions, as a space in which social problems and categories can be investigated in depth free of social pressures, the university represents an important resource for the more intensely political discussions that should take place in the broader public sphere. In the university, social problems and pressing needs can first be perceived and articulated before relatively sympathetic audiences whose members are, at least ideally, open to reason. Even aside from the economic or financial restrictions on admission to this audience, the realities of university politics and conformism have often contradicted this ideal.[31] My concern here,

---

[28] Benjamin I. Page and Robert Y. Shapiro, *The Rational Public* (Chicago: University of Chicago Press, 1992), argue on the basis of extensive meta-analysis of opinion polls that public opinion is stable, coherent, and responsive to new information in a reasonable manner. In *Who Deliberates?* (Chicago: University of Chicago Press, 1996), Page investigates the conditions under which professional communicators can foster public enlightenment. Cf. also Samuel L. Popkin, *The Reasoning Voter* (Chicago: University of Chicago Press, 1991).

[29] See Norman Birnbaum's 1973 essay, "Students, Professors and Philosopher Kings," *Searching for the Light: Essays on Thought and Culture* (New York: Oxford University Press, 1993), 155-233, esp. 158-65.

[30] Birnbaum, "Students," 162.

[31] Charges of conformist tendencies within the university have targeted both the left and the right. See, for example, David Bromwich's iconoclastic *Politics by Other Means: Higher Education and Group Thinking* (New Haven, CT: Yale University Press, 1992). For examples of suppression inflicted by the left, see Bromwich, 9-10, 21-22; also Roger Kimball, *Tenured Radicals: How Politics Has Corrupted Our Higher Education* (New York: Harper & Row, 1990), who records the leftist suppression of alternative viewpoints. Cases of suppression from the right can be found in Russell Jacoby, *The Last Intellectuals: American*

however, is primarily with normative models of university life.

The idea that the university has an important role to play in the civic life of the nation is not new.[32] Nor has the topic been free of contest. In his 1896 reflection on the contribution of higher education to the nation, Woodrow Wilson emphasized the importance of the classics, language, and history as instilling the wisdom necessary for public service, but he rejected a "science of society" as a basis for social reform. By contrast, the AAUP *Report on Academic Freedom and Tenure* (1915) —signed by John Dewey—noted the importance of technical expertise in democracy and accorded the universities an important role in providing such knowledge.[33] The 1945 Harvard Committee Report on General Education notes the tension between such views and attempts to resolve it by arguing that an experimental, critical attitude underlies both the classical heritage and modern science.[34] In any case, there has not been agreement on the specific manner in which the university or college should play its public role. The recent debate over multiculturalism and the curriculum is only the latest episode in a troubled history of self-criticism.

Note that the controversy generated by multiculturalism has centered primarily on pedagogy, and thus on the university's contribution to democracy through its students.[35] To broaden our perspective beyond this one avenue of

---

Culture in the Age of Academe (New York: Basic Books, 1987), 135ff and 176ff. For a critique of the failure of the university and intellectuals during the Viet Nam era, see Noam Chomsky, *American Power and the New Mandarins* (New York: Pantheon-Random, 1969), especially the chapters entitled "Some Thoughts on Intellectuals and the Schools," and "The Responsibility of Intellectuals," 309-21 and 323-66, resp.

[32] See, for example, Woodrow Wilson, "Princeton in the Nation's Service" (1896), in *American Higher Education: A Documentary History,* ed. Richard Hofstadter and Wilson Smith (Chicago: University of Chicago Press, 1961), vol. 2: 684-95; also The American Association of University.Professors "General Declaration of Principles" (1915), excerpted in Hofstadter and Smith, eds., 860-78. For a reflection on John Henry Newman's model of the university and its "social duties," see Jaroslav Jan Pelikan, *The Idea of the University: A Reexamination* (New Haven, CT: Yale University Press, 1992) chaps. 13-15.

[33] "If there is one thing that distinguishes the more recent developments of democracy, it is the recognition by legislators of the inherent complexities of economic, social, and political life, and difficulty of solving problems of technical adjustment without technical knowledge. . . . The training of such experts has, accordingly, in recent years, become an important part of the work of the universities; and in almost every one of our higher institutions of learning the professors of the economic, social, and political sciences have been drafted to an increasing extent into more or less unofficial participation in the public service." In Hofstadter and Smith, 868.

[34] Committee on the Objectives of a General Education in a Free Society, *General Education in a Free Society: Report of the Harvard Committee* (Cambridge, MA: Harvard University Press, 1945), 43-51; the relevant section is reprinted in Hofstadter and Smith, 956-63.

[35] More specifically, these debates have tended to center rather narrowly on curricular changes in English departments; for representative conservative critiques, see Allan Bloom,

influence, I want to suggest three ways the university can contribute to the public sphere. As an institution with a public presence, the university forms a *site* for public debate. As populated by students, professors, and administrators, the university provides *potential participants* for the public sphere. And as addressing particular themes and topics, the university feeds political discussions with *substantive arguments*. Each of these three axes covers a spectrum of possibilities. For example, we find a variety of sites, ranging from the classroom through the campus meeting hall or quadrangle up to officially sponsored public lectures. The kind of participation will also vary, most likely according to institutional role. Administrators make public statements and commitments, professors engage in research and lectures, students rally and occasionally vote. Finally, the arguments and viewpoints will no doubt cover a wide range of different perspectives and contestable political positions. The point is not that they coalesce into a monolithic conclusion, but that positions have a chance to be heard, so that the more convincing views might emerge as the result of critical testing. Like the public sphere itself, the university typically includes a plurality of sites, participant roles, and points of view, which taken as a whole resist ideological unification.

Again, the empirical reality might raise a number of doubts about the feasibility of this model. One might ask whether the university has any real impact on the public sphere.[36] Given the model of the public sphere developed above, however, one should not look for singularly overt or linear paths of intellectual influence. Empirical indicators of contributions can be found, however: Lectures and their attendance, faculty hired for consultations, ideas that originated in the university and find expression in political forums, public discrediting of misinformation campaigns, and so forth.

Catholic Higher Education in the Public Sphere

Questions of identity gravitate toward specific differences, and questions of Catholic identity are no exception. One wants to know, what makes Catholic higher education *different from* the rest of higher education? Although this

---

The Closing of the American Mind: How Higher Education Has Failed Democracy and Impoverished the Souls of Today's Students (New York: Simon and Schuster, 1987), and Kimball, *Tenured Radicals*; for a critique of both sides of the debate as assuming a problematic notion of culture, see Bromwich, *Politics by Other Means*; for a left-wing perspective, see Henry A. Giroux, "Beyond the Ivory Tower: Public Intellectuals and the Crisis of Higher Education," in *Higher Education under Fire: Politics, Economics, and the Crisis of the Humanities*, ed. Michael Bérubé and Cary Nelson (New York: Routledge, 1995), 238-58.

[36] Jacoby, *The Last Intellectuals*, argues that it was precisely the move into the university that took left-wing intellectuals—the activists of the 1960s—out of the spheres of public influence.

question is easily overstated, it strikes me as a valid question that currently challenges educators at Catholic universities and colleges.

Let me start with two tentative assumptions, which I adopt for purposes of exploring answers to the above question. The first is this: The distinctiveness of Catholic higher education will lie in how its Catholicity impinges on the understanding and carrying out of its academic mission. Because our concern here is with the public sphere, this first assumption directs our attention to those aspects of the academic mission that take the university or college into the public sphere. Second, I assume that one's religion does not have to remain compartmentalized from the rest of one's views, but rather has implications for the formation of those views. More specifically, religious ideas and commitments are potentially a resource and an impediment in the formation of publicly tenable political opinions. Religion *can be*—although it often is not—a resource for public reason. Consequently, Catholic higher education can make a specific contribution to the political life of the nation insofar as Catholic universities and colleges learn how to tap that resource in the right way, as universities or colleges.

As formulated above, these assumptions remain rather vague. To arrive at a more precise formulation, I first dip back into political theory. I then turn to a concrete example of one interpretation of these assumptions—a new conception of religious publicity emergent in the last few decades. Third and finally, I draw some more specific, albeit tentative, implications for Catholic higher education.

The vaguely formulated assumption that religion is a resource for public reason allows for a variety of interpretations. In the present context, we want to know how religious ideas and convictions should enter into political debates. One might, for example, hold a very strict view about keeping religious views out of political discourse. On this restrictive interpretation of "neutral dialogue," citizens ought to avoid mentioning their religious beliefs altogether when they discuss political issues. This approach generates a certain dualism: Individuals reflecting in private or with fellow believers may well reach their political views on the basis of their religious convictions, but when they enter into political debates involving the broader public of citizens, they should appeal only to shared political values and principles, or to "primary goods" that any reasonable person desires.[37] According to this restrictive approach, religious convictions have at most an indirect effect on the course of political deliberation. To some extent, then, religious belief remains a resource for public reason, but they do not

---

[37] A number of political theorists at least tend toward this position, which I have stated rather starkly for purposes of presentation; see esp. Bruce A. Ackerman, "Why Dialogue?" *Journal of Philosophy* 86 (1989): 5-22; *Social Justice in the Liberal State* (New Haven, CT: Yale University Press, 1980); "What Is Neutral about Neutrality?" *Ethics* 93 (1983): 372-90; also John Rawls, *Political Liberalism,* esp. lecture 6; and his *A Theory of Justice* (Cambridge, MA: Harvard University Press, 1971).

enter into public deliberation as explicit themes.

A less restrictive approach notes that the more important constraint on deliberation concerns, not what *themes* may enter into discourse, but what *kind of justification* is required to legitimize laws, court rulings, and policy decisions in pluralistic settings.[38] We might dub this the "impartial justification" interpretation to distinguish it from the "neutral dialogue" view. In any case, the key idea is not so much that dialogue itself remain "neutral," as that citizens strive to justify the exercise of power in terms that all reasonable citizens can accept.[39] As long as the decisive justifications remain general or impartial, religious themes are not necessarily excluded from the process of discourse. Indeed, in some cases—rare as these may be—the expression of religious views may help citizens locate the nonreligious grounds for political agreement. [40]

Each of the above two interpretations has a different idea about the relation between religious identity and politics. The "neutral dialogue" view erects a rather high wall between these two spheres. Catholics can accept the democratic process precisely because they can separate their identity as citizens from their identity as Catholics. Thus, neutral dialogue fits quite well with the rigid separation that Catholics once maintained between their religious and civil loyalties—the style of public Catholicism once articulated by John Carroll and dubbed "republican Catholicism" by David J. O'Brien.[41] By contrast, the notion of impartial justification allows religious identities to enter into political dialogue. When Catholics enter into the political arena, they do not simply become American citizens like anyone else, but bring their Catholic identity with them. At least potentially, then, their religious affiliations have public political implications. The religious and civic identities of citizens are somehow combined, or at least not so strongly separated.

The theoretical discussions that have opened up this latter possibility gain some empirical support from the sociology of religion. José Casanova has recently documented a process of deprivatization that has engendered a new style of public religion.[42] To illustrate Casanova's thesis and show how this

---

[38] See Habermas, *Between Facts and Norms,* 308-14.

[39] Note that neutral dialogue is also aimed at achieving an impartial or generally acceptable justification or grounds for political and legal decisions; but it achieves this by precluding certain topics of discussion from the start.

[40] As described here, both approaches—that of neutral dialogue and that of impartial justification—assume that public reason requires agreement on the *same* justifications for political decisions. One can obtain a more complex, realistic conception of public reason by dropping this requirement and developing a notion of "moral compromise" that allows different participants to have different reasons for accepting a common framework of social cooperation; see Bohman, *Public Deliberation,* esp. chaps. 1-2.

[41] See David J. O'Brien, *Public Catholicism* (New York: Macmillan, 1989) chap. 2.

[42] José Casanova, *Public Religions in the Modern World* (Chicago: University of Chicago Press, 1994).

combination of identities might be at least possible, I next examine the practice of the U.S. Catholic Bishops. The bishops' social pastorals—in particular the letters on nuclear deterrence and on the economy—provide a more concrete understanding of the issues in political theory. They thus can serve as a starting point for clarifying our thoughts about how the resources of Catholicism can be tapped for interventions in the political public sphere. [43]

Casanova argues that contemporary religion is undergoing a process of "deprivatization." According to Casanova, this process has led to a new phenomenon in the sociology of religion—specifically, a new kind of publicity.[44] In its primary sense, deprivatization refers to the manner in which some churches have moved from the private to the public sphere while accepting the conditions of intervention in a modern public sphere, that is, accepting universalistic principles of public discourse.[45] Casanova illustrates his thesis with a number of case studies drawn from different countries. Here I am most interested in his analysis of the U. S. Catholic bishops' letters on deterrence and the economy. In Casanova's eyes, the bishops exemplified this kind of shift when they wrote these social pastorals.

The bishops explicitly drew upon their religious tradition—they understood their stance as an outgrowth of their Catholicism—but many of their arguments and conclusions did not crucially depend on that tradition. Their fundamental appeal was much broader, invoking the absolute value of human dignity. Especially noteworthy is the style of discourse practiced by the bishops—the procedure they used in arriving at their positions. The process was broadly consultative and democratic, each letter undergoing significant revision in response to feedback from a variety of quarters. If the letters failed to change policy, they nonetheless were successful as interventions in the public sphere; the big players had to take notice and respond. More importantly, they employed the style of open discourse appropriate to the public sphere. I have already sketched these principles as requirements on informal public deliberation—inclusiveness or openness to a variety of perspectives, a willingness to listen and respond to arguments, and freedom from coercion and other distortions. The bishops' discursive style indicates an acceptance of the principles of a robust public sphere.[46]

---

[43] See National Conference of Catholic Bishops, *The Challenge of Peace: God's Promise and Our Response,* available in Jim Castelli, *The Bishops and the Bomb: Waging Peace in a Nuclear Age* (New York: Doubleday & Co., 1983), appendix, 185-283; and *Economic Justice for All: Pastoral Letter on Catholic Social Teaching and the U.S. Economy* (Washington, D.C.: United States. Catholic Conference, 1986).

[44] Casanova, *Public Religions in the Modern World* chap. 2; for his discussion of public Catholicism, see chap. 7.

[45] *Ibid.,* 221.

[46] For a detailed account of the process and multiple drafts, see Castelli, *The Bishops*

To be sure, the bishops' initiative contained significant internal tensions. According to David O'Brien, the bishops did not completely overcome the dualism associated with the republican style of Catholic engagement.[47] This dualism is clearest in the Pastoral on War and Peace. There the bishops divided their appeal according to the difference between two audiences, the "Catholic faithful" on the one hand and the "wider civil community" on the other.[48] In the Economic Pastoral the dualism is less pronounced but still discernible in the bishops' use of both biblical sources and general ethical principles, as well as in their distinction between their primary aim of guiding Catholics and their secondary aim of affecting public debate.[49] O'Brien sees a deeper conflict of styles underlying this dualism. When addressing the broader public, the bishops employ a republican style. When addressing Catholics, however, the bishops tend toward an "evangelical" style; historically, this approach emphasizes scriptural sources, personal conversion, and the need to separate the faithful community from a corrupt world.[50] O'Brien goes on to argue that this dualism undermines the aim of bringing religious meaning into everyday life. [51]

But these difficulties should not blind us to what is new about the bishops' ecclesial practice. In issuing the social pastorals, the bishops *link together* an authoritative church pronouncement with a deliberative-democratic style of reflection. In contrast to earlier forms of ecclesial publicity, which involved either the establishment of an official church or the mobilization of Catholics as a single bloc for concrete political goals (e.g., Catholic Action, Christian Democratic parties, etc.), the bishops make an argued contribution before a public of citizens who are left free to judge the issue as individuals.[52] According to the republican model, in the political arena Catholics should distance themselves from ecclesial publicity because the forms of such publicity available then would have pitted them either against the state (and its official policy of disestablishment) or against their mainly Protestant neighbors (whose resistance would be provoked by the pursuit of particular group interests). By contrast, the bishops entered the public political sphere with a frank acknowledgment of their

---

and the Bomb.

[47] O'Brien, *Public Catholicism*, 249-50.

[48] *Challenge of Peace* para. 16.

[49] *Economic Justice for All* paras. 4, 12-19, 27, also chap. 2.

[50] O'Brien, *Public Catholicism*, 244-46, 249-51.

[51] "The republican style tends toward another kind of separation between the church and everyday life; by looking upon Christian existence in evangelical terms and public life in terms of natural law ethics, and not religious meaning, it can contribute to the very separation of religion and life it seeks to overcome and thus plays into the hands of those who regard the intrusion of the church into public matters as inappropriate." O'Brien, *Public Catholicism*, 251.

[52] Casanova, *Public Religions*, 61-63, 184-92; Casanova contrasts the bishops' social letters with their approach to abortion; see 192-207.

ecclesial position as pastors.[53] In the first place, then, the novel move consists in the fact that church authorities assumed a *new public role,* one that takes them out of the private sphere and into the informal public sphere.

The texts themselves also display a mode of publicity that differs from the idea of neutral dialogue. The bishops' dual approach to social issues such as nuclear deterrence shows to all audiences how their faith links up with a publicly arguable position on the given issue. This link results from a rhetorical exigency: The bishops want to tailor their intervention for their audiences. At the discursive level, then, the innovation lies in their addressing mixed audiences in a single document, so that each audience, even if not moved by the arguments addressed to its counterpart, can at least hear those arguments and see their consistency with the other set of arguments (assuming the view is consistent). Catholics in particular can see how their faith is consistent with broader moral arguments that appeal to all reasonable citizens. On the republican view of neutral dialogue, one might well be addressing people of different faiths, but the message itself must appeal only to what the hearers hold in common. By contrast, the bishops have juxtaposed *two different kinds of appeal,* each targeting a different segment of their audience, in a single text. Relative to the earlier republican style, this represents a new kind of rhetorical move in the discourse of public religions.

Before moving on, let me summarize in more general terms the key features of the bishops' pastorals. First, they acknowledge their religious identity and attempt to retrieve their particular religious tradition in a public political forum. Second, they are willing to employ a modern discursive process to arrive at their own position—that is, the conditions of public discourse do not just affect *how* they intervene but also the *very position* they defend. In other words, they do not simply use the public sphere to get their message across, but allow its discursive exigencies to affect the message itself. Third, the bishops are willing to live with the tensions generated by their multiple rhetorics and audiences. What lessons for Catholic higher education can we draw from their practice?

Religion and Public Discourse

The foregoing reflections on political theory and the bishops' social pastorals have attempted to open up possibilities for conceiving a style of public religion that would be compatible with political discourse. In this last section I continue to explore possibilities, only now these are possibilities for understanding how Catholic colleges and universities can contribute their Catholic perspectives to

---

[53] On the republican separation of religion and politics, see O'Brien, *Public Catholicism,* chap. 2; note, for example, Cecilius Calvert's admonition to Catholics to keep silent on matters of religion when in the presence of Protestants (12); John Carroll's view that church authorities should stay out of political affairs (17-18). For the bishops' contrasting style, see, for example, *Economic Justice for All* paras. 7-11.

the political public sphere. How these possibilities line up in the current debates over identity within the Catholic academy remains a further question, which I cannot pursue here. Some possibilities, I suspect, are open to both liberal and conservative interpretations, whereas others may fall more clearly on one side rather than another.[54]

Note first how Catholic higher education also exhibits the key features of the new style of publicity familiar from the bishops' pastorals. Among educators working in Catholic schools we find a lively concern to reflect on and maintain the Catholic identity of their colleges and universities. The growing number of books, mission statements, and conferences—both within and between Catholic schools—give witness to this concern.[55] Catholic colleges and universities are much less wary about making their religious identity a visible aspect of their public institutional presence. This in itself is not remarkable, and would not represent the kind of shift in publicity that characterizes "deprivatization," were not Catholic higher education also committed, like the bishops in their social pastorals, to the conditions of modern discourse. Academic freedom is probably the clearest hallmark of this commitment within higher education. Consequently, how a given faculty and administration concretely defines such freedom indicates its level of commitment to modern discourse.[56]

Not surprisingly, the attempt to combine a public acknowledgment of religious identity with a commitment to modern discourse engenders tensions within higher education—the third feature of the bishops' pastorals. Any attempt to answer our leading question—does Catholic higher education have a distinctively Catholic role to play in the political life of the nation? —must face such tensions, which are built into the question itself. However, the nature of the modern university suggests that these tensions will be more sustainable within the academy than they are in the practice of religious authorities. This is because

---

[54] See O'Brien, *From the Heart of the American Church,* for a liberal view of Catholic identity; O'Brien, chap. 6, also provides an overview of the major contributors to the debate. Conservatives tend to be more concerned about the loss of identity through secularization; see, for example, James Turnstead Burtchaell, "The Decline and Fall of the Christian College," *First Things,* 12 (April 1991): 16-29 and part II in 13 (May 1991): 30-38.

[55] For an account of the Holy Cross mission statement, see O'Brien, *From the Heart of the American Church,* chap. 7; the largest inter-school conference I am aware of is the Heartland Conference, which convened for the third time in June 1997; the number and kinds of intra-school reflection groups and courses relating to identity vary from school to school. Saint Louis University, for example, has instituted within the last several years a number of different forums, including a Dean's Seminar on Values, twice-yearly reflection meetings between the Jesuit community and faculty and administrators, a faculty seminar on Jesuit spirituality, and specially designed orientation films for personnel.

[56] Contrast, for example, O'Brien's understanding of the Catholic academy with that of the Franciscan University of Steubenville; O'Brien, *From the Heart of the American Church,* 81-88.

the latter must operate under a higher set of constraints. The Catholic bishops, for example, wanted to speak as one unified group, each of whose members occupied an ecclesial position. Moreover, their instrument consisted of a single document addressed to multiple audiences. Hence the tensions must be contained within the unity of the group and its text. As complex institutions that are defined by their commitment to theoretical discourse, colleges and universities offer an expansive field within which differences and tensions *are expected*—by friendly contest does argumentative discourse live and breathe.

For this reason, I doubt that one can normally expect a Catholic college and university to present a tightly unified "Catholic" front to the public sphere; in keeping with the pluralistic character of the modern university, a specifically Catholic contribution may appropriately emerge only as one kind of initiative among many intellectual endeavors found at the university. Institutions of higher education violate their commitment to discourse if they do not make alternative viewpoints available within their walls. The specific set of tensions for higher education becomes most evident in the practical question: How far can the alternatives go, and what level of institutional support may they receive, before they overwhelm the Catholic character of the school—before the secularization feared by conservatives becomes an inevitability?

In universities and colleges, however, the tensions between Catholic identity and modern discourse are spread out across a variety of fora and levels. Consequently, how one answers the practical question may vary from point to point within the institution. Hence, to grasp how Catholic higher education can contribute to the public sphere, one must attend to the differentiations outlined earlier. I close by recalling these distinctions and briefly noting some of the more obvious possibilities and further questions.

To start with the university as a site for argumentation, then, a university's Catholic presence in the public sphere is realized by the specific fora it sponsors. That is, what speakers does it invite to campus, which research does it fund, what conferences does it host, what discussions does it promote, what courses does it support? To the extent that higher education provides opportunities and forums for attempts to draw upon the Catholic tradition as a resource for public engagement and dialogue, it provides the sites for a specifically Catholic contribution to the public sphere. Positively, a college or university committed to its Catholic identity will foster a variety of such sites.

The controversial practical question connected with this aspect of education is the negative one: To what extent should Catholic schools deny platforms to voices critical of, or at odds with, "Catholic" positions? If no or very little critique is permitted, one preserves a clear identity only at the cost of violating the conditions of modern discourse, in particular the requirement that informal publics be open to one another (and thus that one's views should be formed by engaging with opposed views and counter arguments). The key to a solution, I suggest, lies in the dialogical character of criticism. If one understands critical sites as opportunities for dialogue—rather than, say, chances for the disgruntled to express their cynicism—one can keep the seemingly opposed demands of identity and discourse in healthy tension.

Second, the university contributes potential participants for the public sphere. As already noted, the kind and degree of participation will depend on the role. Because people tend to see administrators as speaking for the university as a corporate body, one might expect tighter constraints on their public participation than on faculty and students. With faculty, one should distinguish their scholarly research, writing, and speaking—modes of participation that normally have only a minimal, indirect effect on public discourse—from their teaching impact on students. To the extent that courses enable students to engage their Catholic tradition as a living resource for their civic reflection in a suitable manner—i.e., in an open discursive manner appropriate to civil discourse—the university is forming potential participants whose Catholicism makes a difference for their citizenship.

One practical question in this context concerns the makeup of the faculty and administration. Must we define the university's distinctively Catholic contribution of "participants" in terms of professedly Catholic faculty and administrators? Certainly a significant level of explicit Catholic commitment or interest must exist among its personnel for a university to maintain a Catholic identity.[57] But I suspect that we do not need to define the university's contribution to political participation so narrowly. One might, for example, consider it a specifically Catholic contribution of participants that some faculty simply gain a greater knowledge and respect for the Catholic tradition through their contact with personnel who are more committed to the Catholic identity. That is, positive contact of this sort could foster a greater openness in political discussions to Catholic participants and their perspectives (assuming their Catholicism emerged as relevant to the issue under discussion).

Finally, the Catholic college or university can contribute substantively to the arguments and opinions circulating in the public sphere. This does not mean that the viewpoints must be explicitly Catholic, but only that they have been informed by the Catholic tradition. The philosophical arguments in the bishops' pastoral letters are examples of this from outside the university. But consider an inside example, which will also help summarize the foregoing points. If a university sponsors a conference on assisted suicide at which the speakers make

---

[57] Timothy O'Meara, Provost Emeritus of the University of Notre Dame, has argued that the Catholic character of a university will be preserved in the long run only if the hiring process makes religious affiliation an explicit issue; informal presentation, Colloquium on Catholic Higher Education, Saint Louis University, May 9, 1997.

the best philosophical arguments they can in keeping with Church teaching, then the university has contributed (1) a public site for argumentation; (2) participants who take their Catholic heritage seriously, but who bring it non-dogmatically to a public discourse open to a variety of viewpoints, Catholic and non-Catholic; and (3) a set of arguments and reasoned opinions, which are put up for critical discussion before a *general* audience.

At a practical level, this last point has a further implication that tests the seriousness of such a commitment to the public sphere: If Catholics presume to put their views forward in public, then they must be willing to have them criticized and rejected. More to the point, they must be willing to revise those views in the light of better arguments. Given the discursive commitment of the university, the dialogical character of critique, and the fact that traditions develop precisely *through* argument,[58] openness to criticism is essential to any Catholic contribution to the public sphere. Granting this point of principle, however, does not fully answer the practical question of how such criticism should best be organized, and how much it should be fostered, at sites provided by Catholic colleges and universities.

In conclusion, I have attempted in this essay to sketch a framework, an organized series of perspectives and questions, for thinking about the role of Catholic higher education in the political life of the nation. Recent democratic theory allows us to conceive one side of that equation—the nature of political deliberation—in more complex, realistic terms without entirely sacrificing the ideals of public reason. I hope to have suggested how we might likewise approach the other side of the equation—the role of Catholic higher education— in recognition of the complexities of the contemporary university. To be sure, the proposed framework is still rudimentary. I offer it simply as a starting point for further reflection on a topic of prime importance for the future of Catholic education.

---

[58] See Alasdair MacIntyre, *After Virtue,* 2nd ed. (Notre Dame, IN: University of Notre Dame Press, 1984), esp. 222.

9

Jesuits and Scholarship

A Reading of the Macelwane Report

William M. Shea

Saint Louis University

The Jesuits

The Society of Jesus is the first and historically the most important modern (i.e. post-Reformation) Catholic religious order of men. Its cradle was the University of Paris where the original companions studied. Begun in the sixteenth century, the Jesuits fell on hard days when, for a variety of political reasons, they were suppressed by Pope Clement XIV in 1773. They continued underground in many places and over ground only in Poland and Russia until they were restored by Pope Pius VI in 1814.[1] As the papal struggle with the Enlightenment and modern European nation states intensified in the nineteenth century, the Jesuits became the popes' "shock troops" in the ideological struggle with modernity. With the blessing of Pius IX and Leo XIII, they helped to initiate the Thomist revival in the nineteenth century.

The Jesuits came to North America with the French. English Jesuits settled in Maryland and Virginia. One of them became the first Catholic bishop in the United States in the person of John Carroll. Here they followed their European pattern, playing the role of educators and teaching chiefly in urban centers and nearly exclusively in preparatory schools and colleges, some of which were chartered by their respective states as universities. But they served

---

[1] For the details see William V. Bangert, S.J., *A History of the Society of Jesus* (St. Louis, MO: Institute for Jesuit Sources, 1972), 363-429.

the church in other ways as well, not least among them foreign missionaries, missionaries to the native Americans and advisors to Catholics entering the abor movement. They were, as it is said, a "presence" in American Catholicism, highly regarded by Catholics for their discipline and superior theological and philosophical training. But they were feared as well, by those non-Catholics convinced that the "Romish" church harbored anti-democratic intentions. Today Jesuits work in twenty-eight colleges and universities in the United States. Some three thousand of over twenty thousand Jesuits are currently involved in higher education world-wide.[2]

Several years ago, having arrived at a Jesuit university as a faculty member and wanting to explore the history and character of Jesuit higher education in America, I read William Leahy's *Adapting to America*. I was caught by the concluding chapter in which he makes the following overall assessment of Catholic higher education:

> But even though improved, Catholic higher education generally remains undistinguished in American intellectual culture, despite nearly four decades of effort and expenditure of millions of dollars. While many Catholic colleges and universities offer at least an adequate undergraduate education, few possess national reputations for academic excellence, and none ranks among the elite institutions in graduate programs, research, and professional scholarship.[3]

Why? He suggests three answers (the lack of requisite funds is not among them!): they are, by circumstance and choice, local rather than national universities; with few exceptions they have not had the quality of presidential leadership required for such high purpose and accomplishment; and, most interesting of all, there is an inverse statistical correlation between religious dedication or mission and scholarly productivity. Leahy concludes that in the nineteen sixties,

> ...most faculty and administrators involved in Catholic higher education emphasized teaching, student contact, and administrative needs. But while important, such priorities often resulted in intellectual stagnation among many Catholic professors and their students. In addition, the focus on the classroom and communication of religious values almost guaranteed the neglect of research and scholarly writing, increasingly the route to distinction in American

---

[2] In 1972, 1,283 American Jesuits (of approximately 6600) were "missioned" to higher education. See Joseph A. Tetlow, S.J., "The Jesuit Mission in Higher Education: Perspectives and Contexts," *Studies in the Spirituality of Jesuits* 15 and 16 (November -January, 1983-84): 49-50. See also General Congregation 34 (1995): D.17, #405 (http://web.lemoyne.edu).

[3] William P. Leahy, S.J., *Adapting to America: Catholics, Jesuits, and Higher Education in the Twentieth Century* (Washington, DC: Georgetown University Press, 1991), 135.

academic culture. ...Studies of faculties in American institutions of higher learning have noted that scholarly production and religious commitment vary inversely and that "stronger degrees of one tend to be accompanied by weaker degrees of the other." Jencks and Reisman commented in 1968 that the low publication rates among Catholic faculty suggest that "it is hard to maximize both piety and scholarship simultaneously."[4]

This remark by a Jesuit set me wondering about Jesuits and scholarship. Alice Gallin's faculty seminar at Saint Louis University in 1996-97 afforded me the opportunity to explore several facets of this topic, and the essay that follows is a fruit of that opportunity.

The American Context and the Macelwane Report

American higher education developed dramatically in the five decades before the Macelwane Report, the center piece of this essay, was written (1930-1932). In 1876 Johns Hopkins was founded as the first American graduate school on the European model (C. S. Peirce taught there, and John Dewey was among the students). Harvard had already begun its climb and quickly became a modern university. By the turn of the century Harvard boasted the finest philosophy faculty in the country, populated with internationally reputable faculty, among them George Santayana, William James, Josiah Royce, and G. H. Palmer. The Rockefeller money that founded the University of Chicago in 1893 was meant to support not just a college but a full-blown research university. By the end of the nineteenth century state universities such as Michigan and Minnesota were already centers of serious scholarship. They were John Dewey's first and second steps on his long career, and he served there with distinguished philosophers, psychologists, and social thinkers. In 1903 Nicholas Murray Butler tempted him from his third step, University of Chicago, to his fourth and last, Columbia. [5]

By 1889 The Catholic University of America had been founded in the nation's capital as a graduate school of the sacred sciences, and soon began branching out from theology to philosophy and the social sciences (1895).[6] In

---

[4] Leahy, 142-143. He cites studies by Christopher Jencks and David Riesman,*The Academic Revolution* (Garden City, NY: Doubleday and Co., 1968) and Stephen Steinberg, *The Academic Melting Pot: Catholics and Jews in American Higher Education* (New York: McGraw- Hill Book Co., 1974).

[5] Steven C. Rockefeller, *John Dewey: Religious Faith and Democratic Humanism* (New York: Columbia University Press, 1991).

[6] The story is told by Philip Gleason in *Contending with Modernity: Catholic Higher Edu-cation in the Twentieth Century* (New York: Oxford University Press, 1995). See also C. Joseph Neusse, *The Catholic University of America* (Washington, DC: Catholic University Press, 1990).

fact, so swiftly were the American institutions inventing their own version of the German research university that they found it necessary to establish the Association of American Universities (AAU, 1900) to exercise some degree of control over the explosion of graduate schools and doctoral programs. The Catholic University, and no other Catholic university, was among its fifty charter members. At the time the doctoral degree was becoming the rule for a career in college teaching, and established as a research degree rather than professional certification. Colleges and the research universities were by then distinct from one another as, by the end of that century, colleges had been distinguished and separated from preparatory schools.

When the Macelwane Report was sent to Wlodimir Ledochowski, the Jesuit Father General in Rome, the American depression was three years along and the pioneer era was over except in the new talkies and wild west novels. The Catholic Church was widely regarded as the enemy of intelligence and democracy, and Catholic educational institutions were perceived as sectarian.[7] The status of the church and of Catholic educational institutions was ambiguous. They had little or no relationship to American high culture and scholarly institutions. Having long been the church of immigrants rather than the church of the Carrolls of Carrollton, it served and saved millions of immigrants. Its people and their leaders, by and large, had neither the money, the leisure, nor the tradition of intellectualism to look to the new research universities and to elite colleges.[8] It would be highly unusual for a Catholic to aspire to a professorship even in the public institutions.[9] Catholics adhered to a church characterized by a powerful, highly articulated anti-modernist ideology.[10] Their few public

---

[7] The Jesuits, as other Catholics, were sensitive to this public reputation. The Macelwane Report shows evidence of this. For another example, see the letter of Frederick Odenbach, S. J., to Jesuit colleges asking them to establish seismological laboratories in "honor of the Church which has been proclaimed an enemy to all modern progress and enlightenment," quoted in Fr. Macelwane's introductory essay to the "Jesuit Seismological Association, 25th Anniversary Volume," Midwest Jesuit Archives. The letter was written on February 2, 1909.

[8] John F. O'Brien, *Catholics and Scholarship: A Symposium* (Huntington, IN: Our Sunday Visitor, 1939). This is a collection of essays made by Fr. O'Brien, chaplain at the University of Illinois and *bete noire* of the Jesuit college people who opposed O'Brien's promotion of state universities as acceptable institutions for Catholic students. The essays include a great deal of data and several positions on the question of Catholic participation in public academic life. For O'Brien's encounter with the Jesuits see Gleason, 143-145 and Leahy, 41. Leahy reports that at the turn of the century twentieth century, two thirds of Catholics attending college did so in non-Catholic institutions. See Leahy, 21.

[9] O'Brien, 18-25. He reports that in the late thirties there were two Catholic professors (out of a total of 207) and 34 other full time Catholic faculty (out of 1,100) in the University of Illinois where Catholics made up a fifth of the state population.

[10] Michael V. Gannon, "Before and After Modernism: the Intellectual Isolation of the

intellectuals were more often than not former Protestants or European Catholics.[11]

During the 1920s some American Jesuits became concerned with the state of their educational work in the wake of the strides being made in other quarters of American higher education. In 1920 the American Provincial superiors of the Jesuit community established an Inter-Province Committee (IPC) to make recommendations for the improvement of their high schools, colleges, and universities. In 1921 the Jesuit General approved the formation of the IPC. From 1920 to 1931 the Committee met annually and made its reports to the Provincials. Very little happened. The Provincials did not publish the IPC reports for the national community of Jesuits. However, the minutes of the meetings were sent directly to the Father General in Rome, keeping him in touch with the problems and the thinking of American Jesuit academic leaders. [12]

In February 1927 the Jesuit Father General was presented with serious criticisms of American Jesuit collegiate and professional education by the Cardinal Secretary of State, criticisms which were based on complaints the Cardinal himself had received.[13] The Cardinal expressed skepticism about the reports and the General expressed astonishment at them, but both men took them seriously enough for the General to launch an inquiry. The Cardinal's questions centered upon the Catholicity of the American Jesuit colleges.[14] The General, in turn, questioned the leaders of the Jesuits in America about those criticisms. As

---

American Priest," ed. John Tracy Ellis, *The Catholic Priest in the United States: Historical Investigations* (Collegeville, MN: Liturgical Press, 1971), 293-383.

[11] For examples, see Peter A. Huff, *Allen Tate and the Catholic Revival: Trace of the Fugitive God* (Mahwah, NJ: Paulist Press, 1996) and David O'Brien, *Isaac Hecker: An American Catholic* (Mahwah, NJ: Paulist Press, 1992), especially chapters 14 and 18. Other twentieth century examples would be Carlton J. H. Hayes at Columbia University, and Jacques Maritain and Etienne Gilson who lectured and taught in leading American universities.

[12] The events from 1921 to 1937 fall into three easily distinguished periods: the work of the IPC, 1921-1931, the Macelwane Commission, 1931-1932, and the establishment and early years of the Jesuit Educational Association under Daniel O'Connell, S.J., of the Chicago Province, 1934-1937. The General was in close touch with all these events, and in fact either initiated or approved the establishment of mechanisms marking each phase. See Paul A. Fitzgerald, S.J., *The Governance of Jesuit Colleges in the United States, 1920-1970* (South Bend, IN: University of Notre Dame Press, 1984), 1-53.

[13] Fitzgerald, 21ff. See Fr. Ledochowski's letters of March 12, 1927 and June 7, 1928 in "Printed Correspondence from the General, 1921-27," Midwest Jesuit Archives, St. Louis, MO. . See also the response by the Missouri Provincial, Samuel Horine, and the reports of the rectors of the three universities - Saint Louis, Marquette, and Creighton.

[14] A copy of the General's questionnaire is attached to the letter of 1927. The Roman concern with the "identity" of the Catholic institutions of the 1970s to 90s is not entirely without precedent. See Gleason, 178-79.

a result of the responses, Fr. Ledochowski issued a directive which, among other things, excluded women from Jesuit colleges and universities, excluded non-Catholics from deanships, and, wherever prudently possible, from chairmanships and faculty positions.[15] The American Provincials and the Rectors of universities and colleges did what they could to meet the directives without harming their institutions. When feasible they appointed Catholics to administrative positions (it was sometimes not feasible for academic reasons), and they found ways of justifying the presence of religious women and other women in the classrooms of their colleges. Authority gradually bowed to practical wisdom, as it has on other occasions.

In response to further expressions of concern, this time about the quality of Jesuit education and its relative standing in the United States, the General wrote another letter on December 8, 1930. The letter asked the Provincials to recommend names for a commission to investigate the state of Jesuit colleges and universities. He soon appointed a commission chaired by Fr. James B. Macelwane.

Fr. Macelwane studied physics at the University of California and wrote a dissertation in seismology. He taught there for two years and returned to Saint Louis University in 1925 as founding director of the department of geophysics. From 1927-1933 he served as dean of the graduate school. His national reputation later led him to the presidency of the American Geophysical Union and to the National Academy of Science.[16] His professional role as scholar fit well his vocation as a Jesuit.

> Although he moved in the circle of scientists of eminent international fame, Fr. Macelwane never lost his simplicity and humility. When presented in 1948 with the William Bowie Medal before geophysicists gathered from many nations in Washington, D.C., and after giving expression to sentiments of gratitude, he said A...in all sincerity I must plead that all my life long I have been on the receiving end, so to speak, of the cooperation which the medal symbolizes. Whatever I am as I stand before you I owe to the Catholic religious order to which I belong. I came to the Jesuits a country boy with only a high school education and even that received under their auspices. They gave me broad

---

[15] The General's letters of 1927, 1928, 1930 and 1934, and responses to them are in "Printed Communications from the General, 1921-1942," at the Midwest Jesuit Archives.

[16] Five others were appointed to what became known as the Macelwane Commission: Charles F. Carroll, prefect of studies of the California province; Charles J. Deane, dean of Fordham University; Albert J. Fox, dean of John Carroll University in Cleveland; John W. Hynes, president of Loyola University in New Orleans; Edward P. Tivnan, procurator of the New England province. Biographical data on them can be found in Fitzgerald. Macelwane's career is traced by William B. Faherty, S.J., in his *Men to Remember: Jesuit Teachers at Saint Louis University, 1829-1979* (St. Louis, MO: Saint Louis University Press, 1997), 82-84.

scholarly training, unusual scientific opportunities, generous support, and unfailing encouragement—the best cooperation a man ever had...[17]

In the final report of the Macelwane Commission in 1932, the General's questions were answered so meticulously that it leads one to recognize his knowledge of the problems and even of the directions that should be taken by the Commission before he wrote the letter of appointment. The General may have been out of touch with the American educational scene in his first letter, but he recovered quickly. The second letter is hardly a request for guidance in an area in which he suffered any absence of knowledge. He knew what the problems were. He consulted with leading American Jesuit educators before he acted. He had before him ten years of the minutes of the IPC, four members of which he appointed to the Macelwane Commission, assuring significant continuity in the effort, already a decade old, to renew American Jesuit colleges.[18]

The 234 page Macelwane Report (MR), submitted in 1932, was highly critical of the institutions and the way they were being run. It made sweeping recommendations sure to arouse internal opposition. Perhaps because of this it stayed in the General's file until, in 1934, the American Council on Education issued a list of sixty-six approved doctoral programs. On the list none of the thirty-four Jesuit programs found a place. This shock caused the General to take the MR out of its file and enact its recommendations.[19] From 1934 on, the Jesuit educators and Provincials, surely not without great difficulty and many setbacks, worked on their institutions in the spirit and with the objectives recommended by the Commission and approved by the General.

---

[17] From *The Newsletter*, Missouri and Wisconsin Provinces 28.25 (April, 1956) in the archives of the Chicago Province under "Macelwane, Fr. James, 1883-1956."

[18] The Commission did rely on the Inter-Province Committee's annual reports. The MR states that "...very many of the points urged in this present report of the Commission had already been proposed years ago by the Inter-Province Committee." The IPC did not achieve its goals because it did not report directly to the General. The MR remarks that "A central authority from above is needed ... else the recommendation for an association of Jesuit schools and a Commissarius would suffer the fate of the recommendations of the old Inter-Province Committee established in 1920 by the Provincials and approved by the General in 1921." There is heavy emphasis on the appointment by the General in order to break the jamb of inertia of Provincials and local superiors in this "critical situation." (MR 23; 27-28) The IPC annual reports, and one of the two quinquennial reports (1927), are available in the Midwest Jesuit Archives in St. Louis. I was unable to locate the second Quinquennial Report (1931), but it is likely present in one or more of the archives of the Jesuit provinces, or in the archives of the Association of Jesuit Colleges and Universities, the successor to the Jesuit Educational Association.

[19] To add insult to injury, five departments at Catholic University and one at the University of Notre Dame were recognized and approved (though not ranked "distinguished"). See *Contending with Modernity,* 182-183.

Trying Times

The Macelwane Commission is important historically because it served to elevate, document, expand and transmit the growing concern among American Jesuit educators with the state of their institutions. It "proved" the case, providing a platform for the General's actions, and detailed the steps which had to be taken if the institutions were to survive and prosper.[20] This essay addresses only one question to the MR: What is the view of the life of scholarship stated and implied in the MR and what does it state and imply about the intellectual life of Jesuit communities? The following summary will be drawn from the point of view of the guiding question on Jesuits and scholarship, and does not pretend to a complete presentation and analysis of the MR and later documents.

The Macelwane Report

The General had asked the Commission in his 1930 letter to respond to four questions regarding the American Jesuit colleges and universities. The MR used the questions to organize its work into four parts: (1) unification of action in the American Jesuits' educational work; (2) the comparative standing of Jesuit institutions in American higher education; (3) their relationship to public accrediting agencies; and (4) improvements in the education of Jesuits themselves (MR 4-5).

At the outset, the MR briefly restated the historical objective of Jesuit education: to help shape the "whole man," not only for this world but also "for the world to come." There is, in the Jesuit view, no "real education without religion" and so religion provides the "very atmosphere of their educational world." This is joined to several other characteristics of Jesuit education: instruction in current Scholastic philosophy, thoroughness in educational planning and execution, personal interest in and contact with students, and training for leadership. Together they provide a "foundation" of a life of dedicated service to God, demanding both "accuracy as the very soul of scholarship" and a "correlation" (integration) of subject matter (MR 10-13; 32). Jesuit education has the classical humanist goal: to train the students to organize knowledge, to stand on their own feet in the world of language, and to express themselves in accordance with high ideals. Much of the MR is meant to improve

---

[20] So important is the Commission and the document it produced that it can only be compared with those decisive years (1967-1972) when Paul Reinert, S.J. of Saint Louis University led American Catholic educators in coping with threatening financial circumstances and nearly universal institutional conditions inhibiting the presidents' freedom to act. See Paul C. Reinert, S.J., *To Turn the Tide* (Englewood Cliffs NJ: Prentice-Hall, Inc., 1972); Paul Shore and Paul Reinert, S. J., *Seasons of Change: Reflections on a Half Century at Saint Louis University* (St. Louis: Saint Louis University Press, 1996); and Alice Gallin, *Independence and a New Partnership* (South Bend: University of Notre Dame Press, 1996); also Gleason and Fitzgerald.

the ability of the Society's institutions to accomplish these collegiate goals (MR 17).[21]

Both the humanist and the religious goals stem from St. Ignatius himself. In the fourth part of the Constitutions of the Society we read:

> ...we must treat of the building up of learning and of the means of using it in order to help them [i.e., the students] the better to know and serve God our Creator and Lord. For this purpose the Society accepts colleges and eventually universities... (MR 17)

The MR quotes the twenty-fifth General Congregation of the Society (1906), 12th decree, to the same effect:

> In drawing up these ordinations it is proper to take account in the first place, of the end which the Society proposes to itself in its colleges. This end is not only to develop all the faculties of our students by good methods of teaching but to educate them in faith and piety, to build up their character, to accustom them to self-control, and to help them acquire habits of virtue (MR 17).

Simply put, education is a means to an end which does not exhaust itself in secular goals but finds its justification in the transcendent goal of human beings. The openness to transcendence is the basic characteristic of Jesuit and, indeed, any religious education.[22] The MR proposes no change in that goal. Rather, it proposes new and reformed means of achieving them in a new cultural and educational context.[23]

---

[21] The historical and historic Jesuit view of education is neatly sketched in George Ganss, S.J., *The Jesuit Educational Tradition and Saint Louis University* (St. Louis, MO: Institute for Jesuit Sources, 1969). Note the contemporaneous debate among Jesuits on graduate education, amounting to rejection of the MR, in George Bull, S.J., "The Function of the Catholic Graduate School" in *Thought* 13 (Spring 1938): 364-80; see his work on *The Function of the Catholic College* (New York: America Press, 1933). Fr. Bull saw little distinction between undergraduate and graduate education, except the latter has more of the same.

[22] Compare the current Saint Louis University Mission Statement in the *Catalogue of the Graduate School, 1994-1996*: "The Mission of the University is the pursuit of truth for the greater glory of God and for the service of humanity."

[23] A massive study of Midwestern Jesuit colleges and universities was being completed at the time under the direction of Joseph McGlucken, S.J. The dissertation, a three volume sociological study, was accepted in 1932. I have no evidence that the Commission used its findings, but find it hard to believe that it did not. See Wilfred Michael Mallon, S.J., "The Jesuit College: An investigation into factors affecting the educational efficiency of the Jesuit Colleges in the Central States," 3 vols., Ph.D. dissertation (Saint Louis University, 1932). Copies are held in the archives of the Midwestern Provinces in St. Louis and in the collection of the Graduate School of Saint Louis University housed in Pius XII Memorial Library.

Part I: Unification of Effort

The Society at the time ran over two dozen collegiate and university institutions independent of one another, set in discrete geographical provinces, highly sensitive to the educational needs of their localities and incapable of coordinated action for the good of the whole. The IPC had been unable, in a decade of its efforts, to spark enough significant cooperation on educational matters among the leaders of the institutions or the Provincials. As a consequence, the MR recommended the formation of a national Jesuit association of universities, colleges and high schools, and the immediate appointment of a "Commissarius" (a delegate of the General) in the role of executive secretary with the authority to carry out "the provisions of this report..." (MR 26 -27). The Commissarius's primary job would be to establish strong graduate schools under recognized academic standards, with some fields special to each of these graduate schools as determined by the association. There would be planned financial cooperation among provinces and institutions. The Report also called for common action among the provinces and institutions in the education of Jesuits in training (MR 29-30). A centralized planning and decision making body might turn the independent institutions into something approaching a Jesuit "system," an intelligent request destined to frustration.

Why the appointment of a delegate responsible directly to the General? An extraordinary task and extraordinary conditions in the Society required this extraordinary step:

> The inertia of local traditions, the inbred opposition of Ours[24] to any change, and the prevailing ignorance of conditions among both inferiors and superiors, all call for energetic action, which can only come from a head exercising inter-province power (MR 42).

These factors continued to feed resistance to the implementation of the MR by the General, his Commissarius, Fr. Daniel M. O'Connell, and the Jesuit Educational Association.[25]

Part II : Comparative Standing

Competitors in higher education, for the purposes of the Commission, fall into two groups: other Catholic institutions, and non-Catholic public and private institutions (MR 34-39). With regard to the first the question is, In what ways do other Catholic colleges and universities (none is named except the Catholic

---

[24] Jesuit communications use "Ours" to refer to members of the Society.

[25] Fitzgerald, 36-53.

University in the District of Columbia[26]) succeed better than the Jesuit institutions and what are the reasons for that success? The MR answered: other Catholic institutions have superior facilities; frank public financial and educational statements; a budget system; loyalty of alumni; and a thoroughly trained faculty whose qualifications are "...revealed by the nature and results of his research work, the measure of inspiration he has given his students, and by his writings." Tenure, rank and retention at these other institutions are determined "...by the efficiency of (faculty) work" (MR 38). Statutes, by-laws, and clear and accurate description of the powers and duties of officials and so orderly procedure in administration are in place. Similarly, more of their faculty have higher degrees, they are more open to the public, more assertive in educational procedure, more published in periodicals and books. Faculty members are prominent in the Catholic Philosophical Association and the Catholic Historical Association ("we are conspicuously few in both membership and in contributions to the publications of these associations"). Finally, "they have the encouragement of their superiors" in all this, "an encouragement which seems strangely lacking in the Society"(MR 42).

The Catholic University is cited as setting standards for hiring, tenure, and promotion.[27] These requirements are quoted at length and pronounced more rigorous by far than those in Jesuit institutions. In Jesuit schools appointments of full time faculty are made without the doctorate and even,

> ...without any graduate training in the subject in a recognized graduate school. In fact, in many cases Jesuits have been appointed to teach college subjects in

---

[26] The MR also calls the General's attention to a contemporaneous row about graduate education between the Catholic University administrators and Jesuit administrators by printing in an appendix to the report letters from Maurice Sheehy, assistant to the Rector of Catholic University, to the Jesuits Wilfred Parsons (*America* editor) and Alphonse Schwitalla of Saint Louis University (MR 198-208). The General addressed the problem in a letter to the Provincials of the American Assistancy, dated August 15, 1934, the same day on which he enacted by letter the recommendations of the MR, telling them in effect to pay more attention to the role of the local bishop in their institutions and to avoid "adverse criticism and unfounded suspicion." For an account of the argument see Gleason, 177-178. The text of the letter is in "Printed Communications from the General, 1921-1942," Box VI, Midwest Jesuit Archives.

[27] The Report notes "the hostile attitude of the Catholic University of America, especially as recently expressed toward our graduate schools" (MR 21, n1) and the "jealousy of many non-Jesuit schools" (MR 22). It also cites the prevalent "hostility" of "non-Catholic institutions and organizations" and the non-Catholic and even anti-Catholic "strain" in American culture (MR 40-41). The worries about and reactions to perceived hostility are part of "contending with modernity" (Gleason) and the general and historical mutual disregard existing between Protestants and Catholics. The sense of competition with Catholic institutions may be part of the Jesuit mentality at the time. However, one should not overlook the political usefulness of this rhetoric when painful changes are being suggested.

which they did not have a corresponding undergraduate major. Instances are known in which they were appointed without having made any upper division college studies in the subject (MR 50).

Students are spoon fed even in philosophy—they are not trained to think philosophically, and even their teachers cannot outline the problems confronting modern philosophers. Students "complain that they were never really taught how to study for themselves, never educated to sustained and independent effort" (MR 59).

The second group of competitors are non-Catholic institutions with graduate schools where

> ...the endeavor is also made ... to secure one or more men whose preeminence in their particular field is well recognized. These men and their accomplishments are continually kept before the public eye. An atmosphere of scholarship is created and emphasized and an interest in fields of higher study is stimulated (MR 38).

In Jesuit institutions, as the Commission's survey of faculty reveals, only 20% of those teaching graduate courses had the equivalent of the Ph.D., only 9% had the actual Ph.D., and only 9% published their research. But 84% of these same teachers considered published research is desirable and 90% that they should have the Ph.D. in order to teach in graduate school. In non-Catholic graduate programs and at Catholic University the professors were required to have experience in research and publication, and to be actively engaged in the field in which the course is given.

> The professor who gives the course must have done sufficient research in that particular field to make him a competent guide. No professor should attempt to give a graduate course outside his own research field (MR 67-68).

In the Jesuit graduate schools where there were 34 departments offering the doctorate, there were 103 faculty with Ph.D.'s, only 19 of them Jesuits. Six of those departments had only one Ph.D. on the faculty, six had two, fourteen had three, and eight had four or more.[28]

---

[28] At the time Saint Louis university had fifteen doctoral departments, seven in science and math. Fordham had ten doctoral programs and Marquette eight. Loyola University in Chicago had a doctorate in education (MR 158ff). Library holdings are also compared. The largest Jesuit library was at Georgetown (224,000 volumes); CUA had 268,000; Notre Dame 143,000; Saint Louis had 134,000. At the same time Harvard's library contained 2.4 million; Yale 1.5 million; Chicago 1 million; Stanford 545,000. Saint Louis among the Jesuit universities had the most periodicals at 877 while Yale had 13,000. "Our Jesuit university libraries ... would be scarcely more than college libraries as regards their administration, books or periodicals" (MR 70-71). Fitzgerald quotes Fr. O'Connell as saying of one Jesuit university

Then the MR asked: What is needed to justify offering the Ph.D.? The MR's answer is that commonly accepted standards must be met in many Jesuit institutions, chiefly: (1) a fully organized and recognized graduate school with dean and board; (2) a competent head of department; and (3) "... an outstanding professor or professors in the particular field." On the last point the MR quotes a highly respected commentator on American universities, J. H. McCracken:

> The factor which chiefly determines the selection of a graduate school is the professor under whom a student desires to study and pursue investigation. Ordinarily the person sought will be known to the graduate student because of his contributions to the literature of his subject and the reputation gained by his scholarly achievements.... The spirit of the American graduate school is not unlike that of the universities of Germany. The entire strength of the professor and of the student is devoted to the search for truth, the recruiting and training of scientists being secondary. Research achievement is indicated in part by book titles and by the character of journals including contributions (MR 83).[29]

Competence in the search for truth is seen as the mark of a genuine doctoral student. In recognized institutions of the American Association of Universities one qualifies not just by doing the minimum but by "...[undertaking] by every possible means to make himself a master of his special field, to locate the frontiers of knowledge of the subject, and to discover those points of attack where he may hope successfully to invade the unknown" (MR 87). The people in charge must be

> ...university men with high ideals of scholarship and first hand knowledge of university practice... [given] the proper measure of academic responsibility for the consistent enforcement of acceptable standards....The graduate schools can hope to exert an influence only if we make it clear that they are conducted by scholars in a scholarly way....our lack of influence has in great measure been due to the practice of plunging into a new enterprise not only unprepared, but without hope of being prepared to carry on the work, years after it has been undertaken (MR 89-90).

To improve the comparative standing of Jesuit institutions, the MR again makes its list of straightforward prescriptions: adequate endowment; a budget system; trained bookkeepers; cost accounting and audits; public disclosure of financial statements; copies of educational statements issued only by competent

---

library space that the sight of it made his "heart contract." Fitzgerald, 47.

[29] J. H. McCracken, *American Universities and Colleges* (Washington, DC: American Council of Education, 1932), 49-50. McCracken recognized the fact that "Publications however are not always a test. Departments vary with respect to practice in the attribution of credit for research" (MR 83).

officials and kept on file; contact with those who can help financially or educationally; statutes and by-laws; norms for appointment, tenure, and promotion; and lay professors with the Ph.D. and recognition as scholars (MR 184).

Part III: Accrediting Agencies

A long section follows regarding accrediting agencies, a matter vital to the future of Jesuit institutions. Only Saint Louis University and Marquette University were recognized as "universities of complex organization" by the AAU (MR 99). In a rebuke to administrators and faculty alike, the MR points out that:

> Our attitude has been one of indifference. We have not been interested in learning what this or other associations have been doing. Regarding those to which we did belong, we have been satisfied with paying our dues. We have been remiss in attending the annual meetings, and have failed to read the proceedings of these meetings....we did not take into consideration the disability thus incurred by our graduates and undergraduates whose admission into other schools was seriously affected (MR 105-106).

The agencies had been viewed by Jesuits as a threat to their educational autonomy, a possibility not dismissed by the MR. But the MR recommended full participation in the work of accrediting associations in the name of self-interest and self-protection (MR 108-111;153). The discussion of the accrediting agencies had been initiated by the IPC a decade earlier.[30] The MR argued that these agencies should be used as a public and objective standard against which the quality and goals of both undergraduate and graduate education should be measured, but in the second instance the MR emphasizes the importance of the active practice of scholarship by faculty and the knowledge of the methods and standards of research on the part of administrators, especially of graduate schools. The indifference of collegiate Jesuits to the professional associations and accrediting agencies is a measure of their failure to understand the forces of development in American higher education. The goal of the MR in this respect is not only a matter of public relations, but an indictment of the attitudes and habits of the Jesuits and a plea to reverse them. The Commission seems to have recognized that in American society professions must regulate themselves if they are to avoid government regulation.[31]

---

[30] The reports of the IPC can be found in "Interprovince Committee," Box VI, Midwest Jesuit Archives, St. Louis, MO. The file contains the annual reports submitted to the Provincials and to the General, including the Quinquennial Report of 1927; the Quinquennial Report of 1931 is not in the file.

[31] The Report expresses concern about the proposed department of education in the national government (MR 109-110).

Part IV: The Education of Jesuits

At the Commission's first meeting in Philadelphia in June of 1931 a questionnaire was planned and subsequently sent to all teachers. The return, summed up in the MR, indicated "a startling lack" of preparation of the Jesuit teachers in colleges and universities as well as an "acute consciousness" of that lack. The MR expressed a hope that Jesuits be allowed to develop "that measure of scholarship which should be the aim of every Jesuit" (MR 5-6). The report concludes that "...we cannot afford to be less trained than our competitors ...we cannot really hope to take our proper place in the American educational field unless we make the attainment of the doctorate the professional goal of every Jesuit in the same sense and to the same extent ... as the Profession is the ecclesiastical and religious goal..." (MR 112-113; 187). There follow fourteen reasons for significant changes in the education of young Jesuits, most of the reasons having to do with competition and public respect and three with the intellectual and spiritual life of members of the Society.

The MR proposed a reorganization of the Juniorate (college years) as the point of specialty training in undergraduate major fields, that is, to make it the "upper division" of college. Secondly, all students interested and competent in a particular major field should be sent to a single institution, no matter their province, in order to assure the quality of training which will prepare them for graduate school and in order to cultivate professional "interest groups" among Jesuits to carry them through their academic careers in communities of Jesuit scholars.[32] It is then recommended that "Ours hold active membership in learned societies in their field, and that such membership be permitted to continue during theology..." training. Jesuits are to be trained not only in a subject but for a specific position in a particular institution which, in turn, should supervise his training (MR 187-191; 161-162).

The many years of Jesuit training, then, should include two new elements: (1) socialization into an academic field; and (2) careful planning for an academic career. The Commission was well aware that reform would run up against ingrained community habits of governance. Yet success in revising the training of Jesuits was essential to their status and performance as educators in the American academic ethos.

The Macelwane Commission posited a series of grave problems relating to academic practice, administrative practice, quality of teaching in both

---

[32] There is no plan here to send Jesuits to secular universities, though Fr. Macelwane himself was a graduate of the University of California; to the contrary, the Commission wanted to "greatly lessen the need of sending Ours to secular universities" (MR 137). But a door is left open to what is now common Jesuit practice.

undergraduate and graduate programs, the absence of research and other professional engagement on the part of faculty, and the education of the Jesuits themselves. If there were a single word to capture its solution to the problems, it would be professionalization: standards of preparation, practice and achievement should be adopted from other American and Catholic educational institutions and adapted by the Jesuits to their own educational aims and traditions. The Jesuits were not close to measuring up in the view of the Commission, and change was imperative.

When the absence of Jesuit doctoral departments from the list of the ACE received public attention in 1934, Father General Ledochowski pulled the MR from storage. He issued directives, established the Jesuit Educational Association, and appointed its executive secretary subject directly to himself. The impact was immediate, especially on the education of Jesuits and on the politics of Jesuit higher education in the United States; it had far reaching effects on the Jesuit education of their students and thereby on the survival and reputation of their institutions. Comparing today's Jesuit colleges and universities with the institutions described in the MR, one is forced to conclude that the cumulative impact of the MR, the IPC before it and the Commissarius after it, was nothing less than monumental even though some developments took a different form than the General, the Commission itself, and the Commissarius Fr. O'Connell, would have hoped.[33] The story of the last sixty years is one of profound change and steady development, driven by the fierce dedication of some of the leaders of the colleges and universities. No matter how we may judge the current status of the Society's institutions, they are in vastly better shape than they were sixty years ago when the Macelwane Commission submitted its report.

The Jesuits and Scholarship

The Report is a remarkably frank document composed by persons who knew a great deal about the direction of American higher education as well as about the peril confronting the Jesuit institutions if their leaders failed to comprehend that direction and its demands. It is important for what is in it (its analyses and its proposals) and for its long range effects, as difficult as it may be to estimate

---

[33] See Leahy, 54-55 and Fitzgerald, 45-53. The cooperation among institutions was fitful even after the MR, and resistance to O'Connell and the Jesuit Educational Association mounted, in part due to O'Connell's penchant for saying what he thought. Fr. O'Connell was removed by the General in 1937 and the JEA had its powers curtailed and was put under the direction of the Provincials. However, professionalization continued apace, along with advanced education of Jesuits. Fitzgerald is convinced that O'Connell was a key figure in the acceptance of public standards by Jesuit educators, perhaps the most important and far-reaching change of all.

accurately those effects. But it is also important for what it reveals about the attitudes within the American branch of the Society itself toward scholarship. A reading of the document calls forth on this score more questions than answers, but the questions themselves need airing. In this regard the MR remains a pertinent document, not only in a history of Jesuit higher education, but in a history of the communities of the American Assistancy. If one starts a reading of this history with the supposition that scholarship is the primary charism of the Jesuit order, one may be surprised that it is not; if one starts with the hope that it is a high priority of the community, one may be disappointed. However, there are factors which mitigate the bleak intellectual situation in Jesuit communities and colleges described in the MR, and which set a context for an evaluation of the MR's statements and implications.

For one thing, high scholarly interest, ability, and temperament are far from common in Catholic university faculty and graduate students to my observation, even with the happy advance of professionalism in faculty and programs over the past half century. We have and turn out all too few genuine scholars, and hope at least for professional competence. In any case, this is not out of line with American colleges and universities as a whole. A very small percentage of the professorate in the United States turns out a very large percentage of scholarly product.[34] This perhaps indicates that faculty and graduate students, while paying homage to the life of research and writing, in fact choose to emphasize teaching and service, and that the general American practice is closer to the Jesuit one than it is to any ideal cosmopolis of intellectuals and scholars.

In the second place, the crusade in the 1930s to formalize and upgrade institutional governance practice and to set higher standards of education for Jesuits and other faculty is completely intelligible in the context of the changing scene in American higher education in general as well as in terms of the development of American Catholicism. Both sorts of improvement are constantly afoot in educational institutions, whether private, church-related, or state sponsored, whether catching up, keeping up, or getting ahead. In this sense the overriding intent of the MR is the professionalization of Jesuit education, a goal

---

[34] During the 1995 and 1996 academic years 72% of American faculty members reported spending less than eight hours a week on research and scholarly writing, while 97% spent the same time on community service and 97% on consulting or freelance work. 20% of university faculty published nothing in the two year span and another 20% published one or two professional writings or conducted performances. 78% of university faculty members keep research among their professional goals while 84.1% intend to be good colleagues and 98.7% want to be good teachers. Based on these statistics, it would seem that there need be very little worry among educators in Jesuit universities that research will bury good teaching and service. See *The Chronicle of Higher Education: Almanac Issue* 44.1 (August 20, 1997): 26, 29.

that has been accomplished to some degree in the intervening years. The Commission itself seemed to follow an established consensus among leading Jesuit educators that the situation was critical.[35] The Commission did an outstanding job of academic self-criticism in a style familiar in American education as well as in government bureaucracy, the military, and corporations. The strategy of the blue ribbon commission has been and continues to be a recognizable event in American society in general.

Thirdly, Jesuit institutions had been colleges, not research universities, and Jesuits for the most part had been collegiate and preparatory school educators and administrators, not scholars. As the MR insisted, a Jesuit must be a scholar of sorts to work in institutions of higher learning, but he works *as a Jesuit* to form and influence souls and cultures. He knows that he will give up his faculty practice of scholarship to take on administrative and other leadership roles as may be required. For him education itself is a means to an end, and scholarship is a means to a means to an end. Individual Jesuits may be scholars, but theirs is not a society of scholars; they are the *socii Jesu* intent on increasing the number of people who can share in this *societas*.

It must be recognized, then, that the Jesuit vocation, before and after the Second Vatican Council, is a *religious* and *practical* vocation, not a vocation to scholarship. Although Jesuits have become scholars (many of the best Catholic thinkers and scholars in this century have been Jesuits, and the roots of this are buried deep in the history of the order), I doubt that men become Jesuits in order to be scholars though I am sure that some who become Jesuits also wish to be scholars. The MR itself evidences among its authors an acute sense of the importance, value, and procedures of scholarship, it pushes the Jesuits in higher education toward fuller participation in it, and it recommends that all Jesuits be trained in the methods of research scholarship. But even in the MR the corporate mission, while it may involve scholarship, is recognized as more and other than scholarship. The Jesuit mission, the Macelwane Commission pointed out, is education for this life and the next, and to that the life of scholarship may well take a back seat.[36]

While scholarship should be the goal of a Jesuit graduate school and, even if only in a preparatory sense, of Jesuit colleges, and though every Jesuit, in the

---

[35] The Commission was not set up to debate whether there was a problem. Therefore no voices from "the other side" were heard. The General himself identified the problems in his letter of appointment. The Commission members had a perspective from which they addressed the General's requests and had every reason to suppose he would be receptive to their strong recommendations.

[36] William Leahy himself is an example of the fate to which members of religious communities in higher education are liable. Shortly after his book was published he was elevated from his research faculty to an administrative post at Marquette University and shortly thereafter to the presidency of Boston College.

ideal order, ought to be a trained scholar, the Jesuit mission is directed toward soul-saving, character formation, and the transformation of cultures. The tension between over-all religious mission, now phrased as "faith seeking justice," and scholarship will become acute in a Jesuit whose dedication to scholarship may seem inimical to the corporate and institutional goals, or in a Jesuit whose dedication to the corporate mission threatens to outweigh his responsibility to scholarship.[37]

The life of a scholar and that of an administrator are not inimical to one another in the abstract (and perhaps sometimes in practice), but it does appear that one will predominate over the other and even effectively eliminate the other in our age of specialization. There are, then, two flash points in the relationship. The first is the tension between the needs of the Jesuit "system" for capable administrators and the requirements of scholarship. In the short run and in terms of this or that individual Jesuit, this is concrete tension is perfectly understandable. In the long run, however, when the community does not house a significant number of men who are dedicated to a high level of scholarship, the Jesuits will become in the eyes of the academic community an order of administrators. In other words, it is not simply the absence of capable administrators which threaten the Jesuit character of their institutions. The less obvious yet in the long run more devastating absence of Jesuit scholars must be taken into account. In the second place, while there seems no intrinsic contradiction between a religious mission and scholarship, there does seem to be trouble reconciling them in the concrete as statistical evidence indicates. In an activist order such as the Society, the love of God may promote directly ministerial service over the love of learning.

Be that as it may, the ironies in the Report are many. It contains no meditation on scholarship and offers no definition of it. The Jesuit documents, including the MR, display no belief in or positive evaluation of any realm of Sacred Scholarship to which the practice of scholars provides entry. They are not

---

[37] The ruling body of the Society is its General Congregation, a representative legislature meeting approximately every ten years. The 31st, 32nd, and 34th congregations (1965-66; 1975-1976; 1995) all reaffirm the mission to and in higher education, and even mention the importance of scholarship to the church and the world. Only one of them offers a nugatory "spirituality" of scholarship, sketching a connection between the life of the Jesuit scholar and the "paschal mystery" (GC 34, D.16, #398; http://web.lemoyne.edu). The Jesuit mission, and therefore the root of overall Jesuit spirituality, is the service of faith, justice and peace, and each individual mission is to be understood in these terms. See also the American Provincials' letter on education, "The Jesuit Mission in Higher Education: A Letter from the American Provincials, Easter 1978," in Joseph A. Tetlow, S. J., *The Jesuit Mission in Higher Education*, 81-95. The Provincials reaffirm the importance of the commitment to higher education at a time when it was being challenged (# 9-12), but again find the "primary identification" of the Jesuit to be "Christian apostle," "agent of change," and "[man] of ethical concern" (# #15, 20, 23).

driven by the desire for a scholars' world important in itself. Their vision is entirely "practical," that is, pragmatic in its aim. The MR delivers a professional critique of the institutions. Philip Gleason, in a summary remark on the MR in his own *Contending with Modernity,* states that "Fundamental to this problem [the inferiority of Jesuit higher education] was the absence of any deep sense of the importance of nurturing scholarship."[38] From an educational point of view this must have been the most difficult criticism to read. Yet, at the same time, we find at Saint Louis University Frs. Macelwane, Joseph McGlucken, and Alphonse Schwitalla, each of whom had a well deserved national reputation in their fields of scholarship and the capacity to evaluate education and to lead the institution in steady improvement over several decades.

The MR states that the colleges and universities were being informally, perhaps badly, administered by Jesuits who knew little of current academic standards or standard administrative and business practice. Yet, at the same time, men with energy and intelligence were in place, or in place to get in place, to work a transformation of institutions which have since deserved their reputation for competence. These men were able to capitalize upon the criticisms delivered by the MR, by Commissarius Daniel O'Connell and the JEA, and by the Father General, and to respond to them for the most part realistically and constructively. Ambition and clear sight has, though with difficulty, won out over philistinism and educational anachronism often enough to give one hope for the institutions and for the Jesuits as a community. When one joins this achievement to the change in the stance of the Society from anti-modern defense of ecclesiastical orthodoxy to leadership of the Catholic creative engagement of modernity, one is brought to realize again the extraordinary resilience of this community and the flexibility of its spirituality.

Nonetheless, the changes recommended by the MR would, according to the MR itself, run up against significant anti-intellectualism in the Jesuit communities:

> It is not pleasant to hear one of Ours who had spent some time in a non-Catholic university state that what he would miss most would be the lack of the atmosphere of encouragement with which he was surrounded while there. The lack of encouragement is a very common and too true complaint of many of Ours who are capable of producing work of merit, but receive no encouragement until all ambition and interest are lost (MR 43).

---

[38] Gleason, 180. Even in the theoretic ethos of Bernard Lonergan's *Insight: A Study of Human Understanding* the crucial notion of Cosmopolis is pragmatic—its value is in its service to the world of commonsense. See *Insight* (New York: Philosophical Library, 1957), 238-241.

In fact, the MR is driven to hope that in the future "...a general attitude of sympathetic encouragement of scholarship and scholarly activities be manifested in our communities; and that Superiors effectively discourage any contrary attitude," something apparently not true at that time (MR 184).

It also finds that mediocrity may be favored in Jesuit recruitment and training:

> ...we have frequently admitted pious but useless men. We have failed or neglected to drive home the fact that talent which is above mediocre is an essential part of a vocation to the Society. Too often Ours have zealously labored to develop a student's vocation without developing his character. ...The Society is not a refuge for fearsome souls....Again and again our Fathers who had taught certain novices during their college days have been dismayed by the effects of the novitiate training on these students. Those who had been sane and normal as students, developed in the meantime a warped and distorted view of life in general, and of life in the Society in particular, that threatened to minimize, if not ruin entirely, their future usefulness in the Society in any capacity (MR 118-122, 124).[39]

Other Jesuit literature bears out a claim that this problem has continued into the present even though the educational demands on young Jesuits have increased. That there remains something quite short of consensus in an understanding of the Jesuit vocation (never mind the Jesuit voices raised against the "desiccated" scholars in universities "cranking out yuppie intelligentia..." and "the spurious free-floating intellectual simply pursuing pure knowledge") is vividly stated by John Coleman:

> American Jesuits at present do not have anything like a coherent operative philosophy or rationale for the intellectual life or for our insistence on a well-trained ministry in all our apostolates. ...I do not find that anything now compels widespread consent among Jesuits to ground our historic and present commitment to the intellectual life and a learned ministry.[40]

Realizing that there is no consensus in society as a whole about the role of the intellectual, Coleman thereupon favors the development of a spirituality which joins the vocation of the Jesuit with the intellectual life, indicating that the

---

[39] It is likely that the term mediocre, if its root in the Jesuit usage of the term *mediocris*, means the English "average."

[40] John A. Coleman, S.J., "A Company of Critics: Jesuits and the Intellectual Life," in *Studies in the Spirituality of Jesuits* 22 (November 1990), 11-12, 29. See a more recent reflection echoing Coleman's call for a deepened appreciation among Jesuits of the intellectual life: Francis X. Clooney, S.J., "Jesuit Scholarship in a Post-Modern Age: A Site for Material Related to a Conversation among Jesuits on the Practice of Scholarship..." (http://fmwww.bc.edu/jspma/).

intellectual life is far from taken for granted among Jesuits:

> ...every Jesuit is called to be an intellectual ...an essential component of each Jesuit's vocation and every apostolate...every Jesuit remains an educator...every Jesuit is called in some form to the ministry of the word, to communication of values, and to education.[41]

Laudable as his prescription undoubtedly is, it reveals that in 1989 the situation of the scholar in Jesuit communities may not have changed much from 1931. In fact Coleman, himself a well known Jesuit scholar, does not discuss the role of the scholar in Jesuit life at all and restricts himself to arguing that the Society is (or should be) a society of culture critics. We are brought back again to the issue of the aim of the Society. Coleman leads us to believe that it not scholarship but education in character and values as well as religion that is the aim of Jesuit life. But he shows that it is not agreed that the Jesuit is to be an intellectual, much less a scholar.[42]

That the Jesuits are not an order of scholars is plain enough, but Jesuit anti-intellectualism and the lack of appreciation of scholarship as a way of life for Jesuits does require explanation. Both their well deserved reputation as educators and their history up to the Suppression of 1773 would lead one to expect something different. So also would the prominence of some Jesuits in American intellectual and scholarly life, among them Bernard Lonergan, John Courtney Murray, and Walter Ong, the latter perhaps the best known and most

---

[41] Coleman, 14-15. There are vigorous Catholic critics of the post-Vatican II social turn in Jesuit ministry and education, some of whom are themselves Jesuits. See James Hitchcock, *The Pope and the Jesuits: John Paul II and the New Order in the Society of Jesus* (New York: National Committee of Catholic Laymen, 1984) and Malachi Martin, *The Jesuits: The Society of Jesus and the Betrayal of the Roman Catholic Church* (New York: Linden Press, 1987). See also Joseph M. Becker, S. J., *The Re-formed Jesuits: A History of Changes in Jesuit Formation During the Decade 1965-1975* (San Francisco: Ignatius Press, 1992).

[42] As the reader must have noticed, I skip over the problems of definition of terms such as intellectual and scholar. I am willing to accept Coleman's usage, namely, an intellectual is a culture critic, and as such needs advanced education and some ability and training for scholarship and knowledge of its methods. On the terms scholar and scholarship, I prefer the tight definition of them suggested by Bernard Lonergan:

> I wish to propose a convention. Let the term, science, be reserved for knowledge that is contained in principles and laws and is either verified universally or else is revised. Let the term, scholarship, be employed to denote the learning that consists in a commonsense grasp of the commonsense thought, speech, action of distant places and/or times. Men of letters, linguists, exegetes, historians would be named scholars.

See *Method in Theology* (New York: Herder and Herder, 1972), 233-34. In Coleman's usage, all Jesuits are called to be intellectuals while some might be scholars, some scientists, and some both. I think the MR holds to the wider convention, using the term scholarship to include both the humanities and the sciences insofar as they methodically seek new knowledge.

influential of the three outside Catholic circles. Scholarship seems adventitious to a Jesuit vocation. It seems that it has not been looked upon with automatic understanding and approval by many Jesuits though the rudiments of scholarship in the form of a research doctorate are now highly prized. The Commission thought that the key to a solution of the problems was to train younger Jesuits in scholarship:

> Setting the doctorate as our normal goal will compel the early study of individual talents which is prescribed in the Society, and will establish intellectual life interests for all of Ours; ...The general possession of the doctorate will lift the intellectual level of our communities....The marked growth in individual scholarship, resulting from this policy will react favorably on the spiritual life of Ours, for the reason that it will remove the indifference, discouragement and lack of interest which now effect many of Ours so adversely both intellectually and spiritually (MR 114-115).

If witnesses such as Coleman and Francis Clooney are to be credited, the Jesuit intellectual and scholar, in that essential aspect of his identity, may find himself without the empathy of his community.

Anti-intellectualism among Jesuits may have been fostered prior to the Council (1962-65) by the general social situation and attitudes of Catholics which Jesuits were sure to share,[43] as well as by the bitter anti-modernism of the leaders of the Catholic Church and of prominent Jesuits.[44] After the Council the same anti-intellectualism may have been fostered by the activist social

---

[43] See O'Brien's introduction and the first chapter in his edited volume. While he is careful to avoid saying that there is anti-Catholicism in the state system, one of his interlocutors and critics, Philip Burke, has no such hesitation (39-50). O'Brien does recount the shortcomings in the Catholic social and intellectual situation in the late thirties, and he does decry the lack of interest among Catholics in the intellectual and scholarly life for several reasons. Understandably, he does not even refer to Catholic anti-modernism as a factor. In that same volume the essay by Justin E. West, "Scholars Have Stomachs," reveals the low estimate of worth administrators put on faculty in Catholic institutions in terms of salary and research support. One is forced to conclude that among Catholic educators in general research and scholarship were not high priorities, even in institutions with graduate schools.

[44] On Catholic anti-modernism see Gannon, note 10 above; R. Scott Appleby, *"Church and Age Unite!": the Modernist Impulse in American Catholicism* (Notre Dame, IN: University of Notre Dame Press, 1992); Lester P. Kurtz, *The Politics of Heresy: The Modernist Crisis in Roman Catholicism* (Berkeley, CA: University of California Press, 1986); David G. Schultenover, S.J., *A View from Rome: On the Eve of the Modernist Crisis* (New York: Fordham University Press, 1993); Marvin R. O'Connell, *Critics on Trial: An Introduction to the Catholic Modernist Crisis* (Washington, DC: Catholic University Press, 1994); Thomas Shelley, *Dunwoodie: The History of St. Joseph's Seminary* (Westminster, MD: Christian Classics, 1993). For a social history of the American Jesuits in this period of anti-modernism see Peter McDonough *Men Astutely Trained: A History of the Jesuits in the American Century* (New York: Free Press, 1992).

engagement of Jesuits in the life of "faith seeking justice" and accompanying suspicion of "mere academics," putting into question the three decade long effort to improve the reputation of the institutions for scholarship. In addition to the presence in Jesuit life (as in all human life) of the general bias of common sense against theory,[45] social and ecclesiastical conditions influenced the community in the direction of anti-intellectualism. But still it remains odd, indeed ironic once again, that the religious community with the best reputation for intellectual leadership should justly suffer criticism by its own confreres for what seems to be a pervasive prejudice against the intellectual life in general and the scholarly life in particular.

As I warned at the outset, many more questions remain. What is the root of the problem which the MR, and later John Coleman and Francis Clooney address? Is it tension between ideals, namely classical humanism versus modern specialization, or between teaching (practice) and research (theory)? Is the cause a division between factions in the Society regarding priorities in its work, more recently between conventional education vs the forwarding of human liberation? Or is the Jesuit situation merely reflective of the universal plight of the scholar and the intellectual, of a constant tension between them and their communities?

Again, why are the novitiates seed beds of anti-intellectualism? Have the admission standards of the Society encouraged or at least abetted anti-intellectualism? What is the attitude toward scholarship among those responsible for the spiritual direction of young Jesuits, and how are their spiritual directors and instructors themselves shaped and picked?

To return at last to William Leahy, is there something about religious dedication itself that lessens one's devotion to the search for "new knowledge," for an understanding that is theoretical rather than or in addition to practical? Religious commitment certainly does not preclude scholarship and scholarly productivity (Walter Ong and Joseph Fitzmyer, both Jesuit scholars, are living proof of that!) but religious communities may not value it sufficiently and may aim so intently at fulfilling religious and educational interests that the connection between scholarship and well-being in this life and the next may be obscured. Does the very spiritual vision and experience of an intensely practical vocation too easily become inhospitable to the detachment and to the contemplative and individualistic qualities of the consciousness of the scholar? Especially in the case of the Jesuits, the person who intends to change the conditions promoting injustice, loss of faith, and suffering in "the present age" is making a different sort of commitment than is the person who spends a life learning things that just

---

[45] Lonergan, *Insight*, 225ff.

may (or may not) make a difference in the social situation of the future. Only the rare person, such as John Dewey, can make and carry both commitments. What a Jesuit he would have made!

CONTRIBUTORS

Michael D. Barber, S.J., is professor of philosophy at Saint Louis University and is author of *Guardians of Dialogue* (1993) and *Ethical Hermeneutics* (1997).

Patrick W. Carey is chairman of the Department of Religious Studies at Marquette University, author of *The Roman Catholics* (1993), and editor of *American Catholic Religious Thought* (1987).

Alice Gallin, O. S. U., has been professor of history at the College of New Rochelle, Director of the Association of Catholic Colleges and Universities, visiting research scholar at the Catholic University of America, visiting professor of theological studies at Saint Louis University, and is author of *Midwives to Nazism* (1986) and *Independence and a New Partnership in Catholic Higher Education* (1996). Her latest book, *Negotiating Identity: Catholic Higher Education Since 1960,* will be published in 1999.

James F. Hitchcock is professor in the history department of Saint Louis University, and author of *The Decline and Fall of Radical Catholicism* (1971) and *Catholicism and Modernity* (1979).

Richard T. Hughes is distinguished professor in the religion division of Pepperdine University. He is author of *Reviving the Ancient Faith* (1996)and editor of *Models for Christian Education* (1997).

Sandra Yocum Mize is associate professor of religious studies at the University of Dayton. She is editor of *American Catholic Traditions* (1997) and author of *Defending Roman Loyalties* (1990).

William R. Rehg, S. J., is associate professor in the philosophy department of Saint Louis University. He is author of *Insight and Solidarity* (1994) and co-editor of *Deliberative Democracy* (1997).

William M. Shea is professor of American religion and theology at Saint Louis University, author of *The Naturalists and the Supernatural* (1984), and editor of *Knowledge and Belief in America* (1995).

221

Paul J. Shore is associate professor of education at Saint Louis University, author of *The Myth of the University* (1992) and co-author of *Seasons of Change* (1996).

Charles H. Wilson was a participant in several of the cases on Catholic higher education argued before the Supreme Court and state courts, in some as counsel of record and others as lead counsel. He was partner in Williams and Connolly, and is now senior staff attorney for the Bazelon Center for Mental Health Law in Washington, D. C.

South Florida Studies in the History of Judaism

240001	Lectures on Judaism in the Academy and in the Humanities	Neusner
240002	Lectures on Judaism in the History of Religion	Neusner
240003	Self-Fulfilling Prophecy: Exile and Return in the History of Judaism	Neusner
240004	The Canonical History of Ideas: The Place of the So-called Tannaite Midrashim, Mekhilta Attributed to R. Ishmael, Sifra, Sifré to Numbers, and Sifré to Deuteronomy	Neusner
240005	Ancient Judaism: Debates and Disputes, Second Series	Neusner
240006	The Hasmoneans and Their Supporters: From Mattathias to the Death of John Hyrcanus I	Sievers
240007	Approaches to Ancient Judaism: New Series, Volume One	Neusner
240008	Judaism in the Matrix of Christianity	Neusner
240009	Tradition as Selectivity: Scripture, Mishnah, Tosefta, and Midrash in the Talmud of Babylonia	Neusner
240010	The Tosefta: Translated from the Hebrew: Sixth Division Tohorot	Neusner
240011	In the Margins of the Midrash: Sifre Ha'azinu Texts, Commentaries and Reflections	Basser
240012	Language as Taxonomy: The Rules for Using Hebrew and Aramaic in the Babylonia Talmud	Neusner
240013	The Rules of Composition of the Talmud of Babylonia: The Cogency of the Bavli's Composite	Neusner
240014	Understanding the Rabbinic Mind: Essays on the Hermeneutic of Max Kadushin	Ochs
240015	Essays in Jewish Historiography	Rapoport-Albert
240016	The Golden Calf and the Origins of the Jewish Controversy	Bori/Ward
240017	Approaches to Ancient Judaism: New Series, Volume Two	Neusner
240018	The Bavli That Might Have Been: The Tosefta's Theory of Mishnah Commentary Compared With the Bavli's	Neusner
240019	The Formation of Judaism: In Retrospect and Prospect	Neusner
240020	Judaism in Society: The Evidence of the Yerushalmi,Toward the Natural History of a Religion	Neusner
240021	The Enchantments of Judaism: Rites of Transformation from Birth Through Death	Neusner
240022	Åbo Addresses	Neusner
240023	The City of God in Judaism and Other Comparative and Methodological Studies	Neusner
240024	The Bavli's One Voice: Types and Forms of Analytical Discourse and their Fixed Order of Appearance	Neusner
240025	The Dura-Europos Synagogue: A Re-evaluation (1932-1992)	Gutmann
240026	Precedent and Judicial Discretion: The Case of Joseph ibn Lev	Morell
240027	Max Weinreich Geschichte der jiddischen Sprachforschung	Frakes
240028	Israel: Its Life and Culture, Volume I	Pedersen
240029	Israel: Its Life and Culture, Volume II	Pedersen
240030	The Bavli's One Statement: The Metapropositional Program of Babylonian Talmud Tractate Zebahim Chapters One and Five	Neusner

240031	The Oral Torah: The Sacred Books of Judaism: An Introduction: Second Printing	Neusner
240032	The Twentieth Century Construction of "Judaism:" Essays on the Religion of Torah in the History of Religion	Neusner
240033	How the Talmud Shaped Rabbinic Discourse	Neusner
240034	The Discourse of the Bavli: Language, Literature, and Symbolism: Five Recent Findings	Neusner
240035	The Law Behind the Laws: The Bavli's Essential Discourse	Neusner
240036	Sources and Traditions: Types of Compositions in the Talmud of Babylonia	Neusner
240037	How to Study the Bavli: The Languages, Literatures, and Lessons of the Talmud of Babylonia	Neusner
240038	The Bavli's Primary Discourse: Mishnah Commentary: Its Rhetorical Paradigms and their Theological Implications	Neusner
240039	Midrash Aleph Beth	Sawyer
240040	Jewish Thought in the 20th Century: An Introduction in the Talmud of Babylonia Tractate Moed Qatan	Schweid
240041	Diaspora Jews and Judaism: Essays in Honor of, and in Dialogue with, A. Thomas Kraabel	Overman/MacLennan
240042	The Bavli: An Introduction	Neusner
240043	The Bavli's Massive Miscellanies: The Problem of Agglutinative Discourse in the Talmud of Babylonia	Neusner
240044	The Foundations of the Theology of Judaism: An Anthology Part II: Torah	Neusner
240045	Form-Analytical Comparison in Rabbinic Judaism: Structure and Form in *The Fathers* and *The Fathers According to Rabbi Nathan*	Neusner
240046	Essays on Hebrew	Weinberg
240047	The Tosefta: An Introduction	Neusner
240048	The Foundations of the Theology of Judaism: An Anthology Part III: Israel	Neusner
240049	The Study of Ancient Judaism, Volume I: Mishnah, Midrash, Siddur	Neusner
240050	The Study of Ancient Judaism, Volume II: The Palestinian and Babylonian Talmuds	Neusner
240051	Take Judaism, for Example: Studies toward the Comparison of Religions	Neusner
240052	From Eden to Golgotha: Essays in Biblical Theology	Moberly
240053	The Principal Parts of the Bavli's Discourse: A Preliminary Taxonomy: Mishnah Commentary, Sources, Traditions and Agglutinative Miscellanies	Neusner
240054	Barabbas and Esther and Other Studies in the Judaic Illumination of Earliest Christianity	Aus
240055	Targum Studies, Volume I: Textual and Contextual Studies in the Pentateuchal Targums	Flesher
240056	Approaches to Ancient Judaism: New Series, Volume Three, Historical and Literary Studies	Neusner
240057	The Motherhood of God and Other Studies	Gruber
240058	The Analytic Movement: Hayyim Soloveitchik and his Circle	Solomon
240059	Recovering the Role of Women: Power and Authority in Rabbinic Jewish Society	Haas

240060	The Relation between Herodotus' *History* and Primary History	Mandell/Freedman
240061	The First Seven Days: A Philosophical Commentary on the Creation of Genesis	Samuelson
240062	The Bavli's Intellectual Character: The Generative Problematic: In Bavli Baba Qamma Chapter One And Bavli Shabbat Chapter One	Neusner
240063	The Incarnation of God: The Character of Divinity in Formative Judaism: Second Printing	Neusner
240064	Moses Kimhi: Commentary on the Book of Job	Basser/Walfish
240066	Death and Birth of Judaism: Second Printing	Neusner
240067	Decoding the Talmud's Exegetical Program	Neusner
240068	Sources of the Transformation of Judaism	Neusner
240069	The Torah in the Talmud: A Taxonomy of the Uses of Scripture in the Talmud, Volume I	Neusner
240070	The Torah in the Talmud: A Taxonomy of the Uses of Scripture in the Talmud, Volume II	Neusner
240071	The Bavli's Unique Voice: A Systematic Comparison of the Talmud of Babylonia and the Talmud of the Land of Israel, Volume One	Neusner
240072	The Bavli's Unique Voice: A Systematic Comparison of the Talmud of Babylonia and the Talmud of the Land of Israel, Volume Two	Neusner
240073	The Bavli's Unique Voice: A Systematic Comparison of the Talmud of Babylonia and the Talmud of the Land of Israel, Volume Three	Neusner
240074	Bits of Honey: Essays for Samson H. Levey	Chyet/Ellenson
240075	The Mystical Study of Ruth: *Midrash HaNe'elam* of the Zohar to the Book of Ruth	Englander
240076	The Bavli's Unique Voice: A Systematic Comparison of the Talmud of Babylonia and the Talmud of the Land of Israel, Volume Four	Neusner
240077	The Bavli's Unique Voice: A Systematic Comparison of the Talmud of Babylonia and the Talmud of the Land of Israel, Volume Five	Neusner
240078	The Bavli's Unique Voice: A Systematic Comparison of the Talmud of Babylonia and the Talmud of the Land of Israel, Volume Six	Neusner
240079	The Bavli's Unique Voice: A Systematic Comparison of the Talmud of Babylonia and the Talmud of the Land of Israel, Volume Seven	Neusner
240080	Are There Really Tannaitic Parallels to the Gospels?	Neusner
240081	Approaches to Ancient Judaism: New Series, Volume Four, Religious and Theological Studies	Neusner
240082	Approaches to Ancient Judaism: New Series, Volume Five, Historical, Literary, and Religious Studies	Basser/Fishbane
240083	Ancient Judaism: Debates and Disputes, Third Series	Neusner
240084	Judaic Law from Jesus to the Mishnah	Neusner
240085	Writing with Scripture: Second Printing	Neusner/Green
240086	Foundations of Judaism: Second Printing	Neusner

240087	Judaism and Zoroastrianism at the Dusk of Late Antiquity	Neusner
240088	Judaism States Its Theology	Neusner
240089	The Judaism behind the Texts I.A	Neusner
240090	The Judaism behind the Texts I.B	Neusner
240091	Stranger at Home	Neusner
240092	Pseudo-Rabad: Commentary to Sifre Deuteronomy	Basser
240093	FromText to Historical Context in Rabbinic Judaism	Neusner
240094	Formative Judaism	Neusner
240095	Purity in Rabbinic Judaism	Neusner
240096	Was Jesus of Nazareth the Messiah?	McMichael
240097	The Judaism behind the Texts I.C	Neusner
240098	The Judaism behind the Texts II	Neusner
240099	The Judaism behind the Texts III	Neusner
240100	The Judaism behind the Texts IV	Neusner
240101	The Judaism behind the Texts V	Neusner
240102	The Judaism the Rabbis Take for Granted	Neusner
240103	From Text to Historical Context in Rabbinic Judaism V. II	Neusner
240104	From Text to Historical Context in Rabbinic Judaism V. III	Neusner
240105	Samuel, Saul, and Jesus: Three Early Palestinian Jewish Christian Gospel Haggadoth	Aus
240106	What is Midrash? And a Midrash Reader	Neusner
240107	Rabbinic Judaism: Disputes and Debates	Neusner
240108	Why There Never Was a "Talmud of Caesarea"	Neusner
240109	Judaism after the Death of "The Death of God"	Neusner
240110	Approaches to Ancient Judaism	Neusner
240112	The Judaic Law of Baptism	Neusner
240113	The Documentary Foundation of Rabbinic Culture	Neusner
240114	Understanding Seeking Faith, Volume Four	Neusner
240115	Paul and Judaism: An Anthropological Approach	Laato
240116	Approaches to Ancient Judaism, New Series, Volume Eight	Neusner
240119	Theme and Context in Biblical Lists	Scolnic
240120	Where the Talmud Comes From	Neusner
240121	The Initial Phases of the Talmud, Volume Three: Social Ethics	Neusner
240122	Are the Talmuds Interchangeable? Christine Hayes's Blunder	Neusner
240123	The Initial Phases of the Talmud, Volume One: Exegesis of Scripture	Neusner
240124	The Initial Phases of the Talmud, Volume Two: Exemplary Virtue	Neusner
240125	The Initial Phases of the Talmud, Volume Four: Theology	Neusner
240126	From Agnon to Oz	Bargad
240127	Talmudic Dialectics, Volume I: Tractate Berakhot and the Divisions of Appointed Times and Women	Neusner
240128	Talmudic Dialectics, Volume II: The Divisions of Damages and Holy Things and Tractate Niddah	Neusner
240129	The Talmud: Introduction and Reader	Neusner
240130	Gesher Vakesher: Bridges and Bonds The Life of Leon Kronish	Green
240131	Beyond Catastrophe	Neusner

240132	Ancient Judaism, Fourth Series	Neusner
240133	Formative Judaism, New Series: Current Issues and Arguments Volume One	Neusner
240134	Sects and Scrolls	Davies
240135	Religion and Law	Neusner
240136	Approaches to Ancient Judaism, New Series, Volume Nine	Neusner
240137	Uppsala Addresses	Neusner
240138	Jews and Christians in the Life and Thought of Hugh of St. Victor	Moore
240140	Jews, Pagans, and Christians in the Golan Heights	Gregg/Urman
240141	Rosenzweig on Profane/Secular History	Vogel
240142	Approaches to Ancient Judaism, New Series, Volume Ten	Neusner
240143	Archaeology and the Galilee	Edwards/McCullough
240144	Rationality and Structure	Neusner
240145	Formative Judaism, New Series: Current Issues and Arguments Volume Two	Neusner
240146	Ancient Judaism, Religious and Theological Perspectives First Series	Neusner
240147	The Good Creator	Gelander
240148	The Mind of Classical Judaism, Volume IV, The Philosophy and Political Economy of Formative Judaism: The Mishnah's System of the Social Order	Neusner
240149	The Mind of Classical Judaism, Volume I, Modes of Thought:: Making Connections and Drawing Conclusions	Neusner
240150	The Mind of Classical Judaism, Volume II, From Philosophy to Religion	Neusner
241051	The Mind of Classical Judaism, Volume III, What is "Israel"? Social Thought in the Formative Age	Neusner
240152	The Tosefta, Translated from the Hebrew: Fifth Division, Qodoshim, The Order of Holy Things	Neusner
240153	The Theology of Rabbinic Judaism: A Prolegomenon	Neusner
240154	Approaches to Ancient Judaism, New Series, Volume Eleven	Neusner
240155	Pesiqta Rabbati: A Synoptic Edition of Pesiqta Rabbati Based upon all Extant Manuscripts and the Editio Princeps, V. I	Ulmer
240156	The Place of the Tosefta in the Halakhah of Formative Judaism: What Alberdina Houtman Didn't Notice	Neusner
240157	"Caught in the Act," Walking on the Sea, and The Release of Barabbas Revisited	Aus
240158	Approaches to Ancient Judaism, New Series, Volume Twelve	Neusner
240159	The Halakhah of the Oral Torah, A Religious Commentary, Introduction and Volume I, Part One, Between Israel and God	Neusner
240160	Claudian Policymaking and the Early Imperial Repression of Judaism at Rome	Slingerland
240161	Rashi's Commentary on Psalms 1–89 with English Translation, Introducion and Notes	Gruber
240162	Peace, In Deed	Garber/Libowitz
240163	Mediators of the Divine	Berchman
240164	Approaches to Ancient Judaism, New Series, Volume Thirteen	Neusner
240165	Targum Studies, Volume Two: Targum and Peshitta	Flesher
240166	The Text and I: Writings of Samson H. Levey	Chyet

240167	The Documentary Form-History of Rabbinic Literature, I. The Documentary Forms of Mishnah	Neusner
240168	Louis Finkelstein and the Conservative Movement	Greenbaum
240169	Invitation to the Talmud: A Teaching Book	Neusner
240170	Invitation to Midrash: The Workings of Rabbinic Bible Interpretation, A Teaching Book	Neusner
240171	The Documentary Form-History of Rabbinic Literature, II. The Aggadic Sector:Tractate Abot, Abot deRabbi Natan, Sifra, Sifré to Numbers and Sifré to Deuteronomy	Neusner
240172	The Documentary Form-History of Rabbinic Literature, III. The Aggadic Sector: Mekhilta Attributed to R. Ishmael and Genesis Rabbah	Neusner
240173	The Documentary Form-History of Rabbinic Literature, IV. The Aggadic Sector: Leviticus Rabbah and Pesiqta deRab Kahana	Neusner
240174	The Documentary Form-History of Rabbinic Literature, V. The Aggadic Sector: Song of Songs Rabbah, Ruth Rabbah, Lamentations Rabbati, and Esther Rabbah I	Neusner
240175	The Documentary Form-History of Rabbinic Literature, VI. The Halakhic Sector: The Talmud of the Land of Israel A. Tractates Berakhot and Shabbat through Taanit	Neusner
240176	The Documentary Form-History of Rabbinic Literature, VI. The Halakhic Sector: The Talmud of the Land of Israel B. Tractates Megillah through Qiddushin	Neusner
240177	The Documentary Form-History of Rabbinic Literature, VI. The Halakhic Sector: The Talmud of the Land of Israel C. Tractates Sotah through Horayot and Niddah	Neusner
240178	The Documentary Form-History of Rabbinic Literature, VII. The Halakhic Sector: The Talmud of the Land of Israel A. Tractates Berakhot and Shabbat through Pesahim	Neusner
240179	The Documentary Form-History of Rabbinic Literature, VII. The Halakhic Sector: The Talmud of Babylonia B. Tractates Yoma through Ketubot	Neusner
240180	The Documentary Form-History of Rabbinic Literature, VII. The Halakhic Sector: The Talmud of Babylonia C. Tractates Nedarim through Baba Mesia	Neusner
240181	The Documentary Form-History of Rabbinic Literature, VII. The Halakhic Sector: The Talmud of Babylonia D. Tractates Baba Batra through Horayot	Neusner
240182	The Documentary Form-History of Rabbinic Literature, VII. The Halakhic Sector: The Talmud of Babylonia E. Tractates Zebahim through Bekhorot	Neusner
240183	The Documentary Form-History of Rabbinic Literature, VII. The Halakhic Sector: The Talmud of Babylonia F. Tractates Arakhin through Niddah and Conclusions	Neusner
240184	Messages to Moscow: And Other Current Lectures on Learning and Community in Judaism	Neusner
240185	The Economics of the Mishnah	Neusner
240186	Approaches to Ancient Judaism, New Series, Volume Fourteen	Neusner
240187	Jewish Law from Moses to the Mishnah	Neusner
240188	The Language and the Law of God	Calabi

240189	Pseudo-Rabad: Commentary to Sifre Numbers	Basser
240190	How Adin Steinstalz Misrepresents the Talmud	Neusner
240191	How the Rabbis Liberated Women	Neusner
240192	From Scripture to 70	Neusner
240193	The Levites: Their Emergence as a Second-Class Priesthood	Nurmela
240194	Sifra	Ginsberg
240195	Approaches to Ancient Judaism, New Series, Volume Fifteen	Neusner
240196	What, Exactly, Did the Rabbinic Sages Mean by the "Oral Torah"?	Neusner
240197	The Book of Job with a Commentary for Our Times	Sacks
240198	Symbol and Theology in Early Judaism	Neusner
240199	The Ecological Message of the Torah: Knowledge, Concepts, and Laws which Made Survival in a Land of "Milk and Honey" Possible	Hütteman
240200	Pesiqta Rabbati: A Synoptic Edition of Pesiqta Rabbati Based upon All Extant Manuscripts and the Editio Princeps, Volume II	Ulmer
240201	Concepts of Class in Ancient Israel	Sneed
240202	The Rabbinic Traditions about the Pharisees before 70, Part I, The Masters	Neusner
240203	The Rabbinic Traditions about the Pharisees before 70, Part II, The Houses	Neusner
240204	The Rabbinic Traditions about the Pharisees before 70, Part III, Conclusions	Neusner
240205	Aphrahat and Judaism: The Christian-Jewish Argument in Fourth-Century Iran	Neusner
240206	Chronology and Papponymy: A List of the High Priests of the Persian Period	Scolnic
240207	The Native Category-Formations of the Aggadah, I. The Later Midrash-Compilations	Neusner
240208	The Native Category-Formations of the Aggadah, II, The Earlier Midrash-Compilations	Neusner
240209	Approaches to Ancient Judaism, New Series, Volume Sixteen	Neusner

South Florida Academic Commentary Series

243001	The Talmud of Babylonia, An Academic Commentary, Volume XI, Bavli Tractate Moed Qatan	Neusner
243002	The Talmud of Babylonia, An Academic Commentary, Volume XXXIV, Bavli Tractate Keritot	Neusner
243003	The Talmud of Babylonia, An Academic Commentary, Volume XVII, Bavli Tractate Sotah	Neusner
243004	The Talmud of Babylonia, An Academic Commentary, Volume XXIV, Bavli Tractate Makkot	Neusner
243005	The Talmud of Babylonia, An Academic Commentary, Volume XXXII, Bavli Tractate Arakhin	Neusner
243006	The Talmud of Babylonia, An Academic Commentary, Volume VI, Bavli Tractate Sukkah	Neusner
243007	The Talmud of Babylonia, An Academic Commentary, Volume XII, Bavli Tractate Hagigah	Neusner

243008	The Talmud of Babylonia, An Academic Commentary, Volume XXVI, Bavli Tractate Horayot	Neusner
243009	The Talmud of Babylonia, An Academic Commentary, Volume XXVII, Bavli Tractate Shebuot	Neusner
243010	The Talmud of Babylonia, An Academic Commentary, Volume XXXIII, Bavli Tractate Temurah	Neusner
243011	The Talmud of Babylonia, An Academic Commentary, Volume XXXV, Bavli Tractates Meilah and Tamid	Neusner
243012	The Talmud of Babylonia, An Academic Commentary, Volume VIII, Bavli Tractate Rosh Hashanah	Neusner
243013	The Talmud of Babylonia, An Academic Commentary, Volume V, Bavli Tractate Yoma	Neusner
243014	The Talmud of Babylonia, An Academic Commentary, Volume XXXVI, Bavli Tractate Niddah	Neusner
243015	The Talmud of Babylonia, An Academic Commentary, Volume XX, Bavli Tractate Baba Qamma	Neusner
243016	The Talmud of Babylonia, An Academic Commentary, Volume XXXI, Bavli Tractate Bekhorot	Neusner
243017	The Talmud of Babylonia, An Academic Commentary, Volume XXX, Bavli Tractate Hullin	Neusner
243018	The Talmud of Babylonia, An Academic Commentary, Volume VII, Bavli Tractate Besah	Neusner
243019	The Talmud of Babylonia, An Academic Commentary, Volume X, Bavli Tractate Megillah	Neusner
243020	The Talmud of Babylonia, An Academic Commentary, Volume XXVIII, Bavli Tractate Zebahim A. Chapters I through VII	Neusner
243021	The Talmud of Babylonia, An Academic Commentary, Volume XXI, Bavli Tractate Baba Mesia, A. Chapters I through VI	Neusner
243022	The Talmud of Babylonia, An Academic Commentary, Volume XXII, Bavli Tractate Baba Batra, A. Chapters I through VI	Neusner
243023	The Talmud of Babylonia, An Academic Commentary, Volume XXIX, Bavli Tractate Menahot, A. Chapters I through VI	Neusner
243024	The Talmud of Babylonia, An Academic Commentary, Volume I, Bavli Tractate Berakhot	Neusner
243025	The Talmud of Babylonia, An Academic Commentary, Volume XXV, Bavli Tractate Abodah Zarah	Neusner
243026	The Talmud of Babylonia, An Academic Commentary, Volume XXIII, Bavli Tractate Sanhedrin, A. Chapters I through VII	Neusner
243027	The Talmud of Babylonia, A Complete Outline, Part IV, The Division of Holy Things; A: From Tractate Zabahim through Tractate Hullin	Neusner
243028	The Talmud of Babylonia, An Academic Commentary, Volume XIV, Bavli Tractate Ketubot, A. Chapters I through VI	Neusner

243029	The Talmud of Babylonia, An Academic Commentary, Volume IV, Bavli Tractate Pesahim, A. Chapters I through VII	Neusner
243030	The Talmud of Babylonia, An Academic Commentary, Volume III, Bavli Tractate Erubin, A. ChaptersI through V	Neusner
243031	The Talmud of Babylonia, A Complete Outline, Part III, The Division of Damages; A: From Tractate Baba Qamma through Tractate Baba Batra	Neusner
243032	The Talmud of Babylonia, An Academic Commentary, Volume II, Bavli Tractate Shabbat, Volume A, Chapters One through Twelve	Neusner
243033	The Talmud of Babylonia, An Academic Commentary, Volume II, Bavli Tractate Shabbat, Volume B, Chapters Thirteen through Twenty-four	Neusner
243034	The Talmud of Babylonia, An Academic Commentary, Volume XV, Bavli Tractate Nedarim	Neusner
243035	The Talmud of Babylonia, An Academic Commentary, Volume XVIII, Bavli Tractate Gittin	Neusner
243036	The Talmud of Babylonia, An Academic Commentary, Volume XIX, Bavli Tractate Qiddushin	Neusner
243037	The Talmud of Babylonia, A Complete Outline, Part IV, The Division of Holy Things; B: From Tractate Berakot through Tractate Niddah	Neusner
243038	The Talmud of Babylonia, A Complete Outline, Part III, The Division of Damages; B: From Tractate Sanhedrin through Tractate Shebuot	Neusner
243039	The Talmud of Babylonia, A Complete Outline, Part I, Tractate Berakhot and the Division of Appointed Times A: From Tractate Berakhot through Tractate Pesahim	Neusner
243040	The Talmud of Babylonia, A Complete Outline, Part I, Tractate Berakhot and the Division of Appointed Times B: From Tractate Yoma through Tractate Hagigah	Neusner
243041	The Talmud of Babylonia, A Complete Outline, Part II, The Division of Women; A: From Tractate Yebamot through Tractate Ketubot	Neusner
243042	The Talmud of Babylonia, A Complete Outline, Part II, The Division of Women; B: From Tractate Nedarim through Tractate Qiddushin	Neusner
243043	The Talmud of Babylonia, An Academic Commentary, Volume XIII, Bavli Tractate Yebamot, A. Chapters One through Eight	Neusner
243044	The Talmud of Babylonia, An Academic Commentary, XIII, Bavli Tractate Yebamot, B. Chapters Nine through Seventeen	Neusner
243045	The Talmud of the Land of Israel, A Complete Outline of the Second, Third and Fourth Divisions, Part II, The Division of Women, A. Yebamot to Nedarim	Neusner
243046	The Talmud of the Land of Israel, A Complete Outline of the Second, Third and Fourth Divisions, Part II, The Division of Women, B. Nazir to Sotah	Neusner

243047	The Talmud of the Land of Israel, A Complete Outline of the Second, Third and Fourth Divisions, Part I, The Division of Appointed Times, C. Pesahim and Sukkah	Neusner
243048	The Talmud of the Land of Israel, A Complete Outline of the Second, Third and Fourth Divisions, Part I, The Division of Appointed Times, A. Berakhot, Shabbat	Neusner
243049	The Talmud of the Land of Israel, A Complete Outline of the Second, Third and Fourth Divisions, Part I, The Division of Appointed Times, B. Erubin, Yoma and Besah	Neusner
243050	The Talmud of the Land of Israel, A Complete Outline of the Second, Third and Fourth Divisions, Part I, The Division of Appointed Times, D. Taanit, Megillah, Rosh Hashannah, Hagigah and Moed Qatan	Neusner
243051	The Talmud of the Land of Israel, A Complete Outline of the Second, Third and Fourth Divisions, Part III, The Division of Damages, A. Baba Qamma, Baba Mesia, Baba Batra, Horayot and Niddah	Neusner
243052	The Talmud of the Land of Israel, A Complete Outline of the Second, Third and Fourth Divisions, Part III, The Division of Damages, B. Sanhedrin, Makkot, Shebuot and Abldah Zarah	Neusner
243053	The Two Talmuds Compared, II. The Division of Women in the Talmud of the Land of Israel and the Talmud of Babylonia, Volume A, Tractates Yebamot and Ketubot	Neusner
243054	The Two Talmuds Compared, II. The Division of Women in the Talmud of the Land of Israel and the Talmud of Babylonia, Volume B, Tractates Nedarim, Nazir and Sotah	Neusner
243055	The Two Talmuds Compared, II. The Division of Women in the Talmud of the Land of Israel and the Talmud of Babylonia, Volume C, Tractates Qiddushin and Gittin	Neusner
243056	The Two Talmuds Compared, III. The Division of Damages in the Talmud of the Land of Israel and the Talmud of Babylonia, Volume A, Tractates Baba Qamma and Baba Mesia	Neusner
243057	The Two Talmuds Compared, III. The Division of Damages in the Talmud of the Land of Israel and the Talmud of Babylonia, Volume B, Tractates Baba Batra and Niddah	Neusner
243058	The Two Talmuds Compared, III. The Division of Damages in the Talmud of the Land of Israel and the Talmud of Babylonia, Volume C, Tractates Sanhedrin and Makkot	Neusner
243059	The Two Talmuds Compared, I. Tractate Berakhot and the Division of Appointed Times in the Talmud of the Land of Israel and the Talmud of Babylonia, Volume B, Tractate Shabbat	Neusner
243060	The Two Talmuds Compared, I. Tractate Berakhot and the Division of Appointed Times in the Talmud of the Land of Israel and the Talmud of Babylonia, Volume A, Tractate Berakhot	Neusner
243061	The Two Talmuds Compared, III. The Division of Damages in the Talmud of the Land of Israel and the Talmud of Babylonia, Volume D, Tractates Shebuot, Abodah Zarah and Horayot	Neusner
243062	The Two Talmuds Compared, I. Tractate Berakhot and the Division of Appointed Times in the Talmud of the Land of Israel and the Talmud of Babylonia, Volume C, Tractate Erubin	Neusner

243063	The Two Talmuds Compared, I. Tractate Berakhot and the Division of Appointed Times in the Talmud of the Land of Israel and the Talmud of Babylonia, Volume D, Tractates Yoma and Sukkah	Neusner
243064	The Two Talmuds Compared, I. Tractate Berakhot and the Division of Appointed Times in the Talmud of the Land of Israel and the Talmud of Babylonia, Volume E, Tractate Pesahim	Neusner
243065	The Two Talmuds Compared, I. Tractate Berakhot and the Division of Appointed Times in the Talmud of the Land of Israel and the Talmud of Babylonia, Volume F, Tractates Besah, Taanit and Megillah	Neusner
243066	The Two Talmuds Compared, I. Tractate Berakhot and the Division of Appointed Times in the Talmud of the Land of Israel and the Talmud of Babylonia, Volume G, Tractates Rosh Hashanah and Moed Qatan	Neusner
243067	The Talmud of Babylonia, An Academic Commentary, Volume XXII, Bavli Tractate Baba Batra, B. Chapters VII through XI	Neusner
243068	The Talmud of Babylonia, An Academic Commentary, Volume XXIII, Bavli Tractate Sanhedrin, B. Chapters VIII through XII	Neusner
243069	The Talmud of Babylonia, An Academic Commentary, Volume XIV, Bavli Tractate Ketubot, B. ChaptersVII through XIV	Neusner
243070	The Talmud of Babylonia, An Academic Commentary, Volume IV, Bavli Tractate Pesahim, B. Chapters VIII through XI	Neusner
243071	The Talmud of Babylonia, An Academic Commentary, Volume XXIX, Bavli Tractate Menahot, B. Chapters VII through XIV	Neusner
243072	The Talmud of Babylonia, An Academic Commentary, Volume XXVIII, Bavli Tractate Zebahim B. Chapters VIII through XV	Neusner
243073	The Talmud of Babylonia, An Academic Commentary, Volume XXI, Bavli Tractate Baba Mesia, B. Chapters VIII through XI	Neusner
243074	The Talmud of Babylonia, An Academic Commentary, Volume III, Bavli Tractate Erubin, A. ChaptersVI through XI	Neusner
243075	The Components of the Rabbinic Documents: From the Whole to the Parts, I. Sifra, Part One	Neusner
243076	The Components of the Rabbinic Documents: From the Whole to the Parts, I. Sifra, Part Two	Neusner
243077	The Components of the Rabbinic Documents: From the Whole to the Parts, I. Sifra, Part Three	Neusner
243078	The Components of the Rabbinic Documents: From the Whole to the Parts, I. Sifra, Part Four	Neusner
243079	The Components of the Rabbinic Documents: From the Whole to the Parts, II. Esther Rabbah I	Neusner
243080	The Components of the Rabbinic Documents: From the Whole to the Parts, III. Ruth Rabbah	Neusner

243081	The Components of the Rabbinic Documents: From the Whole to the Parts, IV. Lamemtations Rabbah	Neusner
243082	The Components of the Rabbinic Documents: From the Whole to the Parts, V. Song of Songs Rabbah, Part One	Neusner
243083	The Components of the Rabbinic Documents: From the Whole to the Parts, V. Song of Songs Rabbah, Part Two	Neusner
243084	The Components of the Rabbinic Documents: From the Whole to the Parts, VI. The Fathers According to Rabbi Nathan	Neusner
243085	The Components of the Rabbinic Documents: From the Whole to the Parts, VII. Sifré to Deuteronomy, Part One	Neusner
243086	The Components of the Rabbinic Documents: From the Whole to the Parts, VII. Sifré to Deuteronomy, Part Two	Neusner
243087	The Components of the Rabbinic Documents: From the Whole to the Parts, VII. Sifré to Deuteronomy, Part Three	Neusner
243088	The Components of the Rabbinic Documents: From the Whole to the Parts, VIII. Mekhilta Attributed to Rabbi Ishmael, Part One	Neusner
243089	The Components of the Rabbinic Documents: From the Whole to the Parts, VIII. Mekhilta Attributed to Rabbi Ishmael, Part Two	Neusner
243090	The Components of the Rabbinic Documents: From the Whole to the Parts, VIII. Mekhilta Attributed to Rabbi Ishmael, Part Three	Neusner
243092	The Components of the Rabbinic Documents: From the Whole to the Parts, IX. Genesis Rabbah, Part One, Introduction and Chapters One through Twenty-two	Neusner
243093	The Components of the Rabbinic Documents: From the Whole to the Parts, IX. Genesis Rabbah, Part Two, Chapters Twenty-three through Fifty	Neusner
243094	The Components of the Rabbinic Documents: From the Whole to the Parts, IX. Genesis Rabbah, Part Three, Chapters Fifty-one through Seventy-five	Neusner
243095	The Components of the Rabbinic Documents: From the Whole to the Parts, X. Leviticus Rabbah, Part One , Introduction and Parashiyyot One through Seventeen	Neusner
243096	The Components of the Rabbinic Documents: From the Whole to the Parts, X. Leviticus Rabbah, Part Two, Parashiyyot Eighteen through Thirty-seven	Neusner
243097	The Components of the Rabbinic Documents: From the Whole to the Parts, X. Leviticus Rabbah, Part Three, Topical and Methodical Outline	Neusner
243098	The Components of the Rabbinic Documents: From the Whole to the Parts, XI. Pesiqta deRab Kahana, Part One, Introduction and Pisqaot One through Eleven	Neusner
243099	The Components of the Rabbinic Documents: From the Whole to the Parts, XI. Pesiqta deRab Kahana, Part Two, Pisqaot Twelve through Twenty-eight	Neusner
243100	The Components of the Rabbinic Documents: From the Whole to the Parts, XI. Pesiqta deRab Kahana, Part Three, A Topical and Methodical Outline	Neusner
243101	The Components of the Rabbinic Documents: From the Whole to the Parts, IX. Genesis Rabbah, Part Four, Chapters Seventy-six through One Hundred	Neusner

243102   The Components of the Rabbinic Documents: From the Whole to the Parts, IX. Genesis Rabbah, Part Five, A Methodical and Topical Outline; Bereshit through Vaere, Chapters One through Fifty-seven   Neusner

243103   The Components of the Rabbinic Documents: From the Whole to the Parts, IX. Genesis Rabbah, Part Six, A Methodical and Topical Outline; Hayye Sarah through Miqqes, Chapters Fifty-eight through One Hundred   Neusner

243104   The Components of the Rabbinic Documents: From the Whole to the Parts, XII., Sifré to Numbers, Part One, Introduction and Pisqaot One through Seventy-one   Neusner

243105   The Components of the Rabbinic Documents: From the Whole to the Parts, XII., Sifré to Numbers, Part Two, Pisqaot Seventy-two through One Hundred Twenty-two   Neusner

243106   The Components of the Rabbinic Documents: From the Whole to the Parts, XII., Sifré to Numbers, Part Three, Pisqaot One Hundred Twenty-three through One Hundred Sixty-one   Neusner

243107   The Components of the Rabbinic Documents: From the Whole to the Parts, XII., Sifré to Numbers, Part Four, A Topical and Methodical Outline   Neusner

243108   The Talmud of the Land of Israel: An Academic Commentary of the Second, Third, and Fourth Divisions, I. Yerushalmi Tractate Berakhot (Based on the Translation by Tzvee Zahavy)   Neusner

243109   The Talmud of the Land of Israel: An Academic Commentary of the Second, Third, and Fourth Divisions, II. Yerushalmi Tractate Shabbat. A. Chapters One through Ten   Neusner

243110   The Talmud of the Land of Israel: An Academic Commentary of the Second, Third, and Fourth Divisions, II. Yerushalmi Tractate Shabbat. B. Chapters Eleven through Twenty-Four and The Structure of Yerushalmi Shabbat   Neusner

243111   The Talmud of the Land of Israel: An Academic Commentary of the Second, Third, and Fourth Divisions, III. Yerushalmi Tractate Erubin   Neusner

243112   The Talmud of the Land of Israel: An Academic Commentary of the Second, Third, and Fourth Divisions, IV. Yerushalmi Tractate Yoma   Neusner

243113   The Talmud of the Land of Israel: An Academic Commentary of the Second, Third, and Fourth Divisions, V. Yerushalmi Tractate Pesahim A. Chapters One through Six, Based on the English Translation of Baruch M. Bokser with Lawrence Schiffman   Neusner

243114   The Talmud of the Land of Israel: An Academic Commentary of the Second, Third, and Fourth Divisions, V. Yerushalmi Tractate Pesahim B. Chapters Seven through Ten and The Structure of Yerushalmi Pesahim, Based on the English Translation of Baruch M. Bokser with Lawrence Schiffman   Neusner

243115   The Talmud of the Land of Israel: An Academic Commentary of the Second, Third, and Fourth Divisions, VI. Yerushalmi Tractate Sukkah   Neusner

243116	The Talmud of the Land of Israel: An Academic Commentary of the Second, Third, and Fourth Divisions, VII. Yerushalmi Tractate Besah	Neusner
243117	The Talmud of the Land of Israel: An Academic Commentary of the Second, Third, and Fourth Divisions, VIII. Yerushalmi Tractate Taanit	Neusner
243118	The Talmud of the Land of Israel: An Academic Commentary of the Second, Third, and Fourth Divisions, IX. Yerushalmi Tractate Megillah	Neusner
243119	The Talmud of the Land of Israel: An Academic Commentary of the Second, Third, and Fourth Divisions, X. Yerushalmi Tractate Rosh Hashanah	Neusner
243120	The Talmud of the Land of Israel: An Academic Commentary of the Second, Third, and Fourth Divisions, XI. Yerushalmi Tractate Hagigah	Neusner
243121	The Talmud of the Land of Israel: An Academic Commentary of the Second, Third, and Fourth Divisions, XII. Yerushalmi Tractate Moed Qatan	Neusner
243122	The Talmud of the Land of Israel: An Academic Commentary of the Second, Third, and Fourth Divisions, XIII. Yerushalmi Tractate Yebamot, A. Chapters One through Ten	Neusner
243123	The Talmud of the Land of Israel: An Academic Commentary of the Second, Third, and Fourth Divisions, XIII. Yerushalmi Tractate Yebamot, B. Chapters Eleven through Seventeen	Neusner
243124	The Talmud of the Land of Israel: An Academic Commentary of the Second, Third, and Fourth Divisions, XIV. Yerushalmi Tractate Ketubot	Neusner
243125	The Talmud of the Land of Israel: An Academic Commentary of the Second, Third, and Fourth Divisions, XV. Yerushalmi Tractate Nedarim	Neusner
243126	The Talmud of the Land of Israel: An Academic Commentary of the Second, Third, and Fourth Divisions, XVI. Yerushalmi Tractate Nazir	Neusner
243127	The Talmud of the Land of Israel: An Academic Commentary of the Second, Third, and Fourth Divisions, XVII. Yerushalmi Tractate Gittin	Neusner
243128	The Talmud of the Land of Israel: An Academic Commentary of the Second, Third, and Fourth Divisions, XVIII. Yerushalmi Tractate Qiddushin	Neusner
243129	The Talmud of the Land of Israel: An Academic Commentary of the Second, Third, and Fourth Divisions, XIX. Yerushalmi Tractate Sotah	Neusner
243130	The Talmud of the Land of Israel: An Academic Commentary of the Second, Third, and Fourth Divisions, XX. Yerushalmi Tractate Baba Qamma	Neusner
243131	The Talmud of the Land of Israel: An Academic Commentary of the Second, Third, and Fourth Divisions, XXI. Yerushalmi Tractate Baba Mesia	Neusner
243132	The Talmud of the Land of Israel: An Academic Commentary of the Second, Third, and Fourth Divisions, XXII. Yerushalmi Tractate Baba Batra	Neusner

| 243133 | The Talmud of the Land of Israel: An Academic Commentary of the Second, Third, and Fourth Divisions, XXIII. Yerushalmi Tractate Sanhedrin | Neusner |
| 243134 | The Talmud of the Land of Israel: An Academic Commentary of the Second, Third, and Fourth Divisions, XIV. Yerushalmi Tractate Makkot | Neusner |

South Florida-Rochester-Saint Louis Studies on Religion and the Social Order

245001	Faith and Context, Volume 1	Ong
245002	Faith and Context, Volume 2	Ong
245003	Judaism and Civil Religion	Breslauer
245004	The Sociology of Andrew M. Greeley	Greeley
245005	Faith and Context, Volume 3	Ong
245006	The Christ of Michelangelo	Dixon
245007	From Hermeneutics to Ethical Consensus Among Cultures	Bori
245008	Mordecai Kaplan's Thought in a Postmodern Age	Breslauer
245009	No Longer Aliens, No Longer Strangers	Eckardt
245010	Between Tradition and Culture	Ellenson
245011	Religion and the Social Order	Neusner
245012	Christianity and the Stranger	Nichols
245013	The Polish Challenge	Czosnyka
245014	Islam and the Question of Minorities	Sonn
245015	Religion and the Political Order	Neusner
245016	The Ecology of Religion	Neusner
245017	The Shaping of an American Islamic Discourse	Waugh/Denny
245018	The Muslim Brotherhood and the Kings of Jordan, 1945–1993	Boulby
245019	Muslims on the Americanization Path	Esposito/Haddad
245020	Protean Prejudice: Anti-semitism in England's Age of Reason	Glassman
245021	The Study of Religion: In Retrospect and Prospect	Green
245024	Jacques Ellul on Religion, Technology and Politics: Conversations with Patrick Troude-Chastenet	France
245025	Religious Belief and Economic Behavior	Neusner
245026	Trying Times: Essays on Catholic Higher Education in the 20th Century	Shea

South Florida International Studies in Formative Christianity and Judaism

242501	The Earliest Christian Mission to 'All Nations'	La Grand
242502	Judaic Approaches to the Gospels	Chilton
242503	The "Essence of Christianity"	Forni Rosa
242504	The Wicked Tenants and Gethsemane	Aus
242505	A Star Is Rising	Laato
242506	Romans 9–11: A Reader-Response Analysis	Lodge
242507	The Good News of Peter's Denial	Borrell
242508	ΛΟΓΟΙ ΙΗΣΟΥ, Studies in Q	Vassiliadis
242509	Romans 8:18–30: "Suffering Does Not Thwart the Future Glory"	Gieniusz